Precarious Labour and Informal Economy

Smita Yadav

Precarious Labour and Informal Economy

Work, Anarchy, and Society in an Indian Village

Smita Yadav
University of Brighton
Brighton, UK

and

University of Sussex
Brighton, UK

ISBN 978-3-030-08588-9   ISBN 978-3-319-77971-3 (eBook)
https://doi.org/10.1007/978-3-319-77971-3

© The Editor(s) (if applicable) and The Author(s) 2018
Softcover re-print of the Hardcover 1st edition 2018
This work is subject to copyright. All rights are solely and exclusively licensed by the Publisher, whether the whole or part of the material is concerned, specifically the rights of translation, reprinting, reuse of illustrations, recitation, broadcasting, reproduction on microfilms or in any other physical way, and transmission or information storage and retrieval, electronic adaptation, computer software, or by similar or dissimilar methodology now known or hereafter developed.
The use of general descriptive names, registered names, trademarks, service marks, etc. in this publication does not imply, even in the absence of a specific statement, that such names are exempt from the relevant protective laws and regulations and therefore free for general use.
The publisher, the authors and the editors are safe to assume that the advice and information in this book are believed to be true and accurate at the date of publication. Neither the publisher nor the authors or the editors give a warranty, express or implied, with respect to the material contained herein or for any errors or omissions that may have been made. The publisher remains neutral with regard to jurisdictional claims in published maps and institutional affiliations.

Cover image: © Christina Sarmiento/EyeEm

Printed on acid-free paper

This Palgrave Macmillan imprint is published by the registered company Springer International Publishing AG part of Springer Nature
The registered company address is: Gewerbestrasse 11, 6330 Cham, Switzerland

To Zen and Alex

Foreword: If Not the State Then Who?

Post-Weberian definitions of a state, and its competences, have gradually added a variety of tasks that a state is expected to perform to be legitimised amongst its citizens. Indeed, nowadays the state is not only the only entity with the monopoly on the use of force, it is also an education provider, helps reallocating welfare and labour force, supports vulnerable citizens and groups, collects taxes to redistribute revenues and, in some extreme cases, protects citizens from their own (unhealthy) wishes—for instance, with higher taxes on alcohol or cigarettes.

What if a state fails to fulfil one or more of the above roles? One could easily think that the state is not functioning properly to the point that it might be considered a "failed state." But, what if the state were not the response to everything? Twentieth-century history has been an escalation of the importance of a state in citizen's life. Rousseau's social contract has complicated to include more obligations from both sides, at least in theory. Interestingly enough, this has also come with a gradual liberation of the state from (some) economic obligations. The neoliberal paradigm that has gradually gained consensus has put emphasis on the role of the state as indirect regulator but overemphasised the role of other non-state economic actors.

This apparently overwhelming consensus on the roles and limits of the state has come under question, fortunately, by what can be regarded as the manifesto for alternative economies. Since its appearance, "The end of capitalism as we know it" (by Gibson-Graham) has been used in a variety of settings, and contexts, to challenge the taken-for-granted omnipresence of the state in virtually all aspects of its citizens' life.

However, not only a state can underperform, fail to deliver what it is expected to deliver, refuse to take care of some aspects of its people's life and this can be due to a series of limitations in the conception of the state or capitalism as it has been designed. Even more important, people, as individuals or as a society, have agency. They have the agency to limit the state, reject its interventions or renegotiate its role in one or more aspects of their life. This happens not only if they want to engage with criminal activities. It can also be the result of political measures that are in contrast with what a percentage of the citizens of a state cannot live with. This could also come from a desire to propose alternative models of governance that are more consistent with a local culture, a context, or that have a more human face, allowing people to live the life they want and not the one that their state imagine. This is, at least, one of the lessons one can draw from seminal works by scholars like James C. Scott or Joel S. Migdal.

What we can see in practice are tendencies, practices or even informal institutions that have come to contrast the neoliberal model by putting the accent on more social aspects of the economy. This could be seen as starting from the very idea behind the concept of sustainable development, for which growth should happen keeping into account also social and ecological factors. However, this vision has evolved in a variety of directions emphasising the social aspect of the economy, the fact that growth is not the response to everything or the paradigm we should all ascribe to, hence the term—amongst others—degrowth.

Smita Yadav's Ph.D. thesis, and the subsequent book here, nicely locates in the above debates. In her detailed account of how a community lives, and survive, precariousness induced by a state that is partly absent, she documents the capacity, by individuals, households and eventually an entire village that is able to survive "beyond" or "in spite of" a state. She unveils a conflictual and contradictory logic according to which a state and its institutions are needed and not needed at the same time. A state is needed, as a general assumption of the twenty-first century, and indeed it can have a role in any community's life. However, the presence of a state as an overarching entity is not sufficient to regulate citizen–citizen, or to manage citizen–institution, relations. A state should not just be a state nominally but in fact also act as a state, being this a distinction that is not always made.

In this respect, Smita's deep, and thick, descriptions of intra-village dynamics, power relationship and the way people live this precariousness do not only ascribe to the larger stream of diverse economies. It also demonstrates that a state is not always needed and people, once they realise its absence, can manage to live without it thus looking for a dialogue. This is, however, not just one way of interpreting her rich empirical material and the analysis she offers. It is also a way to look at her work as valid well beyond the context she works in. This is a book on India but not only. It is likewise an anatomy of how substate units work without a state or, with limited support from it. Do these people still need a state thus? They probably need but what they also need is a dialogue with a state that is willing to listen to their feedback and take measures to meet their needs. If elections and referenda are a way to gather formal feedback, to express a perceived need, measurement and understanding of informality can be used to gather informal feedback and understand unexpressed, or veiled, needs. Informality needs to be understood and become an instrument informing governance mechanisms, rather than being considered an element undermining the (alleged) effectiveness of a given system.

Dr. Abel Polese
Senior Research Fellow (Vanemteadur)
Tallinn University, RASI
Tallinn, Estonia
E-mail: ap@tlu.ee
Academia.edu profile: http://tallinn.academia.edu/AbelPolese

Preface

an adivasi (Indigenous) means to labour but different than a wage labourer

Humans have always strived for freedom and autonomy and have learnt very early on that for this experience, they will have to labour. They choose to experience this through either formal or informal, depending upon their subjective interpretations of the terms, contingencies and conditions that can satisfy the values they seek for themselves and for their families. The story of the Gonds, in their own voices, is covered throughout this book and highlights all the empirical conditions in which the Gonds have successfully experienced this autonomy through precarious forms of work. Even though their rights to forests have been suspended and they are not able to practice autonomy against the autocratic forest department, they are experiencing autonomy in the informal economy. They choose their own wage work, fix their own wages, choose the site of the work and can leave and begin work as and when they desire. Migration is also an example of such an anarchic form of resistance towards the constrained choices due to forest restrictions. The income stream from migration is purely used to maintain status quo within their community even though access to local money lenders is still an option, for example, to afford expense of dowry and marriages which has recently become a major source consumption amongst the Gonds. Thus, through migration and other sources of income combined, Gonds maintain autonomy and stay debt free.

Even if they are unable to read and write, the virtues of labouring have allowed the Gonds to quickly assess their niche in the labour market to do precarious forms of work in the region for cash which is supplemental to their subsistence-based agriculture. At the same time, the institutions of household—family, kinship, division of labour between the sexes, marriages, reciprocity, relations of labour and land exchange, gifts, and mode of production—become the central focus of tribal life as described in this book.

Current scholarship on studying Indian economic growth is divided over how to interpret the growing informality and unorganised nature of its economy. Marxist scholars remain firm that it is exploitative and unfavourably against the labourers. They refer to such jobs as being precarious due to their nature of contract being temporary, irregular, insecured or seasonal. The other concern by current Marxist scholars studying poverty and labour studies of the Indian economy suggest that there is no formal union along the lines of the trade unions as in the west. Consequently, this should make the workers in India vulnerable against undignified wages and working in conditions.

Social development scholars doubt the ability of informal economy to reach social transformation and social change equally for everyone if India's economic growth continues to remain unregulated. Both view the informality as a perverse mechanism by privileged groups of people to hide low wages of the labourers who are also made to work longer hours, in unhygienic working conditions with no security and protection at the work site. They demand for a more transparent and accountable system to replace informality.

The conclusions from these studies are clear: only formal and salaried jobs can ensure dignity, security and lead to a viable form of living. However, this does not account and leaves too many poor in countries like India that rely majorly on informal work and can also experience dignity through independent means of livelihood. The social and Marxist portrayal of poor being in perpetual debt and stuck doing precarious forms of work needs re-examination in the face of the burden of so many people making a living through insecured and irregular forms of informal and precarious work. The book offers an alternative to explaining surplus labour production in the context of poverty out of displacement due to forest policies. In such a context, all rights are suspended and the forest rule has become widespread as a result of two sets of forces: a new round of enclosures that have dispossessed large numbers of rural people from the land and the low absorption of their labour, which is "surplus" to the requirements of primitive forms of capital accumulation—land grab by displacing the poor in the name of forest conservation.

The book also makes a case to re-examine previously held view about labourer's weak bargaining cannot be overlooked. The choices that Gonds have made challenge anthropology of freedom, community, individual and agency and show we still need more rigorous understanding of how and why people can freely choose to labour, negotiate their wages and the terms of their working conditions even if they do not have access to the formal state. Do these virtues have any value and is it even possible to have such virtues which are limitless autonomy through labour in our present capitalist society?

Ironically, institutions of kinship and patriarchy were viewed as constricting freedoms and anarchy of the individual and so formal and organised institutions were preferred for the labourer. However, such formalised unions and associations abstract the labour and make the affiliation to the group as the primary aim. This might certainly work in capitalists and social welfare contexts where work, even if limited, is guaranteed with limited autonomy and freedom as being part of the group takes over than the benefits and the return of the work itself. Thus, being part of the union through race, class and gender quotas has to be introduced for diversity. But this formalised union and organisations might not work in contexts where having work—formal work—is not even an option like for the Gonds. The only option is to remain invisible, unorganised, autonomous, anonymous and stateless until such reliable, formalised and regular but limited sources of income become available.

It shows us the limits of the institution of state and brings in the institution of labour and capital as superstructures that the state cannot regulate. At no time during the fieldwork were the Gonds convinced about the idea of the state and they gave all the evidence of it throughout the fieldwork.

The book tells the story of statelessness, dignity, welfare and autonomy through the voices of one such community—the Gonds. My focus in this book is to offer another alternative to explaining surplus labour production in the context of poverty out of displacement due to forest policies. In such a context, all rights are suspended and the forest rule has become widespread as a result of two sets of forces: a new round of enclosures that have dispossessed large numbers of rural people from the land and the low absorption of their labour, which is "surplus" to the requirements of primitive forms of capital accumulation—land grab by displacing the poor.

Brighton, UK   Smita Yadav

Acknowledgements

This work would not have been possible without the moral support of Zen, a polymath, whom I know since my Mumbai days while studying physics and who continues to influence me intellectually and philosophically.

I am immensely grateful to the people of Panna who at various points hosted me found my fieldwork and advised me to be safe while I was still adjusting to a new climatic and cultural conditions and show patience while I took time to adjust to the rhythms of village life. I am indebted to the Gonds with whom I have built lifelong relations and who have inspired me to appreciate the causes of the migrant workers' rights and to accept me into their lives and to understand the meanings of dignified and decent wages which have now become my own future research interests and inspiring me to explore the relation between work and anarchy.

I am thankful to my supervisors, Katy Gardner and Geert de Neve, at Sussex, my dissertation examiners Janet Seeley and Maya Unnithan, and other faculty members who helped shape the outcome of the book with their patient reading of my drafts of the original thesis which was submitted in 2016. I am grateful to all of those with whom I have had the pleasure to work during the writing. I am also grateful to Andrea Cornwall of Sussex Global Studies to make sure I had the right resource support while I completed the book. Nobody has been more important to me in the pursuit of this project than Alex whose infinite patience is with me in whatever I pursue. Also, to my mother who despite not being part of the formal academic world has finally come to accept and appreciate my academic and career choices since this project started in 2012.

Special thanks to Marloes Janse of SOAS, London; and Raminder Kaur at the University of Sussex for initially planting the idea of a monograph in my head. The various chapters were presented at conferences and workshops such as the Development Studies Association, Association of Social Anthropologists, Mobility Workshop in Freiburg, University of Madras and King's India Institute at King's College in London. I am also grateful to the Royal Anthropological Institute for funding the Ph.D. dissertation fieldwork. I am also grateful to Kuntala Lahiri-Dutt from the Australian National University who first introduced me to the mining villages in the district of Panna. This book has benefited immensely from the careful reading of Janet Seeley and Maya Unnithan who served as my examiners and helped to refine my initial thesis. Also, I want to thank Michael Myburgh and others for offering to edit various portions of the book. A special thanks to the commissioning editor of Springer Publishing to be very patient and to allow me to take my time to complete the manuscript.

Contents

1 Introduction: Urgent Anthropology 1
   1.1 Introduction 1
   1.2 Plan of the Book: Politics of Labour, Methodology and Urgent Anthropology 3
   1.3 Earlier Documentation of Gonds in Panna 10
   1.4 Forest Rights 14
   1.5 Feelings of Frustration, Discontentment and Politics of Livelihoods 18
   1.6 The National Park 22
   1.7 The Gonds Curiosity About the Buffer Zone 24
   1.8 Conflict Over the Understanding of Forest Management 26
   1.9 Democracy and Politics of Withdrawal from Welfare State 29
   1.10 Field Immersion: Settling Down and Village Selection 32
   1.11 Conclusion 39
   References 41

2 Local History and the Postcolonial State: The Invisibility of Gonds 43
   2.1 Introduction 43
   2.2 The District of Panna 44
   2.3 Bundelkhand and Panna 47
   2.4 Webs of Tradition and Modernity in Panna 49

2.5	Caste and Ethnic Lines of Occupation	51
2.6	The Gonds in Panna District	55
	2.6.1 The Fall of the Gonds and the Rise of the Rajputs in Bundelkhand	58
2.7	Collective Memory and Oral History of the Past Before the State	59
2.8	Pauperisation, Slow Change and Gradual Invisibility of the Gonds	67
2.9	The Social Hierarchy Amongst the Gonds and with Other Communities	69
2.10	Gonds and Mining	71
2.11	The Stone Quarry Lease	74
2.12	Political Economy of Stone Quarry	76
2.13	Gond's Experience on Starting a Stone Quarry	77
2.14	The Village Layout/House Structure	79
2.15	Conclusion	80
References		81

3 Basic Income, Forests and Anarchy 83

3.1	Introduction: Anarchic Anecdotes	83
3.2	Labouring Lives	85
3.3	Gonds as Subsistence Farmers-Patriarchy and Kinship Norms	89
3.4	Landholdings, Ownership and Land Grabbing	91
	3.4.1 Types of Farming	92
3.5	Stone Quarries	94
3.6	Working on a Piece-Rate Basis in Stone Mines/Contractual Work	96
3.7	The Labour Contractor	98
3.8	Death by TB	98
3.9	NMDC and Its Relation with the Villages in the Tiger Reserve	99
3.10	The Case of India's Universal Basic Income	101
3.11	Alcoholism	102
3.12	Spirit Possession, Shamans, and Indigenous Healing	103
3.13	Conclusion	104
References		105

4 Family and Kinship: The False Binary of the Subjective and Empirical Definition of a Household 107

4.1 Lineage and Family Systems of the Gonds 107
4.2 Nyaarpanna *(Separation of the Cooking Hearth)* 108
4.3 The Dichotomies of "Household" and "Family" 110
4.4 Marriage 113
    4.4.1 Stages of Marriage 114
    4.4.2 Sharing the costs of the Wedding Ceremony 115
4.5 Types of Gond Women in Mahalapur 117
    4.5.1 Women Married into Mahalapur 117
    4.5.2 Uxorilocal Women 120
    4.5.3 Widows 121
4.6 Inter-generational Participation of Work in a Gond Household 124
4.7 Child Work Participation 124
4.8 Conclusion 129
References 129

5 Narratives of *Kamayee/Dhanda* (Income): Modes of Wages 131

5.1 Introduction 131
5.2 Brief Review of Diversification Livelihood Framework and Social Capital 133
    5.2.1 Livelihood Diversification, Vulnerability and Strategies 133
    5.2.2 Social Capital, Social Networks and Social Protection 138
5.3 Brief Description of Different Sources of Dhanda. Sources of Income/Wage/Trade 142
    5.3.1 Forest-Related Activities 142
    5.3.2 Migration 144
    5.3.3 Road Construction 144
5.4 Case Studies 145
    5.4.1 Leela Bai 145
    5.4.2 Nandlal Adivasi 147
    5.4.3 Multiple Earners and "Older Female Earners" 148
    5.4.4 Emergency and Unforeseen Hardships 150
    5.4.5 Change in Household Development Cycle 152

5.5	*Inter-generational Change in Livelihoods*	153
5.5.1	*Ramcharan*	154
5.5.2	*Nandu*	154
5.5.3	*Gharjamayees*	155
5.5.4	*Gond Women, Work Participation and Hinduisation*	156
5.6	*Conclusion*	159
	References	160

6 State (*Sarkar*) and Society (*Samaj*)   165

6.1	*Introduction*	165
6.2	*Land vs. Social Benefits*	168
6.3	*Politics of the Cards*	170
6.4	*Labelling and Accessing Social Benefits*	172
6.5	*Understanding the Government Programmes in Mahalapur*	173
6.5.1	*Housing in Mahalapur*	175
6.5.2	*Schooling of Gond Children*	176
6.5.3	*The Rural Employment Guarantee Programme*	186
6.6	*Hi-Tech Rural India and Its Paradoxes*	192
6.7	*Conclusion*	193
	References	196

7 Conclusion   199
References   219

Glossary   225

Bibliography   229

Index   251

About the Author

Smita Yadav is an anthropologist interested in power, statelessness/state, anarchy, postcolonial theory, labour, gender, religion, secularism, indigenous knowledge, environment, theory and politics of ethnography, and politics of development and welfare. She has over ten years experience working as a consultant and academic on these topics in India, US, and UK. She is currently preparing a project on religion, secularism, state, and development in India. She is a visiting lecturer in Human Geography at the University of Brighton and is a Postdoctoral research associate at the University of Sussex where she completed her PhD in Anthropology in 2016. The fieldwork on the Gonds in India was conducted from May 2011–May 2012.

ABBREVIATIONS

BPL   Below Poverty Line card
GoI   Government of India
NMDC   National Mineral Diamond Corporation
NREGA   National Rural Employment Guarantee card
UBI   Universal Basic Income

Map of India

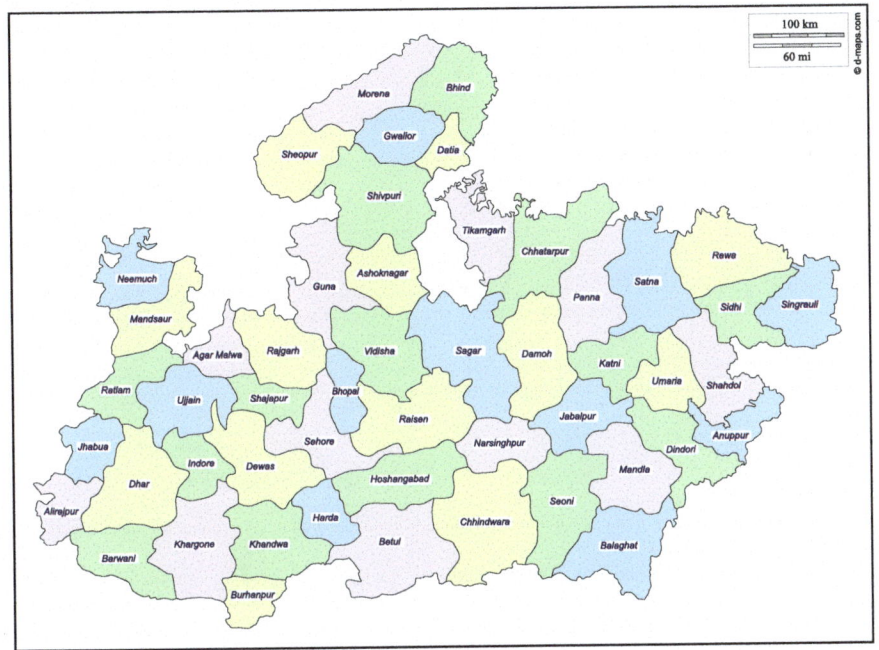

Map of MP State

CHAPTER 1

Introduction: Urgent Anthropology

1.1 Introduction

"We are not poor. Poor means unable to afford food, clothing, and shelter. We have all that, but we are *Majboor* (Vulnerable)," says Aditya, a Sur Gond in the village of Mahalapur, cautioning me not to judge him and his village by their constrained choices of doing precarious forms of work. Aditya is young and unemployed. Despite being a graduate with qualifications and hoping to get a teaching job in his village school, he does casual, unskilled wage work in the stone quarries nearby in order to make a decent wage. The Gonds (who are spread all over the country and speak different regional dialects) have historically been a predominantly forest-based community. However, in 1994 the Panna Tiger Reserve restricted their access to the forests by imposing sanctions, including fines and imprisonment. Today, such villages with predominantly tribal populations are being rooted out of their forests to build dams or for wildlife conservation projects, reducing them to wage labourers. But the Gonds seek to be autonomous, control their own welfare and meet their needs by diversifying their livelihoods even as they battle the state against displacement and resettlement from the forests. Some households engage in multiple occupations, while others survive on a single source of income. Seasonal migration is taken up to work in construction and stone quarries both in-state and out-of-state of Madhya Pradesh. Mahalapur is one amongst many *grams* in India that have been reduced to labour colony for the wider "development" of the region.

© The Author(s) 2018
S. Yadav, *Precarious Labour and Informal Economy*,
https://doi.org/10.1007/978-3-319-77971-3_1

More than half of the older generation in Mahalapur has perished to silicosis because it was incorrectly diagnosed as tuberculosis. Improper diagnosis and treatment of silicosis often led to premature death, typically around the age of 40 (Baviskar 2008). The 27 out of the 71 households that I covered in surveys (table in Chapter 2) are widowed households. The technology, from Switzerland, to detect and diagnose the disease arrived only in 2011 when I started my fieldwork. The stone-quarry workers are being X-rayed for their free medical treatment by the government. Gond children from a young age are found helping family members earn a living in the region. The closure of stone quarries, a crucial source of income for everyone in the region including the Gonds, inside the forest and growing restrictions on forest access affect everyone in the district of Panna. These changes, however, raise particular challenges for Gond households, especially for widowed households who faced greater constraints as they are completely forest depended unlike other marginalised communities. Schooling is the only time children can take a break from various household chores such as preparing dinner or storing water as there is no running water in most houses and modern amenities to keep the cost of living low through woods used for heating and cooking.

Precarious lives coupled with illiteracy make the Gonds unable to articulate their needs and choose to labour and migrate to cities and escape bondage and starvation. Their relations with the forests and state are growing more weaker by the day. Most see integration with the wider Hindu community as the best way forward at the moment. This book therefore makes a strong case for urgent anthropology before the Gonds completely integrate and loose their unique cultural heritage and identity. The Gonds are à Schedule Tribe (ST) community in the Panna district of Madhya Pradesh. The book aims to document how changing political economy in the region, such as the closure of quarries and restrictions on forest access, has led Gonds to engage in a wide range of livelihood activities. Gond migration within the state of Madhya Pradesh and to the major cities of India has intensified since 2011 as they have been banned from collecting wood from the forests. This has had significant effects on their traditional ways of livelihood that was coming from the forests. Finally, the book pays particular attention to differences in household types, namely gender, landholding, age, strategies to secure work and the role of children in households' income generation activities.

While new livelihood activities,[1] such as road construction work and seasonal migration, have led to enhanced income streams for some households, this income is largely consumed by marriage expenses and the pursuit of upward mobility but at the cost of pooling in resources for households from children who have to skip schooling to make their contribution. The readers should note that the Gonds' account in the book is specifically referring to the Sur Gonds and not the Raj Gonds who are the privileged Gond community.

1.2 Plan of the Book: Politics of Labour, Methodology and Urgent Anthropology

The chapters are based around the themes of politics, anarchy, statelessness and autonomy experienced by Gonds. For this, several Gond households have been empirically described in terms of division of labour and access to income sources. The book shares the contention that freedom is an immeasurable virtue experienced through work. The overall aim is to explain the normative and subjective experiences of morals, ethical and virtues out of making a living from precarious and informal kinds of work from multiple sources and sites. Empirical ethnographic account is used to describe the practice of dignity, autonomy and freedoms in the contexts of scant material possessions, especially amongst low-income groups. The Gonds challenge how anthropology of work, family and economy is still Eurocentric. Such approaches to work have focused too much on material aspects of labour such as wages, working conditions and tenuousness of work measured in terms of markets and state but not enough on the household which are the main subjective and ideological focus for agrarian and tribal people such as theirs. The fieldwork revealed that despite modern and postcolonial state in the region, the social institutions of family and kinship are being reinvented and adapted to the changing market forces. In that sense, the Gonds' lives contribute to the anthropology of postcolonial lives in villages across India and how they differ from the unitary and nuclear bureaucratic definitions of households as defined by the social schemes of state. There is also the concern with urgent anthropology raised here

---

[1] Livelihood diversification is conceptualised as an coping strategy (Niehof 2004) to deal with rapidly changing economic environments and as an expression of the Gonds' resilience and entrepreneurship at a time when traditional livelihoods are under serious threat.

using an empirical description and documentation of the Sur Gonds as they are facing a threat to their cultural identity due to forest conservation policies which are driving them out of the forests. Empirical accounts of Gond livelihood profiles have allowed me to cover more diverse and a range of case studies as in Chapters 4–6. Also, empirical accounts have allowed to compare not only Gonds with other Gonds, but also Gonds with other non-tribal communities with whom they coexist like the Dalit communities who are also economically marginalised by the Tiger Reserve in the region. The differences are both subjective and material; however, recently due to integration with the cash economy, the differences between the communities and within the Gonds have become more materialistic with clear empirical differences amongst them.

In Chapter 1, I open the chapter with how a very young Gond expresses his community's current situation. The chapter engages with major current ethnographic framework on social capital, social institutions, state and cash-based transfer. There are not many scholarly works that can show precarious workers in triumphant over the state despite the precarious working conditions such as temporariness, irregularity and insecure forms of work. It shows how Gonds make a choice, even if not always easy and desirable to choose to labour precarious economies so that they can have one foot in the farm which secures their food security and another in the informal economy and supplemental income. The aim of this chapter is to empirically layout the current political–economic situation and a brief discussion of the Gonds' relations with the state and the forest department. I use Tania Li's work on how governmentalities and rationalities run into various problems in postcolonial governance followed by Scott's studies of the Zomia community in Burma that also resist the state control through their agrarian practices. I also engage with Sahlins's work on primitive tribal societies that transform at the material level due to cash economy.

I also refer to the work of Bhrigupati Singh amongst Sahariya tribal communities useful due to his work on the symbolic "death of the forest" as the Sahariyas are forced to deal with the modern state and the forest department. Later, I also refer to Ferguson's work on the impact of social assistance schemes in the form of cash transfer, especially on the poor households in Namibia and how to conceive of the basic income framework when a nation's natural resources are contributed towards global wealth production. I compare that with the Gonds' experience who are bearing the brunt of economic and conservation development projects in the form of displacement without any compensation. Also, the chapter makes it clear that the Gonds described in the book are not all homogenous. Hindu-style caste system is present and leads to three types of Gonds, and the book focusses on Sur Gonds that are residing inside the Tiger Reserve. Lastly, this chapter describes in detail the methodology and the experience of my initial immersion in the field and my own position as an Indian doing an ethnography on other Indians. I also describe how the town people and Gonds interpreted my daily presence differently and how that influenced my fieldwork.

Chapter 2 is an empirical descriptive account of the region and then moves to the description of the Gonds. It first begins by describing the various conquests the region has experienced starting from the Mughals, the Rajputs and then the British. It's not based on archival research but upon the oral accounts from the townspeople as well as the Gonds. All the oral accounts of the forests are all oral narratives from the Gonds that are the main focus of the book. Gonds have been practising subsistence farming for over a century in this region long before the recent cash-based integration, and remnants of the past feudal structure and bondage are still present in the surrounding remote and isolated tribal hamlets. The difference is, as compared to the past that Gonds' practice of subsistence farming was using a bullock as compared to today where they use tractors and an electric water pump. This has radically commercialised their farming even at a small scale. Another difference is that the markets did exist in the past but the Gonds were paid in shells or grains in exchange for their labour and were previously part of a feudal order and bondage/slavery system to the local prince or the big landlords up until 1975 when Indira Gandhi abolished all bonded labourers and redeemed the poor of all previous debts. This chapter locates the Gonds in the local regional history and ethnographically evaluates their current experiences with the state and the forests. The purpose of these oral narratives is also to understand the chronological account of Gonds' relations with different rulers in the region and how it has changed gradually over the years. I believe these are fundamental and evolutionary questions of how the state has treated the Gonds in this region before moving forward to current market and economic conditions in which the Gonds labour. The assumption here is that there is a traceable historical continuity in the ideologies of work and labour, especially based on the observation that Gond women labour as equally as Gond men which is only to practise in the Gond community and not others who are also equally affected by the Tiger Reserve. The chapter also observes how the Gonds are adapting to Hindu and Rajput cultures. This is reflected in their everyday attire and in gender relations where women's bodies and movements are regulated by the wider patriarchal norms. This helps to explain the changing ideologies of family and kinship further in Chapters 4–6.

These empirical accounts of the past life of the Gonds also allow us to compare present Gond lives as they are quickly integrating. What aspects of their lives are changing and which are adapting and which have still been untouched so more future research on their community can be done.

In Chapter 3, I describe the subjectivities arising out of labouring in precarious forms of work in the informal economy. I introduce the subjective concept of *roji* (source of livelihood) and *majoori* (labour) which are the everyday reality of their lives. I ask here what do current observations like alcohol drinking practices (even amongst younger boys), spirit possession, interactions with the labour market and migration help to explain the changing practices of family and kinship ideologies at the household level as they labour for their families. How is the market transforming the household? This is further explained upon in various empirical case studies that are described in Chapters 4 and 5. What institutions of discipline and punishment have Gonds put in their village to resist their integration while also trying to strive for autonomy and freedom from bondage which is always a real threat. It shows the dichotomous but also selective choices that Gonds make in order to remain independent of the state that cannot anymore assure forest-based livelihoods which is a huge blow to their identity, self-preservation and morality coming from the forests. I focus on what newer forms of economies in the surrounds, newer economic actors and institutions of negotiating work have emerged due to rapid infrastructure development like transportation allowing the Gonds to be mobile and for the labour market to fetch the Gonds for work directly from their village. In a way, the ethnographies of labour covered in the book through various case studies are also an ethnography of doing "family," doing "gender," doing "patriarchy" and doing "kinship."

In Chapter 4, my research shows how the Gonds are making a living with constraints. Their strength lied in close-knit family ties and their ability to labour under the hot sun and endure riskier working conditions. I describe the kinship, family systems and lineages of the fonds in the village and how it was formed by one Sur Gond migrating to this region, and what temporal and subjective factors are taken into account by the Gonds. The Gonds and their households labour to maintain the cash flow to meet their basic needs. It is very difficult to find a small "labouring" household. But, modern state tries to reduce the tribal labour into wage labour which further denigrates the values that tribal communities value which is autonomy and freedom to choose work and to diversify. The further complication occurs when the bureaucratic description of households by the state does not take into account these subjective and ideological transformations that Gond households pursue and create actively by doing *majoori* in the informal economy. The promise of non-farm work is false and the Gonds instead create their own forms of entitlements (Leach et al. 1999) through earning. A major portion covered in this chapter is on the Gond widows, who as the female head of their households experience life-changing events after their husband's death as they are suddenly challenged to support their households financially and to meet the needs of their household and are often the only person in a position to earn if their children are too young to support them. This chapter also supports Wilk (1991, p. 3) who points to treat a household as the "black box" rather think in terms of its contents of "who handles resources, makes decision, motivates labor, and distribute the proceeds?" This chapter also demonstrates how to view the "state" from the bottom-up household perspective.

In Chapter 5, I discuss the various case studies to show how Gonds combine farm and non-farm work involving precarious forms of labouring like slicing stones (for men) or carrying load of woods on their foreheads (for women) as being important in stabilising and continuous cash flow and maintain food security for the Gonds. The Gonds appear to be "vulnerable" rather than "poor" going back to my opening quote by Aditya in Chapter 1 who makes this distinction clear. Being able-bodied is their main asset. The chapter follows from empirical descriptions of Chapter 4 to show how the decisions of choosing work are negated and contested at the household level. The chapter shows the Gond families are not a unitary model but is instead organised around multiple generations. The contemporary forms of livelihoods of Gond households involve: (1) the Gonds seeking their own forms of care and security instead of waiting for the state benefits to take effect, (2) Gonds pursuing freedom, independence, resilience and entrepreneurship, (3) Gonds aspiring for upward mobility through newer forms of consumption and wealth and (4) protestations and accommodation of the dominant Rajput identity.

Chapter 6 discusses the impact of various state welfare programmes, for example, housing, employment and education, and explores possible reasons for their lack of impact upon the Gonds' lives by discussing some specific case studies. It will also explore how the Gonds ensure they will be taken care by their kin in their old age. This is done through their families, who prefer to labour in hazardous types of work that allow them to fulfil their social obligations, which in turn allows their children to get married and maintain social status in the village. This chapter will offer explanations as to why it is so difficult for the Gonds to secure formal education and jobs, and will explore the various challenges they face in taking full advantage of welfare state policies, including being absent from their village and the mishandling of welfare funds. These challenges create further distrust of the state and push the Gonds towards the informal economy. The lack of demand for *panchayat* work through the National Rural Employment Guarantee Act (NREGA) scheme makes the Gonds migrate showing that the Gonds are very much aware of the politics of these jobs and how these payments getting delayed and how the funds are being mismanaged. The Gonds value is autonomous and labour instead of going into debt or fake out advance money from their labour contractors or the employers in exchange for informal and oral work contracts. Working for the state too is a form of bondage for them as they have to wait for up to two weeks for the money to be paid after the work is finished and the amount of bureaucracy to receive the payment like going through the *panchayat* to sign the vouchers and then stand in long queues for wages which they can make up by working in the informal precarious economies by taking risks. Their strategy in the informal economy is to attain bargaining power by working in groups (unorganised unions) outside and it has worked for them in securing wages on time.

The chapter will show how the Gonds are materially poor today but do not want to be treated like one and do not accept assistance from anybody including the state unless it comes to them. They have pride in their ability to work to meet all their needs despite several government programmes.

In Chapter 7, the Gonds in Panna are written off by everyone in the region. They are looked down upon by the locals as people who make poor economic choices like by not saving enough, splurging all their income on gambling and drinking, have too many children and living in unhygienic conditions. Also, there is no hope for them. In the conclusion chapter, I revisit these misconceptions and stereotypes on the Gonds. I summarise the book's contributions to the wider debates on the informal economy, welfare state and changing labour–capital relations in rural India and it's relationship with broader economy in India.

The critical evaluation of the state in its discriminatory treatment of the rural population in India needs more careful ethnographic consideration. The blurring division between the state and the society is less obvious in cities as compared to the villages where traditional forms of social inequality predispose the marginalised and the vulnerable to being socially excluded from various development programmes. The poor, like the Gonds, witness the dubious practices of the state through their own experiences of delayed payments for jobs through NREGA. The blurring division between the state and society also raises suspicion of the state when they are allotted poor quality of land for starting their own stone quarry even if the law has given tribal people rights to use forest lands. They are aware of the nexus/bond between the higher caste bureaucrats and officials of the region. The Gonds find security in their family units and rely on their ability to work which gives them their pride, dignity and income. They want a more secure form of social and economic means that they can rely on and feel socially protected by. I also show the meagre amount of money received as pensions, and compensation makes one question the survey methods and assessments done by the Indian government on poverty estimates and it is worth investigating why there are two conflicting reports about the numbers. It raises concerns about whether the centralised governance is an appropriate source for rural and participatory development.

Lastly, it reflects upon how anthropological critique of state assistances in India as a welfare provider for the poor instead helps us conceptualise the poor not as passive receivers but rather as being anarchic and proactive, taking initiatives and producing formidable and coherent forms of care, protection and long-term security for their families, thus being successful in being economically independent and avoiding bondage and debt.

As Bruner (1997) mentions, the narratives of life course and experiences are richer than the discourse itself. Like all sorrow about a community life, the Gonds' stories are also about past, present and history. As an ethnographer, while I have written down the experiences, I also realise the literal life experiences are not possible. Ethnographic voices do not translate all lived life experiences but anthropologists can bring them to life by contextualising and problematising the voices and narratives within the intersection of linguistic and cultural institutions. Thus, voices are also reduced, condensed and fragmented. Gond lives matter because their work ethics and ideals they attain—freedoms and autonomy—make them unique given that their spatial and temporal amalgamation with the life could not be experienced by them.

1.3 Earlier Documentation of Gonds in Panna

There are three main contemporary published sources on the Gonds, namely Fürer-Haimendorf's various studies (1948, 1979, 1982), Mehta (1984) and Sharma (2005). The work of Fürer-Haimendorf and his collaborators has focused primarily on Adilabad, Andhra Pradesh. Mehta's study is located in Bastar, Madhya Pradesh, and Sharma examines Narsinghpur, Madhya Pradesh.

The Gonds' movements, migrations, conquests and defeats have taken place over the course of more than a thousand years but, before the Mughal period, there are no recorded historical accounts (Mehta 1984). Scholars who have studied the regional history document in colonial Gazetteers like Lucie-Smith describing the Gondwana kingdom in Madhya Pradesh and Andhra Pradesh. The Raj Gonds practised settled agriculture and brought large parts of their kingdom into this form of agricultural production. Gond territory came under British rule in 1817, but until independence Gond chieftains still ruled small feudal states on the borders of British-administered districts.

Gonds' movements, migrations, conquests and defeats have taken place over the course of more than a thousand years but, before the Mughal period, there are no recorded historical accounts (Mehta 1984). Most famous are the "Raj Gond" (Koitur) who, from the end of the fourteenth century until a severe clash with the Mughal rulers in 1749 and their ultimate defeat by the Marathas in 1781, ruled four kingdoms in MP and AP, centred respectively on Ggarha, Deodargh, Kherla and, in the south, Sirpur and then Chanda. They were described by the Mughal chronicler Abu-l-Fazl and also Lucie-Smith, a nineteenth-century British administrator.[2] The Raj Gonds practised settled agriculture and brought large parts of their kingdom into this form of production; there was also a system of revenue raising and armies on a large scale. While at times they allied themselves with Rajputs against the Mughals, they were mostly left alone because their kingdoms were seen as isolated relative to the empire's centre in the north. Gond territory came under British rule in 1817, but until Independence Gond chieftains still ruled small feudal states on the borders of British-administered districts.

Incursions by non-tribal settlers and the reservation of forests together resulted in the shrinkage of the tribal habitat, a radical transformation of the Gonds' system of agriculture and a movement towards a cash economy. Fürer-Haimendorf's study of the Gonds in the 1940s in the Adilabad region, AP, documents this transition in detail. Furthermore, his research provides a potentially useful timeframe for the Gonds in the region that I wish to research, which is located in Central India. However, it must not be assumed that there is one common history.

Fürer-Haimendorf notes that "... early in the 20th century it was colonial government policy to open up areas to outsiders and grant them land rights (*patta*) free of charge in return for cultivating the land" (1982, p. 82). In eastern AP, it was large feudal landlords who moved in and extracted land rent. Land deeds were easy to secure for people with political connections (Yorke in Fürer-Haimendorf 1982). By 1940, most of the villages near administrative centres had fallen into the hands of non-tribals (Fürer-Haimendorf 1982). The tribal peoples could also have claimed "patta but concepts of land rights, especially for specified individual holdings, were foreign to the Gonds, who were slow to realise the necessity of obtaining title deeds to land which they had always considered communal property" (ibid., p. 54). Consequently, "they failed to

[2] "A long list of the Gond Kings who ruled from these places is given by Major Lucie-Smith in his Settlement Report of Chanda District, 1869. When he was preparing the land revenue settlement report of Chandrapur, 1863–1869, he compiled a genealogy of the Gond Kings based on oral and written traditions which he had collected." http://mygadchiroli.com/down21.html.

obtain recognition of their claims to land that they and their forefathers had cultivated" (ibid.).

The other side of the land squeeze was the policy of forest reservations. Large evacuations of tribal peoples from forest areas occurred in the 1920s, with "mopping up" continuing until the 1940s. In Adilabad, this reached a crisis in the 1930s (York in Fürer-Haimendorf 1982, p. 247) resulting in the Babijheri incident.[3] "To understand the process of the Gond's gradual displacement by other and more dynamic populations, it is necessary to consider their system of cultivation as it existed before" (ibid., p. 53). As Fürer-Haimendorf recorded of Adilabad, older Gonds in the 1940s still spoke of traditional cultivation methods: "the Gonds of the highlands mainly cultivated the light, red soils of the plateaux and slightly inclined slopes, but not the heavy, black soils on the valley floors" (ibid.). In the past, the Gonds were able to shift the fields they cultivated every two or three years and were free to return to areas of land with little danger of new claimants (ibid.).

Both the granting of *patta* rights and the forest reserves interacted disastrously with this cultivation system. Fallow land—the red soil of the plateau/hills—was claimed by incomers as "unoccupied" and also by the forest department under the reserve scheme.

> In villages with a fair amount of permanently cultivated heavy black soil, this curtailment of the land with light soil did not result in very great hardship, but the Gonds had to lean more and more on the yield of the heavy soils cultivated in the *rabi* season. But there were other villages, situated on the tops of ranges, where the interference with the cycle of rotation created a very serious problem, for the Gonds of some of these villages, who used to move backwards and forwards between two or three village sites, alternatively cultivating the surrounding land, were now pinned down to the one site which they happened to occupy at the time of the forest reservation. (ibid., p. 90)

There is no exact date marking the point at which the Gonds became integrated within the cash economy in the region, the transition was gradual from the 1940s and manifested as a series of changes in the

---

[3] 1860 Gond rebellion, begun by Ramji Gond in Adilabad.

household dynamic. As both Fürer-Haimendorf (1982) and Mehta (1984) have observed, increased contact with outsiders such as moneylenders and work as migrant labourers played a prominent role in changing the Gonds' socio-economic position. Fürer-Haimendorf showed how the practice of modern types of cultivation led to borrowing money for growing commercial crops, which, in turn, meant borrowing money from moneylenders to buy the seeds (1982, p. 98). The Gonds became enmeshed in the "vicious circle of borrowing and repaying the debt, the terms depending on how good the harvest was" (Fürer-Haimendorf 1982, p. 98), and the Gonds soon found it very difficult to find their way out of this debtor–creditor relationship. The integration with a cash economy ended the Gonds' self-sufficient livelihood, and they are not equipped to deal with new types of threat, such as the effects of crop failure on commercialised farming (1982, p. 98). In addition, due to extensive mining, the soil quality deteriorated, leading to a decrease in groundwater, which has caused water scarcity in the region (1982, p. 98). In turn, increased agricultural cost due to scarcity of water makes growing of millets slowly replaced by wheat (which is also the diet of most Hindu population and eating millet is mostly amongst Gonds such as Sur Gonds who still remember growing them). Their diets too which are mostly game meat, wild fruits and herbs have been replaced with whole grain food.

In the regions that Mehta and Fürer-Haimendorf studied, the Gonds lost their lands to moneylenders and are forced to work on lands that they had once owned (Fürer-Haimendorf 1982; Mehta 1984). Patel (1998), describing the significant transfers of land from Gond to non-tribal people in the 1960s and 1970s, explained that this was largely due to defaults on debt.

Integration into the cash economy also brought social changes to the Gond community. Before the penetration of moneylenders, the Gonds' limited needs are satisfied by weekly markets and fairs where communal exchanges took place (Sharma 2005). Sharma suggests that, when this less complicated way of life prevailed, the Gonds did not feel a sense of economic inequality in the way that they do today. However, the influx of a non-tribal population and integration with a cash economy pushed the Gonds to consumerism as their needs multiplied. Family debts increased in relation to these new needs, creating a cycle of debt amidst the tribal community's uncertainties about modernised economic practice (Sharma 2005, p. 18). The sense of injustice felt by the Gonds[4] in the 1980s was all the greater as, within recent years (1980−2000), thousands of acres of forest had been cleared and occupied by affluent non-tribal people, most of whom had only recently immigrated (Yorke in Fürer-Haimendorf 1982, p. 95). It is also important to note here that most accounts of Gonds are on Raj Gonds. There is even less documentation of Sur Gonds[5] and how they are related to the Raj Gonds. Only oral narrative accounts are possible.

1.4 Forest Rights

Previous work on conflicts over forest land in India in which the values of environmentalism, ecology and conservation have focussed on how often these values pitted against tribal peoples' livelihood needs (Rangarajan 2005; Shah 2010; Baviskar 1994, 1998; Mosse et al. 2002). Being poor and illiterate prevents tribal people like the Gonds from organising against the state, which has constructed images of tribal peoples from Hindu civilisation and from the colonial imagination (Srinivas 1997). The Indian elite, colonial administrators and anthropologists have together created representations that have a powerful effect on society and politics in India (Shah 2010, p. 4). The Gonds fall into the "administrative" and "bureaucratic" categories of Scheduled Castes (SCs) and Scheduled Tribes (STs) which treat them as people who need to be "civilised" through their rural development programmes like employment, education and housing. According to the state, the Gonds' identity is complicated. In addition to being tribal, they are also subsistence farmers. At the same time, the book deals with the contradictions and dilemmas of treating indigenous populations that have to be brought into the fold of modernisation as per the Indian state (Beteille 1998).

---

[4] Some of the Gonds had acquired marginal amounts of land because their ancestors were also clearing forest lands through slash and burning activities to make way for subsistence form of agriculture. The various Gond hamlets around the forest were basically a part of the thick and dense forest before the Gonds had settled there.

[5] Scholars studying Gonds of Central India (David Baker, Archana Prasad, Suresh Mishra, Ajai Skaria, Andre Wink, Sumit Guha) have extensively studied tribes of Central India like the Gonds but do not mention Sur Gonds.

Livelihood activities are diversified according to size and household composition of the household and age and gender of the household members. Livelihood diversification[6] has ensured survival and sustaining of income streams and enabled Gonds to participate in different forms of status-related consumption. These newer livelihood activities also perpetuate certain vulnerabilities, inequalities and insecurities. These are specifically: children dropping out of school, engaging in physically demanding hard work that makes them look older much faster, faster experiences of life cycle of the household members, an unequal labour–employee relation of dependency and exploitation, gendered inequalities and poor access to state social benefit programmes. At the same time for the Gonds, newer economic opportunities have also empowered those widows who are sole contributors to their household as will be shown in Chapters 4–6. Only older and widowed women and very young girls are allowed to earn[7] for the household.

The state in the region has constituted various village-based forest communities around the country with the intention for jointly managing the forests with the villagers. However, such efforts undermine the indigenous populations' knowledge of forest management and instead, expect them to comply with western ideas and standards of wildlife and nature. Also, the tribal people are not identified by their tribal status but as villagers as if their primary identity is that of a peasant. As Sundar too has pointed (2000) from her study in the region of Sambalpur, in the state of Orissa, such village-level communities that served to represent the interests of the forest through civil society quickly get dominated by the forest department, and thus, Sundar doubts how far such state-led "joint" ventures are really "joint" when they are in reality and in function, representing state interests, and can hardly be referred to as "civil." Further, the indigenous and village management and control of forest resources, also referred to as a customary right, are being replaced by modern discourse in the form of modern legal structures (ibid.). Bhogal et al. (2013) also show how the forest departments have instituted devolution policies like joint forest management policies (JFM) as

---

[6]According to Katone-Apte (1988), vulnerable households will diversify, save and store food during leaner periods (as cited in Ali 2005, p. 204).

[7]Newly married women do not engage in earning for their families as their primary duties are household chores and nursing.

it is known in various states differently and have only caused to reassert and monopolise over-existing indigenous knowledge of forest conservation, thus ignoring the historical knowledge of forest livelihoods and biodiversity (p. 56). These kinds of devolution institutions are eroding historical and indigenous knowledge of forest conservation and forest-dependent livelihood management (ibid.). With the constant international pressure on the Indian government to commercialise the forests, the livelihood-based activists are loosing their battle (Bhogal et al. 2013). Further, the authors show from the World Bank funding to Uttarakhand's forestry department on tribal communities has been reduced to mere objects of attention rather than active participants and stakeholders in the JFM model.

In another study, Sundar studies the relations of indigenous populations with the naxalites in Dantewada region of Chhattisgarh. It provides an interesting comparison with the Gonds of Mahalapur. In her study, Maoism replaces the dysfunctional and non-existent in similar overtaking of the forest department in her region of study. The functionaries of the radical movement against the state include collecting taxes from the tribes for the use of the forest and exist parallel to the state.

This kind of politically volatile outcome has not happened in Panna. The major reason is that the landed elites, the Rajputs, in the region, are not only in majority in terms of numbers than the Gond population in the region, but they also enjoy a very closer relationship with the state and have the historical institutions in place that do not allow the Gonds' violent expressions of unrest and subjugation to sustain. In that sense, the study of the Gonds on the district of Panna is quite interestingly different than the study of tribals being studied in more mineral-rich states of India which Nandini Sundar looks at. It gives an idea of how the state functions differently in different forest ecologies of India. The relation between the state and the Gonds is different due to the wider political groups and influence of the elites—the Rajputs. Insurgent movements like Maoism are absent in Panna. This also effects social development schemes as there is not the same awareness of politics of development and active participation in various government-run poverty alleviation programmes. As a result, migration is higher in such regions effected by the autocratic forest rule as their authority over the region remains unchallenged and unchecked and is systemic. At the same time, the landed elites in Panna are not as wealthy as in other parts of India.

Like Gonds, even they are direct victims of the hegemonic forest department which, in this part of India, is clearly more powerful than the state. Even the state requires an No Objection Certificate (NOC) from the forest department before any clearance for setting economic and employment generating activity. The state holds power only because it holds land records which has to be consulted when selling of land occurs or when schools and hospitals need to be constructed. The effect of the forest is even stronger than the state in the region in a span of only twenty years.

MP is one of the states in postcolonial India that has experienced the replacement of natural forest by commercial species (Gadgil and Guha 1989; Sundar 2000) and forest destruction and displacement for development projects such as mining, industry and submergence for large dams. In that sense, the experience of displacement of the Gonds in this region is different than the experience of displacement due to mega economic development projects as their weapon of discontent against the state is to withdraw and disengage rather than actively protest. Even, the weekly meeting for the public redressal grievances at the local council hall referred to as regionally, *jan sunwayee*, the Gond voices were missing.

Bhogal et al. (2013) show how the forest departments have instituted devolution policies like (JFM) as it is known in various states differently and have only caused to reassert and monopolise over-existing indigenous knowledge of forest conservation, thus ignoring the historical knowledge of forest livelihoods and biodiversity (p. 56). These kinds of devolution institutions are eroding historical and indigenous knowledge of forest conservation and forest-dependent livelihood management (ibid.). With the constant international pressure on the Indian government to commercialise the forests, the livelihood-based activism is loosing their battle (Bhogal et al. 2013). Further, the authors show from the World Bank funding to Uttarakhand's forestry department on tribal communities has been reduced to mere objects of attention rather than active participants and stakeholders in the JFM model.

Sundar's most ingenious and more impactful study of the Gonds' relations with the naxalites in Dantewada region of Chhattisgarh is far more intriguing comparison with the Gonds of Bharatpur, in Panna district, MP, in this study. In her study, Maoism replaces the dysfunctional and non-existent. Its functionaries include collecting taxes from the tribes for the use of the forest and exist parallel to the state. This kind of politically volatile outcome has not happened in Panna. The major reason is that the landed elites, the Rajputs, are not only in majority in terms of numbers than the tribal population in the region, but they also enjoy a very closer relationship with the state and have all the historical institutions in place that do not allow the Gonds' violent expressions of unrest and subjugation to sustain. The study of the Gonds on the district of Panna is quite interestingly different than the study of tribals being studied in more mineral-rich states of India which Nandini Sundar looks at. It gives an idea of how the state functions differently in different forest ecologies of India. The relations between the state and the tribal people in these forests are different due to the wider political groups and influence of the elites—the Rajputs. Insurgent movements like Maoism cannot exist in Panna as there are not many resources to support such organisations and the only option is to work on stone quarries, which, even though is lucrative, is not of the same economic scale as the ores and minerals that can be exploited from the forests and soils in other ecologies of India. This also effects social development schemes as there is not the same awareness of politics of development and active participation in various government-run poverty alleviation programmes. As a result, migration is higher in such regions effected by the autocratic forest rule as their authority over the region remains unchallenged and unchecked. At the same time, the landed elites in Panna are not as wealthy as in other parts of India. Like Gonds, even they are direct victims of the hegemonic forest department which, in this part of India, is clearly more powerful than the state. Even the state requires an NOC from the forest department before any clearance for setting economic and employment generating activity. The only power the state has is to hold land records which has to be consulted when selling of land occurs or when schools and hospitals need to be constructed.

1.5 Feelings of Frustration, Discontentment and Politics of Livelihoods

Feelings of frustration are related to loss of employment and the growing control of access to forests by the forest department, especially amongst the younger ones. The forest laws prevent hunting, mining, fishing, chopping woods or even casually hanging around or walking around the forest area. The forest reserve, which originally started as a small garden nursery programme—at least as what was told to the Gonds in the beginning about twenty years ago—according to the Gonds, has now converted into a strongly fenced territory under the forest department which can impose penalties like jail time and fine for numerous kinds of intrusion into forest land. Living very close to the forest means that they cannot commercialise their own trees and land in the village. The local variety of a flower called *Mahua* can produce a good quality of wine but it would require an NOC from the forest department because Mahalapur now falls inside the reserve. The Gonds feel they have been scammed out of their forests to create a habitat for the tiger.

The limited access to the forest has caused changes in the household relations, division of labour, gender relations as well as the differences in the inter-generations. The younger generation is now more aware of the uncertainty of their future as they see their parents live a very hard life. A lot of them do not plan on having so many kids like their parents did. The younger generation is now getting prepared to live a life independent of the forest and move to modern ways of living like a pucks house, have cards, seek formal education and formal work for their children. The other source of frustration amongst the younger Gonds to move away from Panna is the lack of access to do any other employment except working on quarries but that is killing them much younger. There are a high number of TB-related deaths and no intervention from the government. Manoj, another young Gond who works on illegal quarries (referred to as *khadaan* regional language), is very frustrated due to the increasing number of TB in the village and says. *"we will all die working in the mines."*

Other sources of frustration for the Gonds are about heightened corruption in the rural administration. They feel very helpless about the situation where they are asked to pay up every time for any identity-based document from the government like voter's ID, Below Poverty Line (BPL) ration cards or getting jobs through NREGA. They get very annoyed when they see privileged communities and upper castes who even though do not qualify for being poor but manage to secure BPL cards by lying to the government about their assets when the census surveys are done and some even influence the authorities to get these cards by paying bribes. Kotram, a Gond who has recently returned from migrating from Jammu working on construction, says, *" We don't have the means in our community to influence the administration like other communities have."*

In Bundelkhand, Panna is the only district which has the largest percentage of forest area over 50% with respect to its geographical area. In addition to the tribal population, the Scheduled Caste population and Yadavs too seem to be dependent on the forests for food like hunting and fishing animals (Planning Commission, GoI). The forests are a source of food security and for the tribes, a livelihood security. During the months from March to June, Gond households depend on collecting, sorting and selling a multipurpose forest product, a fruit called *Mahuwa*. It is also a flower. The Gonds make oil, alcohol and also the fruit as it is sold on the market. Another source of forest-based livelihood is Tendu leaves which are used to make local form of cigarettes called "bidi." The other forest product that the Gonds use as a source of livelihood is *Amla* (Indian Gooseberry).

However, the forests are totally under the autocratic control of the forest department, especially those parts of the forests which yield good quality of forest wood and land for finding stone and diamond mines. In addition, there are regular illegal activities by the mining mafia comprising of rural administration officers, forest guards and the mine-owners carried out inside the forest like killing of animals and illegal stone mining or sometimes, illegal diamond mines, according to the locals and the Gonds.

Dhiraj is a Gond in Mahalapur who never migrates and is totally depended upon the income coming from selling forest woods. Gonds like him are the worst affected as they will not have any other stream of income left. He expresses strongly his feelings against the forest department as his whole family survives on the income coming from the forest. He says, "Unlike others (Yadavs, *Bengalis* and other SCs), Gonds have no land. Our *dhanda* (trade) is forest and that is being restricted.[8] The forests provide woods, stone quarries, mahuwa and food. Woods are used for cooking and for keeping the house warm during the winter. In extreme crisis, we will migrate wherever there is work so we can eat. Nobody helps us. For everything that we need like job card, poverty card, there is so much of paper work involved, signatures involved, we don't understand all that much." For the Gonds, the *panchayat* is useful only for rural employment. Dhiraj continues,

---

[8] They are aware that forests are a source of basic income for them.

We have only one person working for 5 people to feed. Work reaches us through word of mouth. Work is like putting together bricks, guarding the farm, every 5 acre we get 3 quintal of grains in exchange of labour for guarding, planting, sowing, and cutting. And everyday we manage somehow to make up to Rs. 100. Work comes to us.

Dhiraj says that the process of applying for the rural housing schemes is cumbersome and needs "*leka padhi*" (writing and reading) which no one in Mahalapur can, and there is no one to help them fill up these long bureaucratic applications. He looks to me with great hope and that I should take a lead and help them in advocating for their rights and other such benefits that require basic reading and writing skills which they don't have. He says, "The Gond community is extremely poor because we are affected by the national park's creation directly affecting our livelihoods. The other problem is land. Even if we have 10 acres of land, it gets divided amongst 4–5 children and so it's not enough and then our kids have their own kids who too depend on that land."

Nowadays, he is working for the *panchayat* through the NREGA scheme and makes up to Rs. 150 per hour for transporting stone and mud from one place to another. The *panchayat* work money comes after a month. He continues, "If we work in private like through labour contractors then we get paid in weekly. We are *mistry* (professional stone cutters and make up to Rs. 150 per hour and the *beldari* (the apprentice) removes the boulder. The fuelwood for household is collected by children and we have to train them." Dhiraj says that the children have to be trained in fuelwood sorting, collection and chopping from a very young age otherwise how will they know. Men don't do forest wood collection because when they go into the forests then will smoke *beedi* (*an* indigenously produced cigarette) and get caught by the forest authorities and so they send their children or wives. Forests can easily catch fire from smoking. Women are allowed as they are treated as less of a threat as compared to men and comply and do as has been told by the authorities. The women describe the process of wood collection from the forest as *lipke lipke* (clandestinely from the forest guards).

Forests continue to be mainstay for the Gonds sustenance, and not having access to fuel woods from the forests would mean no fuel for cooking and also a loss of Rs. 900 per month which easily covers their food costs of Gonds like Dhiraj.

1.6 The National Park

The Panna forest is divided into three main divisions—Panna North, Panna South, and the Project Tiger Reserve. The reserve, also known as the Panna National Park, is also home to two sanctuaries—Gangau Wildlife Sanctuary and Panna Wildlife Sanctuary (divided over Ken river)—and the north and the south forests are in the territorial areas.

The Panna National Park was built in 1981 and renamed as Project Tiger Reserve in 1994. It is considered to link the north-central with the eastern wildlife trails. The reserve is the 5th in the state and 22nd in the country. The Tiger Reserve also has some forest areas which fall under the territories of Panna North. The forest department all practices western knowledge of forestry, and indigenous knowledge of forestry is dying as the younger generations of Gonds and others who lived in the forest once upon a time complain how their young once cannot defend themselves against tigers and other wild animals, as they have not seen many wild animals.

The forest department has banned mining within the Tiger Reserve. The reasons cited are that mining creates noise pollution that disturbs the habitat of the tiger. However, the government runs a mechanised mine, which is inside the reserve. It is slated to stop by 2022 when their lease arrangement will come to an end. The NMDC mine has a turnover of about Rs. 84,000 carats of diamonds every year. Despite the ban on collecting forest woods, the Gond women continue to go to fetch forest woods everyday negotiating their way with the forest guards who let them off with a weak warning. Due to illiteracy and poverty, they are able to get away from the forest laws and that is one of the main reasons why forest wood collection is a woman's domain. Unlike men who get no respite for breaking forest laws, women, due to their roles as mothers and income earners, negotiate their way through compromising the forest laws.

The villages that I covered for the fieldwork were in Panna North and Panna South, where the Gonds are found to be mining or depending upon forest-based livelihoods. The villages inside the Tiger Reserve had been resettled few kilometres away from Panna, and the villagers have been compensated based upon the size of their house as well as agricultural land owned by them. However, Panna Tiger Reserve does not have a buffer zone yet. A buffer zone is a zone where human use of the forest is allowed but with limitation as it is considered to be eco-sensitive for conserving the habitat of the tiger. These zones are governed by forest laws.

These zones are to regulate the free movement of the tiger into human-dominated areas, and they impose penalties if the animal will be harmed unless it attacks human life. However, these zones are also spaces of man–animal conflict and there is not much regulation from the government to protect the tiger or the villagers who might get harmed in man–animal conflicts. On the other hand, a village cannot come under the buffer zone if the villagers do not desire it according to Mr. Shukla, Forest Officer for the Panna Tiger Reserve. According to the supreme court, all reserves should have a buffer zone allowing more space for the tiger to "roam." The villages that will come under the buffer zones will be on lands that will be "notified" implying that the land will be meant primarily for forest purposes and people living on that land will have to follow laws laid by the forest department in terms of the land use. In these circumstances, the Gonds and other villagers can challenge the authority of the forest department, but the forest department is working out a decent amount of compensation to those villages who will be affected by the creation of the buffer zone. This compensation money comes from the National Tiger Conservation Authority, based in New Delhi and funded mostly by international wildlife bodies. However, according to my field visits, most of the villagers, especially the Gonds, do not understand the full possible implications and consequences of living in a buffer zone.

The establishment of Tiger Reserve was under the Wildlife Protection 1972 in which 694,682 sq km core areas got reserved for the Panna Tiger Project. The buffer zone is territorial to the core area of the tiger's habitat. The buffer zone includes the protected forest area and reserved forest area. Protected forest area refers to forests that are considered to be in a degraded condition and need attention. The villagers, under this act, are supposed to be made aware of the construction of a buffer zone. The main aim of establishing a buffer zone is that the villagers who are living under this area will have to coexist with the wildlife. Killing any wildlife would lead to imprisonment even if wildlife endangers human life who are already living there. Moreover, a separate forest area out of the core area must be exclusively reserved for the wildlife so that any human casualty caused by the wildlife will not lead to legal liability and compensation from the forest department.

However, at the village level, most of the Gonds do not exactly know what a buffer zone means. Even some of the village heads asked me whether I can explain it to them. There are many versions of it. Some say that having a buffer zone would mean following forest laws and that killing any animal near the surrounding of their homes would entitle imprisonment and will be treated as murder. Even now, there are forest laws that control the use of the forest and often the villagers are not completely aware of breaking those laws until someone breaks it or goes into prison or has to pay a fine. I have been told that a lot of time the villagers who are unaware of these forest laws are sent to jail and they have to pay a bribe to clear their names. Clear signboards of not entering the forests by the forest department are missing throughout the region, and even if they are present, the Gonds are unable to read them as most have never attended schools. The schools are a recent occurrence in the village of Mahalapur, only about twenty years ago.

1.7   The Gonds Curiosity About the Buffer Zone

There is a heightened curiosity about the buffer zone—understandably so, as that allows the Gonds to strategise their livelihood plans for their future accordingly. Implementing the buffer zone cannot be done independently by the forest department, because the land that they want to cover in the buffer zone to the state is known as *Tehsil*. Any land area that is under the *panchayat* is considered as part of the state. The forest department needs to consult the state to know where their jurisdiction ends measured in terms of land area and where the forests can take over. The state (local rural administration) is involved in this because the state has all the records of the rural households and the owners of the land as it is also the source of social development and more importantly to hold regular elections. The forest officials blame the illegal mining and the feudal structure in Panna as further delaying the implementations of the buffer zone. They also suspect the state to be complicit in encouraging the illegal poaching and mining as the state has its own politics of development considering it as one of the important vote banks in the region. For the forest officials, the state treats the tiger less important than social development and poverty alleviation of the poor such as the Gonds in the region and they think that the issue of the Gonds' resettlement and compensation has unnecessarily been delayed until the problem of land sharing between the state and the forest department is resolved.

The ethnography on the tribal community of the Sahariyas in Rajasthan by Bhrigupati Singh (2015) also refers to similar problems of how to understand the forests whose role in the postcolonial context of governmentality is caught up into so many material and legal battles and whether forests are even alive anymore in spiritual terms and which had acted as a source and produced the meaning of life itself and describes this entanglement as the "murder of the forest." He is also specifically concerned about the rituals such as *deni* that were sanctified and made real before the complex rationalisation of the forests occurred in the region under the postcolonial state. Previously, the ritual involved offering a sickle to the daughters in their household and gifting her a hill which only she would use. The sickle symbolically referred to her means of security.

While the state government and the forest department are in a deadlock about the human vs. tiger conflict, the insecurity amongst the Gonds is causing them to seek alternatives to their dependency on forests like migration. At the same time, a major part of my fieldwork so far indicates that growing controlled access to the forests has heavily burdened the women and young children of the households to fetch woods illegally from the forests. Because they are not allowed to chop much wood, households will start sending children to collect so that the amount of woods increases per household. As a result, the children start to chop and sell it to the main Panna town from an early age. Forest dependency increases when the men in the house take a break after returning from migration and stay put in the village for up to three to four weeks allowing their bodies to rest. Living in forest woods meets almost all their basic needs of food and shelter and health.

It is not clear if the compensation is a way to bribe the villagers and the Gonds from asserting their rights to forests. There is no active form of resistance against the forest department by them. This lack of active resistance against the forest department is also in anticipation to get cash for displacement. However, the Gonds remain divided over whether to accept monetary compensation or fight for their access to the forests. Even if they had access to forests, some feel that the forest department is permanently here to stay and they will never have unrestricted access as it was in the past. The region is rife with daily stories of how the forest department harasses people by fining them for just being seen near the forest (especially men), or smoking near the forest or overgrazing near the forest, or will impound vehicles that are seen near the forests. For some Gonds, coexisting with the forest is an everyday reality.

Signs of this integration are already seen in the village. For instance, the Gonds have started to adopt Hindu (Sanskritised) names for their children, headscarfing and veiling of women, and Hindu-style weddings. Their modern aspirations for consumption style are also similar to the surrounding Hindu community: for example, the expensive weddings with an orchestra were absent a generation ago. Weddings have become an elaborate symbol of social status amongst the Gonds for which they will do precarious labour and migrate to cities to meet the cost of hosting the wedding guests, serve three to four course meals, arrange for their transportation and accommodate them in their homes. Previously, the concept of wedding was just a matter of couple of hours of a simple ceremony performed in front of their communal deity (in the forest) as compared to now when weddings have become longer and can last up to a week to ten days depending upon the rituals. All these commodification of the tribal life has occurred less than a decade ago. In fact, for the younger generation, the older generation now seems to be backward and illiterate, which coincides with the dominant discourse about the Gonds in the region. The younger generation is aware of its history of exploitation and it resists this by becoming financially independent and autonomous and by engaging with the informal economy, too often at the cost of not finishing education.

1.8 Conflict Over the Understanding of Forest Management

In other forest reserves in India, the forest department has worked successfully with the tribal populations in JFM. This aspect is missing in the Panna Tiger Reserve. What is the role of the Grievance Redressal Office and what kinds of complaints do they receive about forests and tribes, both at the rural administration and at the forest department?

There are now 18 tigers in the reserve. The population has increased in only about 3 years, as before there were hardly any left. The problem with the increase in tiger population is that it gets difficult to track and control their movements, especially if they are venturing into villages and attacking livestock or can sometimes just go into highways and get into accident or get illegally hunted.

The ban on mining inside the forests, a traditional livelihood practice that had supported the entire district, has affected many locals in the region who too were directly living off of forests including those who would hire the Gonds to work on their stone quarries inside the forests. However, most of them blame the autocratic forest department for taking away their livelihoods after they banned the tribals from using the forests to run their households by selling forests woods and other forest products. The region was completely dependent upon a "forest" economy which now is not possible due to the Panna Tiger Reserve. Some of the Gonds also blame the local prince for selling these forest lands to the government. The family of the local prince once used to own up to 4000 acres of forest, but after independence in 1947, they had to give up their three royal palaces plus the 18 acres of the forest land. One of these palaces is now the district headquarters of Panna's rural administration. The Gonds blame the local prince because the national park[9] was created due to his efforts in 1977 when he was the local member of legislative assembly and influenced Indira Gandhi, the then prime minister, to declare the forest as a national park in return of helping her win the elections for the Congress in the region.

Tania Li's ethnography on governance in Indonesia shows how defining modern postcolonial governing categories cannot be easy, despite the good intentions of governments and their will to improve in the form of welfare, well-being, health and education. She further demonstrates that the modern lives of the postcolonial population cannot be provided for without first defining the population in measurable units so that the process is easy to govern, regulate and manage the social welfare and assistances. She raises concerns about government practice and the bureaucracy behind it. Therefore, what kinds of bureaucratic units need to be devised in order to capture useful information about/provide for the entire population, their welfare and wellbeing? Furthermore, how does one condense a very diverse and heterogenous population into

---

[9]There is a precedence to Panna National Park. Out of the 166 national parks in India, 9 are in Madhya Pradesh alone because of the vast forest area.

something homogenous in a manageable form or unit? Do these measurements reflect the various experiences of colonial and postcolonial realities of the diverse populations? How can we identify areas that need improvement and how exactly do we define improvement?

Postcolonial governance is further challenged, not only in terms of scale, for example in a population as large as India's, but also in terms of heterogeneity. Furthermore, in even more historically complex and heterogeneous societies, it is even a bigger challenge to have any set criteria for governance. What should be governed and what should be left out? Who decides and how? Postcolonial governance has markedly been associated with a people-centric approach and with citizenship, in the form of democratic rights and duties. This is different to the colonial style of governance, where the goal was primarily to control and govern people non-democratically at the cost of local resources and labour extraction. In modern and postcolonial governance, the problem occurs in defining indigenous settlements, who pre-date the modern nation-state, in two ways. Firstly, these settlements need to be defined, and secondly, if the choices made by the governments for one set of populations defined in terms of communities, gender, ethnicity, religion, landholding might not work for other groups of populations within the same national boundaries. This book raises similar challenges that the government face in order to define a highly mobile tribal population in Central India, and what difficulties such populations face when the welfare state schemes cannot be easily accessible due to other hurdles, such as illiteracy and material poverty.

Many indigenous populations such as the Gonds exist with precapitalist forms of living and have a historically continuous identity which cannot be captured by modern government rational models of technocracy. Often, in this context, the problems regarding governance and a unitary model of governance run into extreme difficulties as ideologies and cosmologies of their existence with their social life and nature are much older. Colonial Indian accounts, for instance, have portrayed India in a specific historical entity through various district-level Gazette reports. People, animals, flora and fauna have been described as living together in these reports. This empirical documentation under the colonial rule was rich and elaborate in their descriptions, but was partial and biased. This is not helped by the absence of the voices of native populations in those reports. However, in the postcolonial accounts, the descriptions of human settlements have become very complex due to their heterogeneity and the politics.

Contemporary accounts of people in India make a clear demarcation between people and forests. As observed by Townsend Middleton (2015), more recently, postcolonial government, in India for instance, has come to work with their own anthropologists to better understand the populations and their claim to attachments with their land, community and other such identity-based depictions of the population. This is done both to disbursing the good intentions behind the welfare and to control the movement of the population between various states and more clearly define the country's communities along regionalist and ethnonationalist lines. Thus, these projects to improve people's lives make the populations visible by the state for the purpose of politics based on identities and votes which is currently the "democratic approach" in non-western and precapitalist societies such as in India.

1.9 Democracy and Politics of Withdrawal from Welfare State

If democracy is about economic freedom and expanding human capabilities (Drèze and Sen 2013) and if this has to be assured by the state, then, as per my fieldwork, I agree with them that the state has failed vulnerable populations like the Gonds. However, my one year research amongst the Gonds showed that they demonstrated these attributes of capabilities and entitlements in the informal economy by demanding higher wages as well as choosing the labour contracts despite the constraints of low agricultural productivity, the closure of quarries and the low impact of state benefits in the form of employment, housing and education. Thus, this book focuses on the agency and autonomy of and how the Gonds have turned their vulnerabilities into their strength and challenges the observations of our understanding of human capabilities and social transformation as imagined by Sen (1999) and Drèze and Sen (2013). Even as the elections are contested around land reforms and caste-based social change, modernisation fir populations such as Gonds are experienced in the form of displacement from the forests by the autocratic institutions that are even powerful than the state, such as the forest department, as is the case for the Gonds. Such actions by the government only make the Gonds withdraw from the state, as modernisation in tribal and forested areas is only seen as a colonial remnant, since indigenous forest knowledge is replaced by modern and western forms of forest and wildlife management.

Scott shows how the Zomia peasants in Southeast Asia resist the authoritative state control that wants to impose a "visible" structure in order to govern their traditional and ancient farming activities (2009). Similarly, the Gonds resort to precarious labour in the informal economy and disengage from the state. By being absent in the form of migration for most part of the year and being absent during most key political moments such as elections, the Gonds practise their dissent. In that sense, labouring in informal economy and doing insecure and irregular forms of work are also a political choice by the Gonds as they prove to the state their power to be highly mobile, scattered, invisible and remain fluid. In this way, the Gonds go against the state and its fixed state bureaucratic units and ratios, resisting the formalisation and homogenisation to restructure their lives on the pretext of offering the Gonds better life through non-farm and secured forms of work. However, for this, the state also expects the Gonds to accept modern form of relationships with the state such as citizenship in order to access modern education and housing systems so that the Gond lives could be governed. As the book shows, these modern governing structures like schools and modern living amenities lay in complete disuse in the village. The government-built toilets also have been converted instead as a storehouse for livestock food and other such uses but for hygiene purposes for which they were designed as the Gonds instead still prefer their older ways of defeating in the open as was done by their ancestors. This desire to remain invisible and be fluid within an acephalous social structure (Scott 2009, p. 178) is attributive of a body politic of tribesmen who desire a life of less complexity and retain their segmentation (Scott quoting Sahlins, ibid.).

The postcolonial state has to justify why it improves lives in rural and tribal areas, as well as seek the democratic consent from the people to do so. Often, postcolonial governments cannot improve rural lives directly on the pretext of modernisation such as formal jobs or non-farm work, which is why India still continues to be characterised by an agrarian economy. To question agrarian roots of the society and to replace social and informal relations based on trust and kinship with formal, regular and secured forms of work is not so easily done in rural areas. The process of such an overlap involves questioning the entire politics of identity, history, development and poverty. Instead, the population is targeted based on specific demography defined in several terms. Often, for the government, the documentation is to define population and to indicate the size, sex ratio, density and dependency ratio, and other vital statistics include indicators such as birth rate, death rate and natural growth rate, life expectancy at birth, as well as mortality and fertility rates. These indicators help in identifying areas that need policy and programmed interventions, setting near- and far-term goals. They also decide priorities and help to understand them in an integrated structure. However, documenting is only possible if people have the right identification where they can prove their citizenship which is a bigger challenge in rural and tribal areas as most of such populations can go easily unnoticed in such surveys as they live a highly mobile life in search of livelihoods and are often sent from their village when such surveys take place.

One of the main observations of this book is the difference of governance in rural and urban postcolonial contexts of welfare and social assistances. Focussing on India, this book shows how democracy is specially associated with certain kinds of lives, mobilities and consumption methods. While the postcolonial government has had similar success amongst the urban populations in the form of modernisation and formalising of the governed lives, the experience in rural and tribal areas is far from the ideal outcome. The governments usually remain unchallenged as modern ideas of social mobility in India are accepted to be in the form of consumption of formal education, concrete and fixed housing, and formal jobs where the techno-bureaucratic units have fairly better manageability. However, in non-urban areas the governments hardly go uncontested as there is an obvious clash of what is "improvement" and who defines it. For instance, in the postcolonial rural contexts, there are complex webs of social relations, gender ideologies, indigenous communities, cosmologies, divisions of labour and property relationships that are reflected in their everyday practices of sustenance, market and society. Also, the social lives of people in non-urban areas have a different spatial and temporal dimension giving a different rhythm of their love experienced through different life courses and life cycles of the household members where subsistence-based livelihoods are predominant. These spatial and temporal relations challenge. The governmentalities and technocracies of documenting people often come directly into conflict with the postcolonial government's modern ideas of progress and development as it is these very indigenous practices that the postcolonial governments seek to redefine and make them more visible, so that they can reorganise them and make them more manageable. As will be shown in this book, the modern state and its governing structures are viewed suspiciously by the Gonds as they fight to maintain their freedom. The state's social schemes are not integrated well within the lives of the Gonds as will be described throughout the book. Therefore, to protest, the Gonds bypass the state and instead engage with the informal economy where they experienced social mobility, dignity and welfare and meet all their immediate and long-term needs.

While anthropologists have mostly shied away from agreeing with how to define the state, there is a general consensus that its origins are recent. According to Michael Bouchard (2011), archaeological work done by Childe (1950) showed the earlier beginnings of the modern state which was only possible through specific consumption patterns of Neolithic farming communities in Europe, leading to a formation of class as well as elites who wanted to protect their material possessions. These materialities, produced by the hands of blacksmiths and potters, reflected a specific ideology and cosmology of fragmented social lives of indigenous lives which gave birth to early urban metropolis. In this archaeological description, it can be inferred that the state is indeed measurable and an empirical entity that is made out of natural elements like metals, earth, water and fire, and limited only by the imagination of how these materials interact with each other.

1.10 Field Immersion: Settling Down and Village Selection

I arrived in Panna district at the end of the summer season in 2011 amongst severe water shortage and limited electricity. My induction in the town and later in the village could be compared to a plane landing in an unknown destination as I had met Gonds and had never visited the region. The place was not only difficult in terms of severe heat and remaining hydrated and hygienic, but there were also more complex gender and class dynamics which made my presence as a native anthropologist even more intriguing for the locals in the region. In addition, my urban roots and appearance and my untimely, unwanted and uninvited presence were apparent. I had no link to the place either in the form of kinship relation nor did I have any state or official purpose to be there. I was more like a native tourist in the region learning about the place. The difference between my and other ethnographic studies in such places was that like the Gonds and the other people in the town, I too had an Indian identity.

Initially, I had took up residence in Panna town and got acquainted with the field in terms of its geography and distance: for example, the nearest bus stations and markets. I owned no means of transportation, nor did I have any idea of how to lead my day-to-day activity. I started building relations of trust with everyone I encountered during my fieldwork.

Once I settled in a private residence in Panna town, I faced the challenge of selecting a village where Gonds could be found. I was receiving many suggestions from the locals as to where would be best to find them. The Gonds were a common sight all over the region and not just near and inside the forests. Some locals suggested to go inside the forests were given in order to study the Gonds as they were still practising traditional forest-based activities like hunting, adorning tribal clothing and communicating in their ancient Gondi language. It took me time to choose the village that was most easily accessible by the available mode of transportation in the region from town. I also wanted to spend time to arrange and decide on the logistic of transportation while trying my best to follow the local gender norms where it was uncommon to see women unaccompanied by men or without a veil. In such parts, being a single, unmarried Indian woman did not make it easy to blend in with the locals, even though I was Indian like them. My purpose and presence were constantly under scrutiny, especially by the townspeople and mostly by men. In the meantime, the monsoons had already arrived. The first two months after May I had already acclimatised myself in terms of how to dress and where to live. At the same time, reports of mudslides, minor accidents due to slippery road conditions and villagers being temporarily sheltered in schools due to flooding in the villages caught my attention and forced me to choose a village close to the town of Panna instead of choosing more remote villages located inside the forests so I could arrange for regular travel and also arrange to stay amongst the Gonds in their hamlets if required.

While deciding which village to select amongst the Gonds, I had already conducted several questionnaires and household-based surveys, travelling extensively to Gond villages up to 40 km away from Panna within the first six months. My daily routine for the first six months was to observe the Gonds' households and understand their decision-making processes for making a living and how the households differed from each other. I used friendly casual conversations, group discussions, in-depth interviews, oral histories and surveys. In my initial days of village surveys, the Gonds would gather around me earnestly as if expecting my visit with an announcement of a government scheme or an update on a new forest law regarding compensation for their displacement. Some thought I was from the mining department spying on them for illegal mining as most were engaging in diamond mining whenever someone hired them to dig one up. This kind of diamond quarry work was still a lucrative form of labour even if the diamond was not yielded.

Such events were very personal moments that have I carried home from the field. Upon deep reflection, I always feel as if I have let them down by not following up with my work on their lives, especially when they just revealed their very tough, precarious and harsh realities of their working lives to me. I felt it my duty to at least be able to write about them. This leaves me to question my own authority over these voices. How do I represent these voices? Not only is the ethnographic subject interpreting the native object, but the informants are also interpreting the ethnographer.

I decided to base my fieldwork in Mahalapur as it had some basic and reliable forms of transportation. Also, the village was solely comprised of Gonds, unlike other villages inside the forest reserve where there were Yadavs (shepherds) as well as Sahus and Patels (money-lending class). It was only 10 km from Panna town. After studying both the social and the economic aspect of the Gonds in the village of Mahalapur, I knew that there was a lot of potential to conduct good fieldwork there. So I decided to study Mahalapur. My next eight months were spent within a twelve-kilometre radius.

In the beginning of the fieldwork, I would often go to visit the Gonds with Ashraf who is a local whose family once owned a stone mine until 1994 when the reserve was set up. Later, he would work as a labour contractor and still works like one from time to time, so quite a few Gonds knew him very well. I decided to be completely independent of him after as I realised after a few visits in the village that Gonds were for into accepting me into their lives. I found a huge advantage of starting to go alone in the field. Ashraf was happy to accompany me but had never worked with an ethnographer before. I realised that expecting any kind of patience from him would be unrealistic. My academic work demanded that I immerse myself amongst the current living condition of the Gonds no matter how clichéd and banal it may have sounded to someone like Ashraf who would often lead my discussions and interactions in another direction while I was at the very beginning of my fieldwork. Also, the Gonds spoke up less hesitantly in front of me. Because I was an outsider to the Gonds, they could open up to me easily as they found me harmless. Although Ashraf[10] was not known to them individually, they knew he was a local from his body gestures and his familiarity with the local dialect. I realised that there was a lot about him that was not acceptable to my academic purpose as well as my gender, which I will show in the later section; consequently, I decided to go in my own direction. I mainly interacted with the Gonds through participant observation and informal interactions. Participation was in the form of attending festivals, social occasions and evening meals.

It took me a while to win the trust of the Gonds and rightly so. The younger Gonds were not as suspicious about me and they would start talking. The elders, seeing that, would also start participating. After an hour or so of talking to me, they will raise questions that they feel I should have answer especially on how I managed my funding for this project and what was the practical benefit for them if they allowed me to do research on them.

I found that for most Gond households, livelihoods depend upon what resources they can access and how different kinds of work come to them. Almost all the villages, which I found later, were hamlets organised along different Gond lineages and kinships, which were only 2–4 km away from the forest. Being close to the forest meant that forest woods are an essential part of their life which helped in keeping the cost of living low by saving electricity and gas. However, that also meant walking to the forests early in the morning to collect the woods, and then returning just before the sunset, and another 10 km walk the next day, in the town to sell them. Predominantly, it is the Gond women who do these jobs and accompanied by younger children in the household. It is a common sight to see Gond women carrying a load of up to 50 kg of forest wood on their head. Even little girls can be sometimes seen carrying lesser forest wood loads on their heads.

---

[10] Ashraf was one amongst those who acted as agents for the local administration to help in convincing the villages relocating them from the forests about five years ago. These agents got a small commission from the state for doing so. Working out a compensation package and communicating that to the village being considered for relocation is a long drawn process as the villagers have to produce residential documents and identity cards issued by the *panchayat*.

Eventually, the Gonds too had gotten used to my presence and some would ask me my purpose and how my research would benefit them. It was a completely novel thing for them that some outsider would like to stay with them and be like them. They used to think outsiders were in the form of labour contractors, school teachers, vendors, NGOs, government surveyors and rural development workers, but not someone like me who wanted to have an in-depth conversation about their lives, work, kinship, family, household livelihoods and their struggles by immersing myself in their social world. Before me, nobody, not even journalists, was coming there to find out how the village lives were being transformed as their access to forests was being restricted. The media was more interested in the mining mafia because it directly links up the highest rural authorities as well as higher officials in the forest department.

Initially, I befriended Aditya's household. I felt it was easier to interact with them because of Aditya's level of English and his initial enthusiasm in introducing me to other villagers. He had recently graduated in English Literature from Panna College and was preparing for an entrance exam to qualify to become a village school teacher. In the meantime, he was unemployed and I requested him to help me with the surveys. For the first two months, Aditya was my gatekeeper to the world of the Gonds of Mahalapur. I learnt a lot about the Gonds and then as almost a third of the households were closely related to his father's four other brothers and their extended families. However, the households to which he introduced me, which were not his immediate relatives, were equally willing to interact with me. I mainly interacted with the Gonds through participant observation and informal interactions. Participation was in the form of attending festivals, social occasions and evening meals.

During focus and in-depth household head interviews, the first hurdle I faced was to convince the Gonds that I was not from the mining or the forest department. Most of the mining is done illegally. The Gonds thought that I might be an informer from the mining or forest department whose goal was to report their illegal activities. However, later when they saw me with Aditya, another Gond like them, they became convinced that I was not from the mining office, and instead, I was there to research them. They were curious to know how this study would benefit them, and I replied that anybody who was interested in the Gonds would be able to read my work. Of course, I realised that not only were they unclear about the relevance of spending a whole year with them, but so was I due to my inability to communicate my ethnographic purpose in simple language. It was doubly difficult as a native anthropologist as the boundaries between the ethnographic subjects and the anthropologist are not apparent. However, everyday presence and the practice of conducting the fieldwork made my purpose slightly clearer in their eyes. My constant interactions and inability to completely merge and blend despite being an Indian could not go unnoticed. After a couple of months, I had to put less effort into being accepted for my presence in the village and town.

At the same time, I realised it would be beneficial to narrow down my number of households, even if the Gonds had trusted by now that my presence was temporary, due to the fact that the Gonds were finding it difficult to articulate their very complicated livelihoods information. It was also the case where the illiteracy disempowered them to articulate their lives in a sharp, coherent way.

Before arriving in Panna, I had a romanticised, idealised and sacral view of an Indian village. However, after six months, the apparent political and economic dissent and the harsh reality of Indian village life revealed itself to me. The locals in Panna wondered why I chose Panna over other more prosperous places in Madhya Pradesh as I could have been in a more comfortable region considering I moved from Mumbai. They informed me that Panna was not only "backward and poor" within India but it was also considered so within the state of Madhya Pradesh. To illustrate their point, they would say that doctors who failed to pass medical exams could practise in this region. According to the locals, the only reason people outside of Panna seemed to know the place was because of the diamond mines and the Prannath Mandir which attracted many followers from all around the world as a site of pilgrimage. Places like Mumbai and Surat were known to everyone in Panna as places where diamonds from Panna were cut and polished and then sold worldwide. Since I am from Mumbai, many diamond sellers would try to sell diamonds thinking that I was there to buy diamonds. In that sense, my social status was already elevated due to my city roots which meant, to them, that I must be wealthier than them. Everybody in the town appeared to know each if not by name then at least by face. Even though the *panchayat* head was a woman, she was just a nominal entity. Like other Gond women, her main task was her role of being a traditional Gond mother and wife which was more important than being a village head. The village-level meetings were attended by her husband, and it was him who I had met about three or four times in 12 months. He also looked after the administrative side and knew about the entire village better than his wife. Being a woman, she could not openly interact with household heads as she had to wear a veil.

I was keenly noting how the Gonds would talk to each other, how the general spaces of their conversations were and how they related new information in their village. Most of my fieldwork was spent observing personal relations in the households and I would often play with the little ones. I could walk into any Gond household and get some food and drink hot tea. I moved into Kesar Bai's household where I spent the next 4 months from December 2011 to March 2012. At that time, it was much cooler, even during the day. I would conduct my interviews mostly in the evening because most of them would be in the village at that time and were freer to interact with me—except for those who would return to Mahalapur after months of migration. But I had not given up my rented room in the town as I had kept most of my luggage there and carried only the bare essentials to the village. I moved out of the village when people started to return from migration. This was due to personal safety concerns as people indulge in gambling and drinking and even men from the Panna town start coming around to drink because both meat eating and alcohol drinking are considered unholy for the town, and Mahalapur had become a place for practising such "vices" for the townsmen.

Although I did have an advantage being a native anthropologist, especially due to being able to speak Hindi, I still had the challenging issue of gender norms and my urban roots making it difficult to go completely native. It was not my identity as another Indian woman studying Gonds that was worrying the Gonds (and the local people), but rather the question of who I was, and why was I randomly entering houses, living, studying and talking to them? The questions were not as sharp and pointed as they had their own ways of studying strangers. Even as they were sharp in expressing their intrigue, it still took me six months to finally be fully accepted by the tribe and to judge my persistence and consistency. The daily lives of the women labourers looked simple, but there were so many complicated processes and practices at the level of kinship, patriarchy and gender, within which these women were performing these tasks. As mothers and as household earners, their lives seemed to be full with absolutely no time for themselves. It was these aspects that drew me towards three women—Kesar Bai, Leela Bai and Usha Bai. However, except for Leela Bai, both Kesar Bai and Usha Bai were hardly as impressed or as curious about me as I was about them. Also, these two women were much older than Leela Bai and so it was difficult to converse with them. In Mahalapur, the elderly women did not migrate at all and so they still practised the old Gondi style of speaking in Hindi. However, with continued interaction, we started to understand each other.

1.11 Conclusion

After November in 2011, I stopped doing surveys and casual unstructured interaction with the Gonds. After six months, I marked the households I would be immersing myself in on a regular basis. As I had to spend long hours with each family, it was important that I chose families that were happy to adopt and accommodate me and were comfortable with sharing their livelihood practices with me. I had made my road map for the next six months based on these surveys and also sought informal permission from these families for carrying out my research agenda. The most challenging part of the fieldwork was getting any response from female members. There was a mild fear of speaking too much in front of the male members for women who were housed in joint families. Usha Bai and Kesar Bai, aged 40 approximately, had never left Mahalapur and so it was a very fascinating encounter between me and them. In every possible way, our social worlds of gender and work were so different. Even though they were young, they appeared to be older because of their everyday practice of labouring and fetching woods from the forests and leading a very routine life that for outsiders like myself can appear to be mundane. I realised how important it was for these women to practise this habituated lifestyle—it was necessary for them to keep their households running. I couldn't help but ask myself—what kept them going on a daily basis? How was I supposed to learn about gender, politics, contestations or their protestations and resistance against a suffocating kinship and patriarchy? My everyday life in terms of being a participant observer and a researcher became more and more challenging—both on a normative and on a deeper personal level, as I was made to question my own relatively privileged and comfortable life.

The Gonds in the village of Mahalapur are pushed into migration by combination of stringent forest laws and neglect and oversight of rural and tribal welfare by the rural administration and the total absence of rural credit for the poor. The absence of any rural credit factor has given way to "migrating economies" (Stark and Bloom 1985) in places like

Mahalapur with the brokers and labour contractors (*thekedaar*) fetching the labour from the village itself and the practice of bonding through advance payments and an acceptable level of exploitative conditions of working and waging.

The institutions of governance such as the state in India are often associated with welfare of the low-income groups. In rural India, the state does exactly that extends a lending hand in the form of housing, employment and education and those who are literate and available and aware of such schemes that manage to take full advantage of it to improve their and their families' living conditions. However, the low-income groups are not homogenous and have greater expectations from the state, especially in the times of economic hardship and uncertainty, especially if food security is their main threat with vulnerability being another one due to landlessness. Besides, not all vulnerable groups are at the same stage of economic hardship and vulnerability. The ability to manage and manoeuvre out of economic hardship is shaped by the wider political, agroecological and cultural context but also by the inner dynamics of the household agency shaped in terms of educational levels as well as their own perceptions of poverty that conflict with that of state's discourse. The state policies are plenty for the targeted poor to move out of poverty, but in Panna, the poor can access them only if they ask for them or can read them in this part of India where due to illiteracy, most of the state-led assistances remain dormant and unclaimed. Access to most of such social schemes assumes at least basic literacy and requires the poor to be around and to be aware of such schemes to fully take advantage of such welfare schemes. Similarly, the accounts of the Gonds' experience with the welfare state show the growing tension as they become aware that the state is weakened by the autocratic forest department. Anarchists draw upon the struggles of the indigenous populations and voices of the marginalised; as described later in this book, it is how they challenge the state in an anarchical sense in the form of disengagement and disenchantment. The practice of the politics of withdrawal from welfare state is also to be understood as a pure and genuine struggle against interruption of their cultural ways of depending on forest-based livelihoods. I will show how the Gonds' withdrawal from the welfare state is a reflection of an anarchist act seen as pure and genuine. As Robinson and Tormey (2012, p. 155) observe on the presence and hold of such anarchic causes such as non-engagement and withdrawal from the formalising government structures, "It reflects a distinct social logic, albeit one which, by very virtue of its cooperative basis, sharing of power and collective approach to organising social life, poses a threat to the hyper-real logic of global capitalism, with its relentless war against gift, cooperation and solidarity in the name of the commodification of the world." In this book, I will also show how such anarchic voices are articulated in the pure and genuine struggle of the indigenous populations, the Gonds, against the forest department as well as the weak welfare state in the form of various precarious forms of work. The monograph also shows how indigenous populations such as Gonds revive their own traditional forms of governance such as *panchnama*, a precapitalist form of justice and discipline. The practice of the politics of withdrawal from welfare state is also to be understood as a pure, anarchic and genuine struggle against interruption of their cultural ways of depending on forest-based livelihoods.

References

Ali, A. (2005). *Livelihood and Food Security in Rural Bangladesh: The Role of Social Capital*. Ph.D. Thesis, Wageningen University, the Netherlands, p. 203.

Baviskar, A. (1994). Fate of the Forest: Conservation and Tribal Rights. *Economic and Political Weekly*, 2493–2501.

Baviskar, A. (1998). Tribal Politics and Discourses of Environmentalism. *Contributions to Indian Sociology, 31*(2), 195–223.

Baviskar, A. (2008). Contract Killings: Silicosis Among Adivasi Migrant Workers. *Economic and Political Weekly, 43*(25), 8–10. Retrieved from http://www.jstor.org/stable/40277579.

Beteille, A. (1998). The Idea of Indigenous People. *Current Anthropology, 39*(2), 187–191.

Bhogal, R. K., Sundar, N., Singh, N. M., & Sarin, M. (2013). Devolution as a Threat to Democratic Decision Making in Forestry? Findings from Three States in India. In *Local Forest Management* (pp. 71–142). Routledge.

Bruner, E. M. (1997). Ethnography as Narrative. In L. P. Hinchman & S. Hinchman (Eds.), *Memory, Identity, Community: The Idea of Narrative in the Human Sciences* (pp. 264–280). Albany, NY: SUNY Press.

Bouchard, M. (2011). The State of the Study of the State in Anthropology. *Reviews in Anthropology, 40*(3), 183–209.

Childe, V. G. (1950). The Urban Revolution. *Town Planning Review, 21*(1), 3–17.

Drèze, J., & Sen, A. (2013). *An Uncertain Glory: India and Its Contradictions*. Princeton, NJ: Princeton University Press.

Gadgil, M., & Guha, R. (1989). State Forestry and Social Conflict in British India. *Past & Present*, (123), 141–177.

Katona-Apte, J. (1988). Coping Strategies of Destitute Women in Bangladesh. *Food and Nutrition Bulletin, 10*(3), 42–47.

Leach, M., Mearns, R., & Scoones, I. (1999). Environmental Entitlements: Dynamics and Institutions in Community-Based Natural Resource Management. *World Development, 27*(2), 225–247.
Mehta, B. H. (1984). *Gonds of the Central Indian Highlands, 1*. Concept Publishing Company.
Middleton, T. (2015). *The Demands of Recognition: State Anthropology and Ethnopolitics in Darjeeling*. Palo Alto: Stanford University Press.
Mosse, D., Gupta, S., Mehta, M., Shah, V., Rees, J. F., & Team, K. P. (2002). Brokered Livelihoods: Debt, Labour Migration and Development in Tribal Western India. *Journal of Development Studies, 38*(5), 59–88.
Niehof, A. (2004). The Significance of Diversification for Rural Livelihood Systems. *Food Policy, 29*(4), 321–338.
Patel, M. L. (1998). *Agrarian Transformation In Tribal India 1998*. India: M S Publishers.
Robinson, A., & Tormey, S. (2012). Beyond the State: Anthropology and 'Actually-Existing-Anarchism'. *Critique of Anthropology, 32*(2), 143–157.
Rangarajan, M. (2005). Fire in the Forest. *Economic and Political Weekly, 40*(47), (Commentary).
Scott, J. C. (2009). *The Art of not Being Governed: An Anarchist History of Upland Southeast Asia*. New Haven: Yale University Press.
Sen, A. (1999). *Development as Freedom*. New Delhi and Oxford: Oxford University Press.
Shah, A. (2010). *Shadows of the State: Indigenous Politics, Environmentalism and Insurgency in Jharkhand*. Durham: Duke University Press.
Sharma, A. (2005). *Tribes in Transition—A Study of Thakur Gonds*. New Delhi: Mittal Publications.
Singh, B. (2015). *Poverty and the Quest for Life: Spiritual and Material Striving in Rural India*. University of Chicago Press.
Srinivas, M. N. (1997). Practicing Social Anthropology in India. *Annual Review of Anthropology, 26*(1), 1–24.
Stark, O., & Bloom, D. E. (1985). The New Economics of Labor Migration. *The American Economic Review, 75*(2), 173–178.
Sundar, N. (2000). Unpacking the 'Joint'in Joint Forest Management. *Development and Change, 31*(1), 255–279.
von Fürer-Haimendorf, C. (1948). *The Raj Gonds of Adilabad, Book-1, Myths and Ritual*.
von Fürer-Haimendorf, C. (1982). *Tribes of India: The Struggle for Survival*. Berkeley: University of California Press.
von Fürer-Haimendorf, C., & von Fürer-Haimendorf, E. (1979). *The Gonds of Andhra Pradesh: Tradition and Change in an Indian Tribe*. Vikas Publishing House Private.
Wilk, R. R. (1991). *Household Ecology: Economic Change and Domestic Life Among the Kekchi Maya in Belize*. University of Arizona Press.

CHAPTER 2

Local History and the Postcolonial State: The Invisibility of Gonds

2.1 Introduction

In this chapter, I build the local regional history which shows how slowly the Sur Gonds were gradually transforming into wage labourers and became invisible to the state even though there are visible remnants of the Gondwana kingdom in the form of forts and historical accounts of their rule in the region and ancient Gondi scripts which are in possession with some educated and elite Raj Gonds in the region. This chapter shows the gradual process of how Sur Gonds became invisible in the region and how today they are leading a life of a wage labourer.

At the same time, I also discuss the social lives of other local people with whom Gonds coexist. Even though my research focuses on how the Gonds manage their livelihoods as a poor community, the condition of the other communities, like the Scheduled Castes (SCs) and the Other Backward Castes (OBCs), is not any better, including Muslims, Dhamis[1] and members of higher-caste Hindus. In fact, most people, including the higher castes, live in economic hardship. Many able-bodied young men from all communities, ethnicities and religions are unemployed and remain equally effected by the Tiger Reserve which hinders the growth of any industry the region. If they are not unemployed, it is because they are running traditional family occupations as ascribed by the Indian caste system such as tailoring, running a dairy business or any other

[1] Dhami is a sect of Hinduism which was discovered in Panna region.

© The Author(s) 2018
S. Yadav, *Precarious Labour and Informal Economy*,
https://doi.org/10.1007/978-3-319-77971-3_2

trade like barbers and cobblers. On the other hand, not all Gonds that I found in Panna were marginalised or poor. The Raj Gonds, the highest amongst the three types (Nand, Sur and Raj), were in fact seen driving modern vehicles, working in government jobs and banks and staying in modern homes. Most of the young leave the town to go to nearby bigger cities, like Bhopal, Indore or sometimes to cities' outside, such as Pune, Mumbai and Delhi. Migration as a source of livelihood is attractive not only to the Gonds but also to other locals of the town of Panna.

2.2 The District of Panna

The district of Panna is a "Zilla" (district), and Panna town is the Zilla/district headquarters. Panna district itself is comprised of five *Gram panchayats*: Ajaigarh, Gunour, Panna, Pawai and Shahnagar, in which there are 1048 villages and 6 towns. It is very easy to skip Panna district as it is sandwiched between two semi-industrial districts—Satna and Chhatarpur—as seen in the district map above. The temple of Khajuraho, a current UNESCO World Heritage site mentioned in the Kama Sutra, is located in the Chhatarpur district, roughly 40 km away from Panna. The contrast between Chhatarpur and Panna can be illustrated by the fact that a new International Airport is being built in Khajuraho where tourists can fly in directly instead of coming by train or by road via New Delhi. By contrast, Panna does not even have a railway station. Geographically, the whole of Panna district falls within the border area of Madhya Pradesh and Uttar Pradesh called the Bundelkhand Region. The name of the region signifies the "Bundela kingdom," referring to the (Rajasthani) Bundelas who ruled the area during the sixteenth and early seventeenth centuries. Social relations in Bundelkhand are still based on feudalism and its remains. *Thakurs* or zamindars and Brahmins dominate the traditional power structure. Trade and business is controlled by Banias and Jains. Panna is primarily famous for sandstone and limestone—and as the only place in India where diamonds are found. It is also a holy place for a sect of Hinduism, the Pranam[2] is, for whom it is the birthplace of their religion. There is a myth amongst its followers that their founder blessed Panna with diamonds. Panna is also a name of a type of diamond. The Pranamis, spread all over the world in places like Nepal, Burma and even in America, visit

---

[2] The followers of Dhami are called Pranamis.

the holy temple at different occasions throughout the year. The religion is an amalgamation of Hinduism, Islam, Christianity and Sikhism. A national park was created in 1977 under the active initiatives of the last Rajput King who was also the Member of the Legislative Assembly (MLA) for 15 years. Even now, he is still considered to be the richest man in Panna. The current rural administrative building known to the locals as *kachari* belonged to the Maharajah's family until independence. Even today, his three palaces are still taller than any new building in town. The Gonds have lost respect for Panna Maharaj as they think he has snatched their livelihoods after he founded the Panna National Park for Wildlife Conservation and later, the creation of the Tiger Reserve Project. The Gonds think that the Maharaj has cheated them and left them orphans as he gave away his forest lands to the government to make money out of tourism. The local townsmen in Panna too seem to not have any feeling of honour for the Maharaj and told me that even though he was an MLA for Panna district for 15 years, representing both Congress and BJP as per his own political interests, there is absolutely no sign of road safety neither is there a well-equipped hospital. The district looks in absolute neglect with an open sewage system, dumped trash littering the side of the road and no reliable means of transportation for the locals. General safety of women is in quandary, and there is a lack of hygienic conditions for toilets, not only in the villages, but also in the town area. The general hospital, called Panna Hospital, caters to only snake and scorpion bites and some other minor illnesses. Most of the locals go either to more prosperous districts nearby in Satna or Chhatarpur and, if need arises, further away to Bhopal or Jabalpur.

Panna district feels so steeped in history, with its strong rural architecture and practising the traditional Hindu way of life, that it seems like a setting for an Indian folk tale involving a *Rajah*, dacoits, diamonds and tigers. It is not surprising then to find out there are plans underway to convert the place into a major tourist destination. The district of Panna has religious and historical significance for the Hindus as it is mentioned in the Puranas, a sacred Hindu text. However, it is not referred to as Panna—it is instead named after a Goddess, Padmavati. The district included a much wider area in the past. The myth, according to the Indian epic of Ramayana, is that Ram, Lakshman and Sita (the young Indian prince, his brother and his wife) had rested here while they were in exile in Chitrakoot, which is a few kilometres from Panna. Even today, the locals believe that Lord Ram can be seen or felt there.

The story goes that the Indian prince was so hungry while travelling through the forests that he did not care that the wild berry fruit he ate from an "adivasi" woman had already been defiled by her as she served berries to make sure they were sweet enough for the prince. The woman's name is mentioned as Shabri. The Gonds believe that the adivasi woman mentioned in the epic was a Gond woman. There are also archaeological sites here that are of interest to religious Hindus. There is an archaeological museum in the town, but it appears to be poorly maintained. For the majority of the Hindus, Panna is considered to be the fifth *dham* (holy pilgrimage) after the four major ones—Badrinath, Dwarka, Puri and Rameswaram. However, Panna is not as popular as the other four *dhams*, mainly because the River Ganges, the holiest river for Hindus, passes through the other four, but not through Panna. The local administration in Panna is also desperately trying to promote the place as a Pavitra Nagri (Holy Place). The local Hindu deities for which it is considered sacred are known as Lord Jugal Kishore, his wife, Kesar, and his brother, Baldev. As a result, even those who sell eggs cannot do so during certain major Hindu festivals.

The town is also organised along caste and religious lines. Occupations like barbers, tailors, housemaids, trash collection and laundry services are still done by Scheduled Caste groups. The Hindu settlement areas are different to the Muslim ones. Hindu casteism is not actively practised in the region except on occasions such as marriages where caste identity can be of some importance. Hindu–Muslim tensions are always felt since their different festivals seem to be very close together throughout the year. Often the police have to come out on religious occasions in case of an outbreak of communal riots, and the young unemployed Hindu and Muslim men will get into petty quarrels with each other. Rivalries and gun violence between different mafias involved in illegal mining are also common. These people are often seen carrying guns in public spaces. There is also a gun shop in Panna.

The villages that I covered for the fieldwork were in Panna North and Panna South, where the Gonds are found to be mining or depending upon forest-based livelihoods. The villages inside the Tiger Reserve had been resettled in "denotified" land called Pokhra, a few kilometres away from Panna, and the villagers have been compensated based upon the size of their house as well as agricultural land that they must have owned. However, Panna Tiger Reserve does not have a buffer zone. A buffer zone is where human use of the forest is allowed but with limitation as it's considered eco-sensitive for conserving the habitat of the tiger.

2.3 Bundelkhand and Panna

Bundelkhand is an area made up of several districts in the north of Madhya Pradesh where the Bundela kingdom used to rule. The demand for creating a special state named Bundelkhand arose after the creation of Jharkhand and Chhattisgarh, and recently, the creation of Telangana in Andhra Pradesh has created more hopes for this state to be created. This includes the border of both Uttar Pradesh and Madhya Pradesh states Panna falls under this as the last Bundela kingdom was here. As a result, the history of Gonds is found only when one searches for Bundela history. The Gonds in this region have not been studied and researched as extensively as the Rajput history. The rationale of the people demanding this separate state is that they were once a prosperous region and now suffer from chronic poverty. They hope that a separate state will create a better administration and management of resources. However, some also say that the separation of Chhattisgarh from Madhya Pradesh has significantly reduced its economy as it was rich in minerals. Incidentally, just the same year that I left, the government had come out with a special package for the proposed Bundelkhand region for up to Rs. 2000 crore.

The Bundelkhand region is a Rajput-dominated region. In the Hindu caste hierarchy, the Rajputs are identified as the warrior community and are positioned after the priestly community—the Brahmins. Their cultural ways of life including marriage, social mobility, food consumption, conceptions of gender and family are distinctly different than the Gonds. A year in Panna allowed these differences to be compared. I could not escape observing the cultural ways of life of the locals in Panna town as well as observing the contrasts and seeing how the Gonds were being gradually influenced by the dominant Hindu ways of life. Additionally, the state treated the Gonds in Mahalapur village as Hindus while also considering them as Scheduled Tribes (STs). I found the assumption that the Gonds are Hindus to be contradictory, especially in the state's deployment of housing, education and employment schemes. By contrast, I noticed that Gond households were allowing their women to do unskilled labour, which is not so in other Hindu homes. In that sense, there is both accommodation and resistance towards the Hindu influence amongst the Gonds. The Gonds seem to find themselves slowly experiencing identity shifts as they are integrating with the dominant Hindu culture of the region.

Hinduisation is also reflected in the state's practices of development programmes. Bundelkhand is an area made up of several districts in the north of Madhya Pradesh where the Bundela kingdom used to rule. The demand for creating a special state named Bundelkhand arose after the creation of Jharkhand and Chhattisgarh, and recently, the creation of Telangana in Andhra Pradesh has raised hopes that this state will be created. These states were created in line with the recent trend in India to align ethnolinguistic identities of the marginalised population and their local cultural histories and to have more control over their resources and development. Bundelkhand covers the border of both Uttar Pradesh and Madhya Pradesh states. Panna falls under this as the last Bundela kingdom was here. As a result, the history of Gonds is found only when one searches for Bundela history. The Sur Gonds in this region have not been studied and researched as extensively as the Rajputs (Hindus) and *Thakur* Gonds (or Raj Gonds as they are referred to in Panna). The rationale of the people demanding this separate state is that their region, under the previous Rajput rulers, was once a prosperous region and now suffers from chronic poverty. The Hindus hope that a separate state will create a better administration and management of resources. However, some also say that the separation of Chhattisgarh from Madhya Pradesh has significantly reduced its economy, as it was rich in minerals, and such similar concerns might delay the creation of Bundelkhand as well, because the entire region is rich in minerals and Panna is the only district in the entire country where diamonds are found. Incidentally, the same year that I left, the government had come out with a special package for the proposed Bundelkhand region for up to Rs. 2000 (about 20 million GBP) and already many reports in the media have alleged that it has disappeared into the pockets of the corrupt bureaucracy (*Hindustan Times* 2013).

An alternative prospect of income is often the diamonds. Gonds and other people in Panna aspire to find a diamond but think it's a matter of fate and destiny. Setting up a diamond hunt can cost up to Rs. 50,000, including the cost of labour and water. It takes a month to dig a pit deep enough where diamonds could be found, this digging is done manually. The process involves digging a very deep pit, sifting the mud with water, drying and finally separating diamonds from the gravel. The locals have some idea of where the diamonds might be found based on old folk tales. For this, some people will pray to local deities to bless them to help them find one before they gamble with their fate. It's expensive to be in

Panna—all food-related products are expensive for an average man. Fruit consumption is found in a limited number of households, and milk is watered because the animals are not able to yield much and the milkman adds water to increase the quantity. Milk is essential for the local dominant Hindu culture. The conditions of the poorest in the town are not any different than that of the Gonds in the villages. A housemaid, who is a lower-caste Hindu, retired after working in the government's Public Works Department constructing roads for almost 40 years. She is now cleaning homes and washing utensils of higher-caste Hindus to meet her living expenses and continues to support her married, unemployed son who has married twice and has four children of his own. She is 70 and is illiterate. There are many able-bodied males like this in Panna who have no work and feel embarrassed to labour hard like the Gonds. However, poor women have no choice and will support such men by working as housemaids in higher-caste Hindu households. Unemployment is a major concern for most, both including the Gonds, the rich and the poor in the district. Mild practices of untouchability are still prevalent. The region is a vote bank for major political parties due to high illiteracy. Most of the media news is about the national government and some news from around the town, but, remarkably little news about the surrounding villages.

The everyday lives of the poor like the Gonds are a complete mystery to the town people. There is not a major hospital here in Panna town, the largest being at least 300 km away. Instead, people travel to nearby prosperous districts like Satna and Chhatarpur for extreme emergency cases. Everybody seems to be going about their way to make a living based on their social, educational and economic circumstances.

2.4 Webs of Tradition and Modernity in Panna

Even though Panna town is district headquarters of Panna district, the traditional way of life of the people still dominates. Change is taking place but at an extremely slow pace, despite successive political parties that have ruled the place since Panna district was created in 1950. The pace of change has slowed, especially since 1981, when the Panna National Park was created. The slow rate of change has left the city difficult to reach for people outside the district. Last year, there was a protest march against the local government, calling for them to at least build a railway station. However, all major infrastructural projects, like building a railway station or airport, require an No Objection Certificate (NOC) from the forest department, which is difficult to obtain. In Panna, people appear to be managing their livelihoods with whatever local resources are available which suit the rural way of life. At the same time, they are very aware of modern changes happening in the nearby districts of Chhatarpur and Satna. Even if the locals desire change, the forest laws can prevent them. That said, the forest laws apply even in some parts of Chhatarpur district, but the socio-economic consequence on the poor is not as immense as in Panna district. There is both a railway station as well as an airport in Chhatarpur as it is the location of the UNESCO World Heritage Monument of Indian erotic temple—the Khajuraho temple. According to local gossip, in the future, there are plans to "notify" the whole of the Panna district through the forest department—meaning forest laws will be applied even in the town areas. However, that will take a while because the process involves resettlement and compensation by the forest department. The town of Panna still bears most of the characteristics of traditional Hindu practices, for example their consumption needs, their habits of dress, commensality, customs, religious way of life and fasting—nearly 100% of inhabitants live vegetarian lifestyles. Indigenous forms of non-alcohol-based intoxication, like *paan* (betel nut leaf), *gutkha* (tobacco) and *beedi*, are consumed more than those which are imported from nearby cities.

Other signs of rural life in Panna town are the way women gather in temple compounds for *paaths* (devotional songs), or just local gossiping about outsiders, including myself. Running water is scarce and is available for only two hours daily. The young in the household will be seen queuing up every evening near the water pumps to fill buckets of water and loading them in their bicycles. Most of the houses are not equipped with taps—instead stored water is mostly used in houses. Water is collected for most, even in the town, from hand pumps or from wells. Some running water comes only two hours per day, and only those who can afford to have electricity for installing a water pump can afford to have water.

Life in the town is more difficult than life in the village because Mahalapur, and other villages where Gonds live, gets unlimited electricity and water supplied by the mining corporation which is in the vicinity of the forest where the Gonds live. Most of the needs of the households are met by local markets. All modern consumptions are imported here. Local people associate Panna in material values depending upon what is "imported" and what is "exported." According to them, Panna exports diamonds, stones, forest products and labour and imports modern education, television and the English language. Nobody reads English-language newspapers. There are a couple of newspaper agencies which can arrange to get an English newspaper, but it arrives the next day as they are transported from another city. Hindi is the language used for daily life. There are no signboards in English in the entire town of Panna. Even English speaking classes are advertised in Hindi. Except for those in government jobs, the majority of the town does not have a regular income source and, therefore, they work as labour contractors for the illegal mines under unfortunate circumstances. Commodification of life in Panna with limited sources of income makes life difficult for everyone in the region.

2.5 Caste and Ethnic Lines of Occupation

Few in Panna town are employed in government jobs. The majority of the townsmen, irrespective of their community, do not have a regular source of income. Therefore, they either find work as labour contractors for private stone quarries or join family retail businesses. The local business, jobs and economy are run along ethnic and religious lines. Most Hindus, except for the SCs, are in government jobs as well as diamond trading. The local businesses are still mostly practised by the traditional business classes, namely the Dhamis. The Dhamis are a modern Hindu sect. They identify themselves as Hindus with a higher social status akin to Brahmins, and thus, there is no caste-based hierarchy. They are strictly vegetarians and do not practise drinking alcohol. The Dhamis are found only in Panna.

The other trading communities are Banias, Jains and traditional Muslims. The main occupations for Muslims are butchering, repairing vehicles and modern appliances—in addition, some work as drivers—transporting people from Panna to Satna, the closest train station from Panna. There are no Muslim labourers or stone cutters as all Muslims reside in the town and are involved in occupations in the town. Most Muslims have sold their farms and have migrated to cities or towns.

Other businesses such as cobblers, hair salons, launderettes and tailors are run strictly along traditional and corresponding caste lines. All of the later occupation practitioners are from SCs. From their last names, both their caste and their corresponding ascribed occupation are easily discernible.

There is no, for instance, *Thakur* or Brahmin who will cut hair or stitch clothes. Household maids also belong to the SC community including manual scavengers and will never be invited into anybody's house because they deal directly with human excreta. The other businesses are fruit sellers, small convenience stores, many small beauty salons, small clothes shops, about 4–5 vegetarian restaurants and 3 major hotels to cater to the tourist population coming for pilgrimage or seeing a tiger. The only occupation which is common and open to all castes in Panna is more modern occupations that have opened up due to transportation. New occupations such as engine drivers and conductors of local buses carry people daily of Panna in and out of Panna.

Even though modern occupations of the state, like traffic policeman, were seen, there was never enough traffic to man most of the time. There were not even any traffic lights. However, there were modern SUVs. Cattle and people walked together on the road. I picked up some new vocabulary for certain kinds of dishes, references for Gods and social etiquette. After staying in the field for a year, there is no doubt that the livelihoods of the Gonds and other villagers in Panna town are under threat due to increasing control from the forest department which does not allow any formal industry to operate. The people fear that the forest department will continue to disapprove any projects that could generate employment for the locals as it would disturb the habitat of the tigers. Even though my research focuses on how the Gonds manage their livelihoods as a poor community, the condition of the other communities, like the SCs and the OBCs, is not any better, including Muslims, Dhamis and members of higher-caste Hindus. In fact, most people, including the higher castes, live in economic hardship. Many able-bodied young men are unemployed. If they are not, it is because they are running traditional family occupations like selling clothes, milk businesses or any other retail shop. On the other hand, not all Gonds that I found in Panna were marginalised or poor. The Raj Gonds, the highest amongst the three types, were in fact seen driving modern vehicles, working in government jobs and banks and staying in modern homes. Most of the young leave the town to go to nearby bigger cities, like Bhopal, Indore or sometimes to cities outside, such as Pune, Mumbai and Delhi. Migration as a source of livelihood is not only attractive to the Gonds but also to the locals of the town of Panna. The Gonds' work in Panna is mainly agricultural, whether cultivating their own plots or working as paid labourers. The stones (limestone and sandstone) provide livelihood sources for most of the poorest in the Panna town, including the Gonds. They are part of the unorganised economy, as well as the Mafia syndicate that is involved in illegal mining inside the forest. Even though migration is a long-term livelihood strategy for the Gonds in Panna, most of their immediate needs still continue to be met by the local economy, especially selling firewood which is the main source of food security. In addition, most Gonds do the following types of daily wage work: house-repairs, laying tiles, constructing new rooms in homes or redecorating houses. Through the rural employment scheme (National Rural Employment Guarantee card [NREGA]), the Gonds work in rural infrastructure, for example building wells, hand pumps and canals for their fields, and constructing roads and highways. However, such work is unreliable because jobs through NREGA are only available for three months a year at a rate of one per household which is never enough for the current household size of the Gond families, who are therefore forced to migrate. For the locals, the Gonds are known as "*majdoors*" (labourers) who work in surrounding stone mines and come to the town to sell firewood. Gonds are associated with low literacy, poverty, drinking and gambling; they don't save up money, and they have too many children and are wife beaters. There is also a perception that even though the Gonds are "*majboor*" (desperate lot), they have money because people are aware of the rate that the Gonds charge per day for their wages, which is about Rs. 150. A normal person in Panna also earns a similar amount and sometimes even less—the only difference being that Gonds do unskilled work while the average person either works as a labour contractor or runs a shop. Those Gonds who will break stones can make up to Rs. 250 a day and more if they undergo a contract with the stone mine owner. In a week, a *maistry* (a professional stone-cutter/slicer) can make up to Rs. 5000 at a time. This is the easiest way for most Gonds to raise money for their children's marriage expenses or to meet their debts. The Gonds work sporadically, in a staccato fashion. The labour contractors have a strict business relationship with the Gonds and will punish them if they do not work for the money that has been taken as advance before beginning the work. One stone mine owner, who often works with the Gonds, told me that the Gonds cannot be trusted because they take advance money and leave the work half done, and until they are chased around or beaten or abused verbally, the work does not get completed. He says that sometimes the Gonds will begin work in a new mine before completing mining in the older one and restart the cycle of taking advance money from the new mine owner and, again, leaving the work unfinished.

This shows how forest laws protecting animals are favoured over the forest rights act which continues to remain controversial when it comes to forest lands occupied by the indigenous/tribal populations of India. It is only since this year in August 2013 that the government replaced the Land Acquisition Act of 1894 under colonial times. The current bill is called "Land Acquisitions and Resettlement and Compensation Act 2013" source which will compensate those who are affected by industrialisation. However, this does not include land lost due to environmental and forest conservation reasons, and whether the old Land Acquisition Act of 1894 is still valid in such cases is still too new to discuss. The situation of the Gonds in relation to land continues to be uncertain and with illiteracy and poverty, their awareness of land ownership is becoming even more unpredictable and untenable as some of the Gonds who unfortunately couldn't avoid getting into debt and had to sell their land to rich and landed elites.

Panna town (pop ca 50,000) is the site of India's largest and only mechanised diamond mine, which is state-owned and managed by the NMDC. Also it is known as The Majhagawan diamond belt that covers about 1000 sq km and lies about 20 km from Panna town. Set up in the late 1960s, production went up 20 times in the first ten years of operation and was further upgraded in 2001—"but this is a minuscule amount in the global market. Further, less than a third of the diamonds in the Panna mines belong to the prized gem variety" (CSE 2008).

In 2005, the Supreme Court ordered the mine closed and it only reopened in 2009. Conditions of reopening included contributing 5% of its total capital cost towards afforestation (CSE 2008, p. 215). In May 2010, it was re-granted its licence to operate on forest land. Their current production capacity is at 84,000 carats of diamond.

The contribution of the NMDC mine to the local (or national) economy is not large. In 2003–2004, the Panna unit of NMDC made a profit of little over Rs. 3 crore on a turnover of around Rs. 36 crore; in the same year, India's export turnover from imported diamonds, after cutting and polishing, was around Rs. 40,000 crore (CSE 2008). The latest workforce figure is only 240 (although that is April 2009, before it returned to full strength; before the closure, it was ca 500 (CSE 2008). Shortly after reopening, the NMDC announced plans for major diamond prospecting in other parts of India; within a year, it announced it was suspending exploration projects.

2.6 The Gonds in Panna District

The Gonds comprise of the highest tribal group in the district of Panna.[3] Panna was originally a Gond settlement up to the thirteenth century. Map of India showing Madhya Pradesh in Pink and Panna district in black.

The Gonds in the region of Panna are indigenous settlers (Imperial Gazetteer of India 1908),[4] and they coexist with other communities, like the SCs and OBCs, but the Gonds are the majority in these villages. There is not much of a difference in their income profile or even in their religious and social customs, as all of them are Hindus. The significant difference in village where SCs and STs live together is that they do not intermarry. The Gonds in my fieldwork site Mahalapur are all Sur Gonds. The differences between the groups are mythological and socio-economic status. In the Gond myth, the Raj Gonds descend from the elder sister and the Sur and Nand Gonds descend from the younger sister. The Raj Gonds are wealthier, possess more land and are economically better off than Sur and Nand Gonds. Unlike the Sur and Nand Gonds, the Raj Gonds do not use "Gond" or "adivasi" in their last name. They signal their landedness and literate position by using "Singh" (lion) the title that was bestowed on them by the local Bundela kings for helping them in the fight against the Mughals as per local oral history.[5] The idea of social mobility amongst the Raj Gonds is described as "sanskritisation" (Srinivas 1980) or to become like Hindus and to choose Hindu names. This practice has begun since a generation ago. Being a Hindu also means that the Raj Gonds have moved away from their "forest" roots and have joined the "*samaj*" (society) for progressive reasons. Progress is associated with cultural and economic transformation, and women are a centre of such transformations as their mobilities and their bodies becoming spaces and symbols of transformation. Moving out of

---

[3] http://panna.nic.in/history.html.

[4] I was lucky to get a copy of this in Panna town. A local *Thakur*, the only one who spoke in English, was also interested in the history of Bundelkhand, and he shared this with me.

[5] The Gonds in the past had allied with the Rajputs to strategically defeat the Mughals, but these alliances did not trickle down to the whole Gonds community. In fact, the Rajputisation and Hinduisation led to the creation of caste system within the Gonds as the Rajputs would reward those Gonds who helped them to defeat the Mughals. These divisions have solidified in postcolonial times due increasing monetisation of life in the region.

their courtyard is regulated, and their outfits become more "modest" in front of elderly men of the household.

The Sur Gonds of Mahalapur are also "Rajputised" in their social outlook and appearance as I show in the chapter on Family and Kinship. "Rajputised" is not much different from being "Sanskritised" with a major difference that Rajput culture is also influenced by Mughals as they had to fight and also align with them in most of north-west and Central India. "Sanskritised" cultures will have very limited Mughal influence as is seen in Southern India where women do not veil or headscarf even on their wedding days which is strongly practised in north India. The old Gond names based on nature, animals, seasons and trees are being replaced by Sanskrit names. Along with partial forms of "sanskritisation," there is also partial "Rajputisation" in the form of women being veiled in front of other male members of the household. This is unlike a generation ago when Gond parents would name their children based on nature, season of birth, animals, plants and trees. These transformations are partial because the Sur Gonds cannot afford to allow their women to not contribute towards household income unlike in the Raj Gonds and other Hindu communities where women do not labour or go to forests to fetch woods. In the context of studying Gonds as a tribal community different than the mainstream Hindu caste order, I suggest we use the concept of Rajputisation which is not the same as Sanskritisation as defined by Srinivas (1980). Sanskritisation, explains as defined by Srinivas, is sparse in its discussion of gender, class and education. It refers to Dalit communities, and its mechanics is similar to what David Mandelbaum (1970) has described about Hindus as becoming "westernized" mostly through the route of education. Sanskritisation is still of those who are already Hindus but belonging to the lower castes which is not the case for the Gonds because historically they are not part of the caste system as *adivasis* or indigenous settlers.

Bundelkhand region is a Rajput-dominated region. The various rural schemes too assume that the Gonds are Rajputs, although this is not the case as almost all Gond households allow their women to do unskilled labour work which is not so in other Rajput homes. In that sense, there is both accommodation and resistance towards the Rajput influence amongst the Gonds. The Gonds seem to find themselves slowly experiencing shifts in their identities as they are integrating with the dominant Rajput culture of the region referred to as Rajputisation of their culture. This Rajputisation is also reflected in the state's practices of development schemes how and the cultural ideology of kinship and gender. The Gonds have started to adopt Rajput-influenced names for their children, headscarfing and veiling of women, Rajput-style weddings, and their modern aspirations for consumption style is also similar to the surrounding Rajput community, for example the expensive weddings and the cost of an orchestra which was absent a generation ago. In fact, for the young generation, their elderly generation now seems to be backward and illiterate which coincides with the dominant discourse about the Gonds in the region. The younger generation are aware about their histories of exploitation, and they resist this by becoming financially independent too often at the cost of not finishing education.

Even though the Gonds in the region of Panna are indigenous settlers, they coexist with other communities, like the SCs and OBCs, but the Gonds are the majority in these villages. There is not much of a difference in their income profile or even in their religious and social customs, as all of them are Hindus. The only significant social norm followed in a village where SCs and STs live together is that they do not intermarry.

The major ST group in the district is the Gond. The Gonds are titled as "Scheduled Tribes," and they are not directly linked into the hierarchical Hindu caste-based society. After independence, they have been grouped into the same social category as SCs and OBCs. They are popularly known as "*adivasis*," meaning those who reside in the forests. It is not clear if they are below or above the untouchable or the polluting caste, because there is not much history of their direct contact with the higher-caste Hindus for whom purity and impurity matter. For the majority of the population, who are Hindus, the Gonds share the same social status as the Muslims. Also, like the Muslims, the Gonds can eat meat which the majority of the population in Panna does not, including eggs.

There are three kinds of Gonds found in Panna: Raj Gonds, Sur Gond and Nand Gond. The Gonds where I did my fieldwork, Mahalapur, are all Sur Gonds. The differences between the groups are based on socio-economic status, the Raj Gonds, being wealthier, possessing more land and being economically better off than Sur and Nand Gonds. Raj Gonds also tend to not use Gond as their last name. The Raj Gonds are also more literate than other Gonds and have acquired a higher social status, because their ancestors had helped the Rajputs in their fight against the Muslims about couple of centuries ago. The idea of social mobility amongst them is what Srinivas (1980) describes "sanskritisation" or to become like Hindus and to choose Hindu names for their children. Along with "sanskritisation," there is also "rajputisation" in the form of women being veiled in front of other male members of the household. This is unlike in the past where Gond parents would name their children based on nature, season of birth, animals, plants and trees.

Even as the Gonds have been reduced to their current poor and neglected state, I have found them to have lot of pride in their ability to labour hard despite harsh working conditions, including spending time away from their beloved families. My fieldwork has revealed that the Gonds avoid being dependent and want to be self-reliant as much as possible. This also includes refusing help for free from their own close relations, unless they are really desperate, as this reduces their social status. Maintaining their reputations is important socially, and they look favourably on people who work hard as a prerequisite for social advancement.

2.6.1 The Fall of the Gonds and the Rise of the Rajputs in Bundelkhand

The Bundelkhand region, a historical and cultural association for the people of Panna, has witnessed both Mughal invasion and British rule, with the last King of Bundelkhand ending as a British pensioner. Varied online and vernacular sources on Gondwana kingdom in Central India exist. Scholars have documented the kingdom of Gondwana in Central India. According to the Jhansi district gazetteer report, the region where Panna falls is also known as Bundelkhand region. "Bundela" comes from the name of a Rajput King called Bundela. Before the Rajputs in Panna or the region of Bundelkhand, which is how the locals refer to the region covering the borders of MP and UP in the map above, the Gonds were the rulers and their capital was named as Garh-Mandla. However, the major Gondwana kingdom, of which Panna is also a part, fell victim to the Mughal rules. Prior to that, the Gond King, Dalpat Shah, in this region won the marriage of Rani Durgavati, a Rajput princess, by defeating her father in a fight. During her reign, she had to fight against the Mughal emperor Akbar.

The story goes that when Dalpat Shah died, Akbar sent a proposal to marry her and to subsequently annex Bundelkhand. However, she refused the offer and decided instead to fight, which she lost. She eventually decided to kill herself and her small boy, rather than surrender to the Mughals. However, the Mughal rule too came to an end when the Bundela Prince, Chhatrasal, a Rajput working as an army chief for the Mughals, turned against them by aligning with the Maratha dynasty (under Shivaji) from Maharashtra. Eventually, Bundelkhand region came under the Maratha dynasty, and infighting amongst them along with seeking help from the British to defeat each other led the British to finally bring Bundelkhand under their British rule. Under the British, the region of Bundelkhand experienced unfair taxation and land revenue systems. However, soil and climatic conditions were unknown to the British who did not compromise the land tax imposed on the peasants and marginal subsistence farmers. Under the British, the forests in Central India used for laying railway lines in India were causing environmental damage. The tenancy practice under the British in Bundelkhand reduced the region to bankruptcy. When there was resistance against commercial logging of the forest, the British categorised the rebels under Criminal Tribal Act.

2.7 Collective Memory and Oral History of the Past Before the State

In the collective memory of the Sur Gonds, the place was under the rule of the Rajput *Rajah* and the land and forest were part of his estate. The *Rajah* later sold this to the postcolonial state and reduced the Gonds to pauperisation or "orphans." The Gonds also concede that they never owned the forests, and the ideologies of forest-ownership are missing. The oldest person, known to them as *dabloodukariya* (an obese old woman), was about 102 years when she died. The Gonds say that she settled this village and the Gonds inside the forest. According to the oral histories, the Gonds were brought by the Rajputs, the Bundelas, to work for them. Historical documents suggest that the Gonds were originally bought from the Garh-Mandla, a region not too far from Mandla which used to be part of the Gondwana Rajan the state of Madhya Pradesh. However, memories of the Gondwana kingdom are now forgotten. Only the Raj Gonds have the living narratives of their ruling past. The way the Gonds of Mahalapur connect their relationship to the forests is through how they are forest-dependent for firewood, stones, *Mahuwa* and *amla* (Indian Gooseberry).

The documented histories of the Gonds in Bundelkhand do not mention hierarchies within the Gonds. If the Gonds were once rulers before the Bundelas, I found no evidence of this from my interactions with the Sur Gonds of Mahalapur as compared to my interactions with the Raj Gonds. Jagat Singh is a Raj Gond who is literate, with a job in Panna town. He showed me documentation of the Gondwana kingdom and how the society had its own alphabet, language, numerical system, coins and vocabularies used for agricultural purposes. He wanted to contradict the claims of Elwin Verrier, one of the first missionaries to conduct early studies of tribes of India. Elwin Verrier (Guha 1996) was also the first European anthropologist to study tribes in India. Later, Verrier became an Indian citizen and was the first Minister of Tribal Affairs under former Prime Minister Jawaharlal Nehru. According to Jagat Singh, Verrier did a disservice to the Gonds by assuming that the Gonds were fond of living in small hutments and were originally forest dwellers. He said:

> Looking at my own living condition, can anyone say that Gonds like me like to live on trees and mud huts?

According to Jagat Singh, in the past, the Gonds were forced to retreat towards the forest when they felt threatened by outsiders and invaders—the Mughals and later the Bandits under the Bundelas (the last ruling Rajput Kings)—and sought to protect their women from being molested or kidnapped. This contrasts with what is documented about the Gonds as being natural forest dwellers. Important funeral rituals performed cannot be completed without involving the forest deities. Jagat Singh is planning on taking up the issue of Gond heritage for his political ambitions in the future. He keeps in touch with these villages because there are so many Gonds there. He came to Mahalapur about few months ago and told them about the Gondwana ancestry and kingdom. He told them about how the Hindu deity—Ram—had destroyed the Gonds who are the descendants of Ravana—mentioned as a monster in the Indian epic of Ramayana. Kotram says, "Our most sacred gods are not idols like Ram and Krishna but it's in the form of nature like water and sun." The Gonds originally never accepted human-borne deities like Ram.

Considering this, it is very difficult to accept the current exclusion of the Gonds from the forests and to accept that they are one of the perpetrators in the loss of tigers. Through oral histories, one gets a full picture of how Gonds were not only knowledgeable about forests, but also revered the forests, as it comprised a salient aspect of their cultural ideology and their identity as forest dwellers. The Gonds remember days of eating game meat hunted from the forest, but that was on a very small scale. Even today, the Gonds of Mahalapur will not dress in red when they go to the forests as it is considered offensive to the forest deities as it's their colour of power. However, the current forest management discourse and tiger conservation overlook the indigenous knowledge that Gonds possess about the forests and instead treat it as a hindrance to their ambitious project of protection of the forest rather than to work together with the Gonds in jointly managing the forests. The older generation of the Sur Gonds recall the days of unrestricted access to forests under the *Rajah*'s rule. When I wanted to know about the Sur Gonds prior to 1947, they would say that the right person to tell me was the oldest person, known to them as *dabloodukariya* (an obese old woman), who was over 100 years old. Unfortunately, she had died a couple of years before I arrived in 2011. The Gonds say that she and her husband, with their extended families, were the oldest settlers of Mahalapur and the Gonds inside the forest. According to them, the Gonds were brought from outside of Panna district by the Bundelas to work for them. The Gonds of Mahalapur connect their relationship to the forests in terms of a dependency on the forest for firewood, stones, *mahua* and *amla*. This shows how identities of the past are used to create strategic positions with respect to their social status in present times. In the past, the Gonds worked in artisanal manual stone quarries for the kings and obtained a portion of grain from the *Rajah* in return. In those days, there were only three or more households in the village of Mahalapur, which was surrounded by heavy forests. The oral histories of the Gonds show the politics of documentation—what gets documented and what does not, and whose histories are represented by whom and for what. The formal documented history of the Gonds is that of the Raj Gonds and how they ruled the region until they were defeated by the Rajput in the thirteenth century. This hierarchy of the Gonds, with the Raj Gonds being higher than the Sur Gonds of Mahalapur, which was historically based on the birth order of their mythical ancestors, has now morphed into a socio-economic hierarchy. The Raj Gonds are financially better off, as they have become landed elites, enjoying the same social status as the landed elites of other communities, contrasting severely with the Sur Gonds, who are the poorest and mostly landless. The Sur Gonds, as poor people, could not afford to focus on the politics of creating a past when they had urgent, real current needs. All that interested them was complaining and blaming the forest department for snatching a source of livelihood and reducing them to their current plight. In that sense, the past matters to the Gonds as there were no forest restrictions then. I shifted my attention to the past that mattered to them. Ethnographic writing entails the mission of writing about the people first (Biehl and Petryna 2013). Ethnographers often argue that order should emerge from the field rather than be imposed on the field (Silverman 1985). I found that for the Gonds, memories of the past were about how there was an unlimited access to the forests and about an abundance of flowers, animals and fruits. However, bondage and dependency to the local *Rajahs* were also found in these narratives. Below, I discuss four such narratives: three are from Sur Gonds and one from a Raj Gond.

Bhola Lal, one of the oldest Gonds in Mahalapur, is totally paralysed and bedridden for the last 40 years and is without his left palm. He lost it during the mining about few kilometres away from Mahalapur. This was before marriage. He had four daughters and two sons. All the daughters are married. He went into debt with his close relatives to come up with the expenses for the marriage. They cannot recall the amount of the debt, but she says that they haven't finished repaying it. His wife says, "*Main apna pet katkar bhar dongi*" (I will repay by eating less).

He recollects a lot of things about Mahalapur Village. Before, when the *Gram* (village meeting) was held in Mahalapur village, there were no concrete roads. He has worked for one *anna* (1/100th of 1 rupee), two *anna* and twenty-five *paise*. He says how valuable those *paisas* used to be unlike today, where even one lakh rupees is not enough!

He says that in the past, Panna was the centre of the local market of grains and wheat. At that time, rationing (controlled distribution of essential grains and kerosene or Public Distribution System of food) was not present. The concept of rationing basic/staple food started only when the *panchayat* institution was introduced in the 1980s.

Previously, he says, almost all the Gonds were only practising a subsistence economy and everyone had a bullock. The subsistence activities were organised around "bullock economy," where hallowing of the land was done by bullocks as the yield was meant for self-consumption. Also, a bullock signals speed with which people engaged with trade and the markets in those days. Nowadays, the Gonds hire tractors for cultivation, and there are more options to earn a livelihood besides practising subsistence economy.

Although he personally never experienced bondage (*Begari pratha*), he says that bondage was in the form of accompanying the royal ministers and officials who were travelling from one village to another through the forest. Those were the days when there were no buses. The only way to walk from one village to another village was to trek or bullock carts especially in the forested area. The Gonds as chaperon would walk from dawn until dusk. The Gonds were forced to accompany them and walk miles from one village to another against their wish.

I asked why they were required to escort these officials. He says:

> Because the ministers had to cross a large chunk of forested and unknown areas and they wanted someone to protect against wild animals. In the past, the forest was plentiful and abundant with animals and flowers. In those days, there were not so many forest officers and guards in the forest, and the forest was still well conserved and protected. And today, look at the condition, they have at least one dozen forest guards (Barakha) but still the forest is being destroyed every day. This as the age of doomsday (kalyug).

I was interested to know if he could tell me about how the Tiger Reserve was formed. Bhola Lal says that the land which is now the Tiger Reserve was originally the property of the local prince who then later sold it to some foreigners who converted it into a national park for wildlife. This park was later declared as a Tiger Reserve by the Central Government. Bhola Lal thinks that the past was more secured than the present because it was so easy to access and live with the forests. The diamonds, the stones, the flowers, all were easily available and they could enter the forest unrestricted.

Bhola Lal recalls that the value of today's hundred rupees is equivalent to the value of Rs. 5 of his time. Earlier, they were working in the mines, and the labour contractors would come to fetch them for mining. In those days, they were not paid in cash but in terms of conches (shells). Bhola Lal worries about the future of the Gond society. "I wonder how it would be in the future. In the past, it was so nice when they had unrestrained access to the forest. Now, with so many rules and regulations, how are we going to survive?"

These kind of romanticisation of the past are important as partial truths. As Gardner observes amongst narratives by elderly Bangladeshi migrants in London,

> The narratives of the elders are not coherent wholes or necessarily wholly 'true'. Frequently ambiguous, they are filled with silences, illusive references and contradictions. Indeed, we would probably be misguided if we assumed that oral histories ever produce coherent or objective accounts of the past. Instead, it may be more useful to think of them as myths. This does not necessarily mean they are false, for the unconscious shaping of life stories does not jettison the truth, but rather, involves a recognition that memory is inherently revisionist; what is forgotten may be as important as what is remembered. (1999, p. 65)

Jagdish, another senior Gond who seems to be in his 60s, also recalls how, in the earlier days, the wages were calculated based on the number of shells. One shell would represent one task completed, and its value would be very little, and they were paid in grains. However, that was never enough, as Hari Ram, another Gond around in his 40s, recalls how many Gonds were dying because of starvation. According to Jagdish, the people from this village have been migrating only in the last 5 years. He says that migrating for livelihood and labouring amongst only started in the last 5 years when the roads were along the constructed outside of their village to connect other neighbouring districts.

Jagdish's family is one of the original settlers in the village of Mahalapur. At that time, there was only his family who almost started the village life. Now, there are about 5 generations in the village. He knows a lot about the *panchayat* because it was conceived in front of him. He recalls that unlike now, in the past they grew jowar and bajra, forms of millet, as against today where they grow wheat. However, now they have stopped cultivating millets as it requires a lot of water which is scarce these days. He is concerned that today, the Gonds living beyond 40–45 because of TB and heavy intoxication. He is suffering TB himself. He does not know how he got it. He has been on medication for the last 3 months and so he has a lot of relief. He thinks that he got it from others. The medication is free. According to him, half of the village is suffering from TB (approximately 100 households).

He recalls that when the government diamond mining company, National Mineral Development Corporation (NMDC), opened in the late 1950s, they were first offered jobs. But none of them wanted to work there as they thought that they will undergo bondage. He is also very upset by the current state of the forests nowadays. He says that his son was once caught by the forest department for casually hanging around in the forest.

Kishore Singh, a Raj Gond, is 69 years old. He has retired about 7 years ago from Panna Administration Office as a peon. I asked him about what was the economic and livelihood of the Gonds during the *Rajah*'s time. He mentioned that he does not remember very well, but he knows there was the "Begari Pratha" (forced labour system in India). In the past, all the land of Panna or the estate belonged to the King, especially the land where the tribal population lived in the Panna block of Panna district. All Gonds in the Panna block were landless and had to work for the King. Under the Begari system, the Gonds had to carry loads on their head. These loads could be anything that the *Rajah* wanted to be carried, and their labour would be unpaid! He said that in this system, there was no flexibility and they were forced to escort the Maharajah whenever he wanted their service.

During the Maharaja's days, Mandal, another very old Gond, around in his 80's, says that he was part of the Begari system where they had to carry heavy loads of the *Rajahs* and the landlords without being paid. They would be beaten if they refused to do the work of the Maharajah. Sometimes, the Gonds under the Begari system would have to go hunting, against their wishes with the *Rajah* because of their knowledge of the forests. Mandal has also seen *goras* (Europeans) during his time that would normally stay in the forest going on a tiger-hunting trip with the Maharajah.

Previously, there was also untouchability. The tribal communities and other lower-caste people would place their shoes on their foreheads if a man of a higher caste was nearby. In the past, the *Rajah* had not put any limit to how much of wood can be chopped. There were no forest laws in those days as there is today. Mandal said the system was a tumultuous moment of his life.

Nowadays, he only receives a senior citizen's pension of Rs. 275 every three months! It was supposed to be monthly, but nowadays it comes less frequently. Presently, he does nothing for livelihood and is completely dependent on his neighbours for food and everyday needs.

The Gonds' history is not coherent in the memories of the Gonds. The Raj Gonds will have a different Gond history than the Sur Gonds. The Sur Gonds of Mahalapur have no memories of the Gondwana kingdom unlike the Raj Gonds—like Jagat Singh, a Raj Gond and literate with a job in Panna town. When I met him, I was shown some documentation of the Gondwana kingdom and how the society had its own alphabets, language, numerical system, coins and terminologies for agricultural purposes. He does not agree with the social correction measurement that was proposed by Dr. Ambedkar and said there must be some other alternative. There was also mention of Elwin Verrier. According to Jagat Singh, Verrier did a disservice to Gonds by assuming that Gonds are fond of living in mud huts. He said that looking at his own dwelling can anyone say that Gonds like to live on trees and mud huts. According to Jagat Singh, in the past, the Gonds were forced to head towards the forest as they felt threatened by outsiders and the invaders.

On the other hand, speaking to Sur Gonds, the narratives of the past are all about bondage and subjugation under the Maharajah. From the narratives of Bhola Lal, Jagdish and Mandal, one gets an image of the Gond society that was always under some ruler. In my section on reflection, I show the different styles of narration that I recorded. The older Gonds' styles of narration and memories are embedded in a different spatial and temporal context, and recollecting them in contemporary times means to put together many individual and personal narratives. The narratives of Jagat Singh, a Raj Gond, are that pride of being a Gond which is different than the "sons of soil" pride as seen in the Sur Gonds. The Sur Gonds' attachment to soil is stronger as they are still practising subsistence farming for survival while the Raj Gonds are now mostly educated and have formal jobs and regular source of income.

The Sur Gonds might have "forgotten" about the Gondwana kingdom, but that also implies that they have unconsciously chosen not to remember some deep-seated memories which are more personal and can affect more strongly than the political and historical significance of it. Their relationship with the Gondwana is personal in some way because in their myths, the Raj Gonds are descended from the elder sister and the Sur Gonds of the younger one. Somehow, they feel betrayed by then

Raj Gonds who got closer to the Hindu elites and benefited the most from the state social schemes.

From the interactions with Sur and Raj Gonds, it appears that the Sur Gonds preferred the times after the independence which they refer to as "Indira Raj," after the late Indian prime minister, Indira Gandhi, who abolished the Bondage system as well as removed all previous debts that the Sur Gonds owed to the money lenders until that time. This shows that the Sur Gonds' everyday lives in the past were around bondage to other higher-caste Raj Gonds and *Thakurs*. Some of the Raj Gonds also maintain that the *Thakurs* (the Bundelas) never wanted the Gonds to progress and would always send bandits to loot their villages due to which the Gonds had to escape to the forests to protect their wives and children and their personal valuables. The younger Sur Gonds in Mahalapur seem to view their past as a life of simplicity, minimalism and lack of literacy. For them, the fact that they once ruled Panna has not much meaning. Says Kotram, "We don't know much about our history and heritage. Wished we knew then we could claim our rights. Our ancestors were very simple and docile people. It is in our nature to get carried away by sweet talks of Brahmins and other higher communities. Some of us in the past have given our lands willingly. Our ancestors would easily trust the educated and the royal families."

Upon learning that I was originally from Mumbai, some of the younger Gonds were very curious to know about metropolitan city lives like Mumbai and were in awe with Bollywood. They would ask me questions if I have seen any film stars and what I can tell them about the life in big cities. They will ask "Can you please tell us about your big city life? What can we see? Buildings, Filmcity. Is there an ocean? We have only seen it on television. Have you seen our river?" says Manoj. Kotram wants to know whether there are real Dons in Mumbai like they show in the movies and if there is an underworld and how does it function and why does it exist in a city. Both Manoj and Kotram are from the younger adult generation of Gonds.

2.8 Pauperisation, Slow Change and Gradual Invisibility of the Gonds

Pauperisation amongst the Gonds is taking place despite being a landed community as slowly all the sources of income and livelihood are disappearing around the mines, forcing the Gonds to migrate or else they would starve as they would not have resources to buy raw materials for agriculture. Gonds, although not recently, have been experiencing poverty.

But, it was not without resistance in the form of dacoit groups in Central India. These dacoits arose out of social injustices like caste system and would often target *Thakurs* or dau communities and were mostly Robin Hoods of their days, but some of them would misuse the power of inflicting the terror on the villages.

Later, under the colonial times, Bundelkhand soil and climatic conditions were unknown to the British who did not compromise upon imposing tax on the peasants and subsistence farmers. Also, a lot of forest from Central India was used for laying railway lines in India causing environmental damage. The tenancy practice under the British in Bundelkhand reduced the region to bankruptcy. When there was a resistance against commercial logging of the forest, the British categorised the Bundelkhand people as there. As many scholars (Nigam 1990; Major 1999; Tolen 1991; Kennedy 1985) have pointed out, many north Indian states were placed under criminal class by the British because of resistance and those same regions continue to be marred with poverty, famine, drought, low-agricultural productivity, strong traditional social customs and high rural population even today.

To understand the pauperisation of the Gonds in Panna, one has to understand the overall poverty in the state of Madhya Pradesh which is considered to be very poor in comparison with other states in the country. That said, the region is much cleaner, greener and more spacious than other Indian states. The air in Panna is clean because there are no industries or factories. The controlled operation of the mines by the forest department too has reduced pollution. There are quite a few government and private run holiday homes as well as lodges for tourists who come to see tigers.

The state is the main source of change in the Panna district region, and the prejudices and stereotypes that the majority of the population has against tribal population are also reflected in rural administration. For instance, the local officials label the Gonds as unclean, "dehati" (rural), "*majboors*" [desperate], "drunkards" and "gamblers." These terms are frequently used to refer to them as being inferior to the rest of the non-tribal population. Another way they are made to feel unequal with the non-tribal population is by their social status of ST (Scheduled Tribe).

In my initial days of village surveys, I interacted with the Gonds from other villages who told me that there are political leaders who pay them Rs. 1000 to vote for them. However, the benefits of being elected soon become a fiction once the leader comes into power and forgets them until next election when a new leader appears and repeats the same cycle. This appears to be the reason that the Gonds have lost trust in the state and are keen to be more self-reliant, depending only on their ability to labour. The local village *panchayat* is also politically interested in helping the Gonds in issuing their BPL and NREGA card. If the Gonds elect the opposition party member to power, then it's unlikely the *panchayat* leader will help them to issue or renew new social benefit cards. The land in the region constantly appears to be in conflict between the forest department and the Land Revenue Department which is under the Rural Administration. The former wants the land clear of humans, whereas the land revenue wants to build a school, a hospital, or build a water-hand pump for the villagers. It was only about 15 years ago that Gonds started experiencing any kind of formal schooling with paid teachers and a concrete school building.

2.9 THE SOCIAL HIERARCHY AMONGST THE GONDS AND WITH OTHER COMMUNITIES

In terms of social hierarchy, the Raj Gonds are socio-economically better off than the Sur Gonds of Mahalapur. Says Aditya, "the Raj Gonds abuse the reservation system. We are the real marginalized people and not them. They instead are going ahead by taking advantage of the ST quota when actually it's meant for real poor people like us." On the other hand, the Raj Gonds have a living memory of how they once used to rule the region, even before the Bundelas and how they are now reduced to serving the Bundelas. The Mandalisation in the early '1990's (a political process which bought reservations in jobs and education for the marginalised populations—STs, SCs and OBCs) has bought benefits for Raj Gonds to access jobs and education. However, this has to be taken with a pinch of salt because on the one hand the Raj Gonds have been reduced to the same social status as Sur and Nand Gonds and on the other hand, the Sur Gonds think it's not justified that the Raj

Gonds should seek ST reservation quota because they are already better off like upper-caste Hindus. The other communities, the *Bengalis*, Yadavs and other SCs, are also poor like the Gonds and have the BPL cards, but there is still a significant difference in the perception of poverty. For instance, it is forbidden for women to work for the household unless they are formally educated and seek jobs as teachers which is the only option for most employed people in the district. The women from these communities never go to the forests to collect wood or even sell it. The roles of the women from these communities are confined to household chores even if they are very poor, and it is mostly Gond women who work in the farms of these communities alongside the men of these communities. These communities refer to the Gonds as being "majboor" (a distressed lot). My interactions with the Raj Gonds show the dichotomy the Raj Gonds created to delineate themselves from being a poor marginalised community like the Sur Gonds of Mahalapur while shared the ST status to access the various social benefits aimed at STs. The Raj Gonds identify themselves more with the dominant Hindu community for social mobility as they want to assert that they have moved away from their "forest" roots and are now "civilised." As a result, being adivasi has come to mean as being "uncivilised." The social and symbolic meanings of gender with respect to access to different livelihoods and intra-household relations are themes that the book addresses in its later sections. I show how newer economic opportunities for the Gond households influence the gender and kinship relations, as Gond women earn equally as men. Women's movement out of the confines of the courtyard is regulated, and their outfits become more "modest" in the presence of the elderly men of the household, Sur Gonds of Mahalapur which the older generation Gond women had not experienced before. The Gonds coexist with other communities, such as the SCs and OBCs. There is not much of a difference in their income profile or even in their religious and social customs, as all of them are Hindus. The significant difference in villages where SCs and STs live together is that they do not intermarry. The Gonds of Mahalapur are all Sur Gonds, and they will marry with other Sur Gonds. The differences between the groups are mythological and socio-economic status. In the Gond myth according to oral accounts, the Raj Gonds descend from the elder sister and the Sur and Nand Gonds descend from the younger sister. The Raj Gonds are wealthier, possess more land and are economically better off than Sur and Nand Gonds.

Unlike the Sur and Nand Gonds, the Raj Gonds do not use "Gond" or "adivasi" in their last name. They signal their landedness and literate position by using "Singh" (lion), the title that was bestowed on them by the local Bundela kings for helping them in the fight against the Mughals, as per local oral history.

2.10 Gonds and Mining

According to the Center for Environmental Studies (CSE) report titled («Rich Land, Poor People»), MP "has 335 operating legal mines (excluding coal) spread over 34,000 ha. Main minerals include copper (28% of nation's reserves), manganese (10%), coal (8%), bauxite (4%), limestone (3%), dolomite, ochre, diamond and gold. Limestone accounts for the most number of mines (503) covering 73% of the state's mined area, followed by dolomite (131 mines). Of the 45,80,336 carats of deposits, 31.5% are located in Panna district, an area witnessing a spate of illegal diamond mining activity." NMDC is part of the recently incorporated International Coal Ventures Ltd (ICVL), along with domestic steel majors, which will be looking out for coal properties in target countries such as Australia, Mozambique, Canada, Indonesia and the USA.

In Panna district, here are "over 3,000 illegal mines… and an estimated 90 per cent of diamonds mined in the area are sold illegally" as per India's childhood in the "Pits" Report (2010, p. 95). Small-scale mining/quarrying, often illegal, in Panna district does involve Gond labour by both men and women (and children). There are estimated 4000 small shallow mines run by private operators. Only around a third of these mines are legal (CSE 2008). Artisanal mining of a basic sort goes back to the sixteenth century in the area, and at an individual or family level, many local tribes carry out small-scale panning and recover diamonds from alluvial and colluvial places. However, the proliferation of small-scale mining enterprises in Panna has had major consequences for the Gond population, who are the main labourers. For most of them, it is their sole or main source of income-cash or non-cash (India's childhood in the "Pits" report 2010).

Some of these small mines are operating legally with a government licence. There are at least 121 leases in Panna district 150 for diamond extraction (ibid, p. 35), but the large majority are illegal. While private mines extracted around 16,000 carats of diamond in 2005, only 335 carats were deposited at the government diamond office (CSE 2008, p. 215).

According to industry sources, illegal mining accounts for over 4000 carats of diamonds, mostly from shallow mines spread over 50–90 sq km. An estimated 100,000 people work in these shallow mines. The diamonds are smuggled out of the state to polishing units in Surat in Gujarat and Mumbai in Maharashtra (CSE 2008, p. 216).

The normal wage for working in the artisanal mine is Rs. 120 per day for women and Rs. 160 for men. Most of the illegal mining is done in forest land as "it is far easier to break the laws and mine inside the forests." The mining is done under the protection of dacoit gangs, and "the police don't dare enter the forest when mining is going on" (CSE 2008, p. 216). Many dacoit gangs are also themselves involved in illegal diamond and sandstone mining in the forest areas. In areas around the Reserve, there is not only diamond mining but also sandstone quarrying. "Project Tiger"[6] reports that: "Repeated efforts by the management to curb mining activities, especially in regular forest area, by approaching licensing authorities have been unsuccessful."

In Shahnagar subdistrict of Panna, "there are dalits as well as *adivasis* quarrying stones from a stretch of land which the forest department claims to be under its supervision" (Ramagundam 2005, p. 5). According to Mr. Dinkar, the Minister of Mining and Diamond for Panna district, there are in all 325 small diamond mines and about 121 flagstone mines. These are operating legally. In addition to leasing for stone quarries, the government itself auctions mining areas at twice to thrice a year and the highest bidder gets to mine the land. Most of the stone mines are shallow mines and are in patches. Government Diamond mine, NMDC, is now reopened after being closed for 4 years. According to Mr. Sridhar, a geologist with Environics Trust, there are only about 20% of legal mines in Panna, meaning that the land owned by the Zilla *Panchayat*, i.e. rural administration (meaning outside of the Reserve or the authority of the forest department). The NGO's report states that local miners and traders have said that over 90% of the diamonds mined in the 24 villages are sold illegally or smuggled out of Panna to polishing units in Mumbai and Surat. However, upon further enquiries, it was found that often the mining lease gets delayed because there is an ambiguity between whether the land belongs to the rural administration or the forest department.

---

[6] Project Tiger website: www.projecttiger.nic.in.

According to India's Childhood in the "Pits" (2010) (whose interviews were carried out in Panna in 2009), the level of child labour in the mining is shockingly high and increasing. Children work alongside their parents in the mines but may also become the breadwinners when mineworker parents succumb, as many do, to work-related illness. The incidence of tuberculosis TB is also very high. Schools, including primary schools, in some villages in the district are barely functioning because children are working in the mines (the starting age is about 10). School dropout rates are also high because of migration. These statistics are a reflection of Panna district, but I must add that according to my fieldwork, not all the children in a given household will be involved in mining and working in mines is a characteristic feature of households that have at least five to six children kids and can afford to send one or two children. In Panna, diamond mining is taking place at places called Ramkhiriya, Majhgaon, Itawa and Sejdan. Stone cutting and quarryingare under the total control of contractors, coming mostly from the upper caste and carrying the feudal relations into this business. It is hazardous and a large number of TB cases and other such respiratory diseases can be noticed amongst the workers involved in this business.

Mining and quarrying are the major non-farm activities in the region and provide employment to a large number of manual labour, mostly coming from SCs and tribes. Semi-feudal relations still hold the ground in these relations. The closure of stone quarriesis a loss to the Gonds but a much bigger loss to those families who owned these quarries and are being forced to either relocate or switch to other non-stone quarry-based income because there is no land left to quarry and new leases have stopped being sanctioned and despite being literate, they have no other permanent secured job in Panna as there are no industries. Some still manage to get leases through the mining mafia that operates in the forest department and the mining department, but that has become very risky and is a financial loss ultimately because either the quality of the stone mine is not going to yield quality stones and even if it does, the royalty rates to the state are so high that the mining mafia has become inactive. It is very difficult to get the stones out of the forest without passing through the check posts of the state and the forest department especially in today's modern-day electronic surveillance of the forest boundaries. If any truck with a stone load coming out of the forest does not produce proper documents, the penalty is extremely high and it is not worth the risk.

Bundelkhand is rich in mineral ores like limestone, diaspore and diamond (Panna) apart from building materials. In Panna, the mineowners are at the mercy of the Gonds to get any work done. The Gonds know that most of these mines are illegal, and the owners have no choice but to give them advance payments and wages that the Gonds demand or lose the labour. The Gonds even if they are almost dying cutting stones in hazardous conditions and sweating out under the sun, they have more bargaining power, as I will show later in Chapters 4–6 in the negotiation than the owners who have to almost chase them to get any work done. Those Gonds who trek to nearby places to work, about 60–80 km from Panna, in the quarries are especially the ones who make a decent amount of money because it's almost guaranteed that it's an illegal mine and they can demand more.

Applying for a legal stone mine is a very bureaucratic and cumbersome process because it requires approval from the *Panchayat* Administration. If the land belongs to the *panchayat* (means the state), then the next step for the mine owner is to get an NOC for the forest department because the forest department in this region is even more powerful than the state. In either case, almost all applications need an NOC from the forest department anywhere in the district of Panna. Locals say that if the stone mine is in any of the north or south divisions of the forest which are outside of the reserve, then it's almost guaranteed to get an approval but after a long wait. Getting a lease for the stone quarry for mining inside the Tiger Reserve is impossible.

2.11 The Stone Quarry Lease

Any stone mine lease needs about Rs. 1,40,000 as a deposit to the government. This is like a penalty as well as compensation for the environmental damage caused due to stone mining. On the other hand, a lease to start a diamond mine is less bureaucratic because the environmental damage is very minimum. The application cost is also very low, and there is no need to pay any deposit. In Panna, one is more likely to find good quality limestone and sandstone than a diamond. There are many varieties in a diamond as well. There is no guarantee that the diamond found would fetch the same cost as the total investment in starting a diamond mine which can go up to Rs. 50,000. The local average person in Panna knows from myths and legends about where diamonds can be found, but he will not have Rs. 50,000 to invest in the venture.

Even if they do find any diamonds, it could too small or might not be of the right size and colour to fetch maximum profit in the market unless they are lucky to sell it to find outsiders like me and merchants who might not have any knowledge of diamonds and will pay any price asked. The other problem with a diamond mine is that of trust because it is likely that the labour hired to dig the pit deep enough to locate the diamond might steal it while in the process especially during the sieving process where the gravel is separated from the diamond. If the person who has paid the labourer is not attentive, the labourer might hide it away. And, diamond mines cannot be operated by a person alone. Everyone has to hire labourers, usually the Gonds, to do so. The other difficulty for an average Panna person to start a diamond mine is water. A diamond needs to be separated from the gravel using lots of water, and there is huge scarcity of water in the district. The costs keep adding up in a diamond mine due to the high cost of labour (at least 4 people required depending upon the depth of the pit) and the cost of water. So the stone mines are a more profitable venture. Besides, Rs. 1,40,000 is not a very large amount if you are a Brahman or a *Thakur* with some amount of land and contacts in the rural and forest bureaucracy, like Malay Singh, and a stone mine can reap in a very large profit. He can make up to Rs. 40,000 per month. One needs both capital and networking with the bureaucrat-mine owner syndicate to own a stone mine.

Each mine is about 8 by 4 hectare in size, and the owner will then rent out to a thekedar (leasor) who will lease a small portion of the mine and find labour to mine stones, and he will make profit out of the yield. It takes up to average of 2–3 days to mine stones that can fill up a truck. The profit is shared between the stone mine owner or the leasor, the labourer/miner and the accountant (*munshi*). The *Munshi* keeps a log of the labourer and the stones mined by the miners. The wages depend on the number of stones mined by him and the size of the stone. On an average, the rates are 25% on each slab of a stone for the labourer with almost 70% kept by the leasor. The rates for the labourer range from Rs. 160 to Rs. 250. In a week, with 10 labourers breaking 10 stones for 7 days at the rate of Rs. 250 per stone, the mine owner can make up to Rs. 43,000 per week. The former is on the basis of a daily wage, and the later is when the labourer works on a piecemeal basis and gets paid based on the output (more clearly and in detail). The other part of the mine is crushing of stones. If the lease is illegal, then the owner will also take out

Table 2.1 Mahalapur in numbers (number of households = 71)

Number of landless	50%
Size of the landholding per household	Average 2.5 acre
Number of households with more than 2.5 acre	Two households
Male-headed households	70%
Female-headed households (widows)	27
Kuccha (made out of cow dung and mud) house	99%
Pucca (bricks) house	1% (semi)
People with BPL card	12
People with NREGA card	52
Average number of children in each household	4
Number of forest-based livelihoods (only collecting woods and no migration)	7
Stone quarry-based livelihood	49
Only migration (going out of Panna district to work in brick kilns, home construction)	15
Number of households who collect woods in addition to other forms of livelihoods	71
Average monthly expenditure per household	Rs. 2500
Average annual saving	Rs. 10,000

the share of the bureaucrats who help him to get away from breaking the law (Table 2.1).

2.12 Political Economy of Stone Quarry

Almost all the labour working in the stone quarry in Panna is made up of the Gonds according to Subhash Raja, a well-known stone-quarry owner in the district of Panna. His current lease of the stone quarry expires in 2017. He first got the lease sanctioned in 1997 for up to 2007, and the next one got approved for the next ten years. He does quarrying over a land of ten acres and has a hydraulic evacuator to remove the debris before the stones are dug out. He is not sure if after 2017 he will get another renewal because now the government has changed the rules. Instead of allowing people to apply for lease directly, the government will invite land bidders and Subhash says that small stone-quarry owners like him will be phased out as only those who will offer higher bids will get the lease. Also, the environmental and rural development departments have become stricter. The quarry has to be 250 m away from the forest and 250 m away from villages, hospitals and schools which he says leaves no land for quarrying at all because finding that kind of space is impossible. Subhash Raja is popular to work for in Mahalapur for the Gonds because he pays them on time and treats them well unlike other stone-quarry owners. This is another reason why the Gonds are extremely worried about their financial future.

The closure of the quarries will not affect other poor communities like the *Bengalis*, Sahus, Yadavs in the same way because they are not a labouring community. They have small capital to start other businesses like poultry, fishing, milk and alcohol. In fact, it's only the Gonds who complained bitterly against the forest department because their livelihoods were directly coming from the forests unlike other communities who have non-forest-based livelihood and also do farm work and have a much smaller family to support than the Gonds. By the time I arrived in May 2011, the Gonds told me that there is no work left in Panna. Later, I found out that they meant that in the future, there will be no more work if all the quarries expired and no new quarry is sanctioned. Even collecting forest woods is penalised in some cases by the forest department if the woods are dry as they are important for the wildlife. The Gonds can only collect wet woods as that is considered to be dead and rejected by the forest. The current stone quarry leases will all expire by 2020 including the National Mining Department Corporation run diamond mine which lies much further inside the Tiger Reserve. However, that will not happen without environmental and legal formalities and at least not until 2020.

2.13 Gond's Experience on Starting a Stone Quarry

It's interesting to note that how there is a provision for the Gonds by the state to run a stone quarry if they can organise themselves in the form of a trust or a society. In fact, by law, the Gonds, due to their tribal status, have been given such privileges, but there is a complete lack of awareness as well as nobody who can explain to them the business model of owning a stone mine. These privileges are regulated by laws which state that none of the members of the society should be kins of each other and should have proper legal residential documents. This is an impossible constraint because all of them are somehow linked to each other through kinship structure and there are no seven people, the minimum number required to start a society, in the village not related to each other. Besides, the Gonds don't have enough capital to start such an economic venture. Any stone mine lease needs about Rs. 1,40,000 as a deposit to the government. This includes a penalty as well as compensation for the environmental damage caused due to stone mining. On the other hand, a lease to start a diamond mine is less bureaucratic because the environmental damage is very minimum. The application cost is also very low, and there is no need to pay any deposit.

I interviewed some members of such societies who somehow managed to start a society in the past, and they told me that they could not sustain one due to lack of trust in each other in terms of financial management and agreeing in the distribution of the profits. However, the most discouraging factor from starting the stone mine is that the state will allot them a land which will not yield good quality of stone as most of the good ones are inside the Tiger Reserve where mining is completely banned. Another problem they face is that they don't know the political economy of the mining trade and how the market functions. They know that at some point they will have to depend on brokers and middlemen to help them negotiate the market rate which also keeps changing. In that sense, the Gonds feel more secured relatively speaking, to work as stone cutters and stone-quarry workers as its cash in hand and a clean transaction.

The labour contractors have a strict business relationship with the Gonds and will punish them if they do not work for the money that has been taken as advance before beginning the work. One stone mine owner, who often works with the Gonds, told me that the Gonds cannot be trusted because they take advance money and leave the work half done, and until they are chased around or beaten or abused verbally, the work does not get completed. According to him, the Gonds will begin work in a new mine before completing mining in the older one and restart the cycle of taking advance money from the new mine owner and, again, leaving the work unfinished.

The stones (sandstone) provide livelihood sources for most of the poorest in the Panna town, including the Gonds. The Gonds are part of the unorganised economy, but not of the mafia syndicate that is involved in illegal mining inside the forest. The mafia is made up of forest and mining department officials and rich landed elites of the region. Even though migration is a long-term livelihood strategy for the Gonds in Panna, most of their immediate needs still continue to be met by the local economy, especially selling firewood which is the main source of food security. In addition, most Gonds do the following types of daily wage work—house-repairs, laying tiles, constructing new rooms in homes or redecorating the house in the local areas around Panna town. Through the rural employment scheme called Mahatma Gandhi National Rural Employment Guarantee Act (NREGA, often referred to as NREGA), the Gonds work in rural infrastructure, for example building wells, hand pumps and canals for their fields and constructing roads and highways. However, such work is unreliable because jobs through NREGA are guaranteed for only three months a year at a rate of one per household which is never enough for the current household size of the Gond families, who are therefore forced to migrate. I discuss all this in detail in Chapter 5 on the state.

2.14 The Village Layout/House Structure

The Gond homes in Mahalapur are low-rise, made of clay mud mixed with cow dung and supported by rudimentary lumber. Roofs are made of heavy stone chips arrayed in a conical shape, and, because it is low-rise, it helps the Gonds to use the roof as a storage space to keep daily staples. Some of the houses have also been provided with modern (non-western style) toilets by the *panchayat*, but no Gond household appears to have a functioning one. The *panchayat* only gives them money for such construction. The *panchayat* has also provided water connections to the nearby drainage for the toilets. However, the Gonds prefer to use open-toilet. Women usually go to toilets either early at dawn or at dusk as it is less embarrassing. Similar practice is common even amongst the ladies in the town. There are only a couple of households who have household entrances where there is no need to bend to enter the house. The house is used for sleeping and keeps valuables, if any. Cooking and socialising are done in the courtyard. Bathing is done at the site of the hand pump, and depending upon the weather conditions, they bathe in the nearby lake. Washing hands with soap is uncommon but can be seen in some homes. Although some Gonds have started to use soaps just like using shampoo and conditioner and other make-up items but only as a fashion.

The houses remain cool throughout the year, and the women and girls do *pottai and lippai* (replacing the worn-out cow dung and clay mixture of the house with a replacement layer as it keeps the indoors of the house cool especially during the festive occasion). The men are also often seen working and repairing the house as the house structures are built on a seasonal basis and have to be redone each season to suit rainy and sunny conditions. During the planting season, people busy themselves with fencing their fields to protect their crops from animal damage. Fences are made out of soiled wood brought from the forest and known as *jhariya*. The walls bordering their homes are made out of small blocks of stones that are adjoined with each other. Except for one house, none of the Gond households in Mahalapur had chairs.

They return home after toiling hard for the day and have nothing to sit on except on the ground in a squatting position. The Gonds are a fit and physically active people, and thoughts of sitting on a chair or buying any other forms of comfort are not their priority even if some households can afford it. They inculcate the same habit in their children, who start to squat at an early age. I was so impressed by their ability to be in that position and also talk to me for hours without changing their posture. I tried to sit like that but failed, and they would make fun of me saying that I am too used to comfort and urban ways of living. With long-term stay with the Gonds, I have learnt that they consciously avoid dependency on any form of comfort saying that it will make them lazy and sick and unable to do laborious work. The Gonds' life choices of less comfort and less consumption of indulgent food are to suit their working lives as any illness in the form of physical immobility or laziness or depending on comfort is seen as a threat to their current physically demanding lives where everything is done with hands. Some also cannot simply afford it. It was hard to find anyone in the village who could be considered of a healthy weight. Both men and women of all ages seem to be extremely skinny, and it showed that their labouring lives had taken its toll on their bodies. At the same time, the only main illness in the village was silicosis. Another example of their ability to lead a physical and strenuous life is walking and trekking, which is the preferred mode of transportation unless they have to go to the market to buy and carry things, or when time is an issue.

2.15 Conclusion

In this chapter, I have portrayed the context in which the Gonds make their living. I have tried to locate the Gonds' journey out of poverty and to remain debt free and independent in the wider local economy.

The growing threat to their livelihood from forest restrictions and mine closures is a running theme throughout in the book. I laid out the forest-dominated rural economy of Panna, which is a key to understanding the tribal communities, as the Gonds are facing conservation-based threats to their livelihoods (Bates 1985; Baviskar 1994; Beazley 2011; Corbridge 1988).

Gonds' everyday struggle lies with the forest department as well as with the myriad rural development programmes which have not done much to empower the Gonds. On the other hand, rural poverty in forest-dominated states like Madhya Pradesh (Chakraborty 2007) needs urgent attention and that not all kinds of poverty are homogenous phenomenon but need to be contextualised to a specific history of the region as well as the class relations which produce it. The Gond households are undergoing household level economic changes as they diversify, take up newer livelihoods for the younger generations, along with which come newer forms of aspirations, how they create their own forms of aspirations, their relation with the state and their own social protection. I discuss these key themes in the next chapter.

References

Bates, C. N. (1985). Regional Dependence and Rural Development in Central India: The Pivotal Role of Migrant Labour. *Modern Asian Studies, 19*(3), 573–592.

Baviskar, A. (1994). Fate of the Forest: Conservation and Tribal Rights. *Economic and Political Weekly*, 2493–2501.

Beazley, K. (2011). Spaces of Opportunity: State-Oustee Relations in the Context of Conservation-Induced Displacement in Central India. *Pacific Affairs, 84*(1), 25–46.

Biehl, J., & Petryna, A. (2013). *When People Come First: Critical Studies in Global Health*. Princeton, NJ: Princeton University Press.

Centre for Science and Environment (CSE). (2008). State of India's Environment: A Citizen's Report. *Rich Lands, Poor People—Is Sustainable Mining Possible?* New Delhi: CSE.

Chakraborty, P. (2007). Implementation of Employment Guarantee: A Preliminary Appraisal. *Economic and Political Weekly*, 548–551.

Corbridge, S. (1988). The Ideology of Tribal Economy and Society: Politics in the Jharkhand, 1950–1980. *Modern Asian Studies, 22*(1), 1–42.

Gardner, K. (1999). Narrating Location: Space, Age and Gender Among Bengali Elders in East London. *Oral History, 27*(1), 65–74.

Guha, R. (1996). Savaging the Civilised: Verrier Elwin and the Tribal Question in Late Colonial India. *Economic and Political Weekly*, 2375–2389.

Kennedy, M. (1985). *The Criminal Classes in India*. New Delhi: Mittal Publications.

Madhya Pradesh Human Development Report. (2010). *India's Childhood in the Pitts: A Report on the Impact of Mining on Children in India*. Downloaded on 15 November 2010 from http://www.samataindia.org/documents/childrenandminingstudyindia.pdf.

Major, A. J. (1999). State and Criminal Tribes in Colonial Punjab: Surveillance, Control and Reclamation of the 'Dangerous Classes'. *Modern Asian Studies*, *33*(3), 657–688.

Mandelbaum, D. G. (1970). *Society in India: Continuity and Change* (Vol. 1). Berkeley: University of California Press.

Nigam, S. (1990). Disciplining and Policing the 'Criminals by Birth', Part 1: The Making of a Colonial Stereotype—The Criminal Tribes and Castes of North India. *The Indian Economic & Social History Review*, *27*(2), 131–164.

Ramagundam, R. (2005). The 'State' Revealed in Newspaper Headlines. *Economic and Political Weekly*, 100–102.

Silverman, D. (1985). *Qualitative Methods and Sociology: Describing Social World*. Aldershot: Gower.

Srinivas, M. (1980). *The Remembered Village*. Berkeley, CA and London: University of California Press.

Tolen, R. J. (1991). Colonizing and Transforming the Criminal Tribesman: The Salvation Army in British India. *American Ethnologist*, *18*(1), 106–125.

CHAPTER 3

Basic Income, Forests and Anarchy

3.1 Introduction: Anarchic Anecdotes

My daily visits were filled with anarchic anecdotes which were invoked either by comparing my sluggish urban and city life with their more healthier, clean, stress free, rural, and idyllic life and by their own recent migrations to cities even though if this anarchy failed against the forest department. Says Aditya, "…the labour contractors have money and we have the perseverance to work hard. When the two meet, a new economy is born." Similarly, Kotram says, "Other communities are jealous of our hardworking ability." He continues, "Even if the government provides us food and shelter for free, we will still work/labour or else we will fall sick. That is why we want to work. Our blood will not flow properly. Our condition is such that we want to do laborious work so we can remain healthy. Unlike you people, you need tablets for everything. We cannot live like that. When we work hard, we feel hungry, we can even sleep well. We don't have to jog nor do any physical work outs in gyms like you do. When we return in the evening, we eat the same thing. Our people live very simple and '*bindaas*' (carefree) life."

His brother, Brijesh, however says that jealousy of the positive kind is good. He shares his philosophy of jealousy for the Gonds in Panna and says, "it's good to be jealous because that helps you to work hard and earn through decent means and live a more civilised life. I don't like the negative type of jealousy that destroys others."

Such is the anarchy expressed by the Sur Gonds who despite the economic gloom in the region, labour, even if precarious, in the new economy as they know that without their labour, the mine owners and the landed elites cannot do any form of trade and experience growth in the mines or lands that they have invested in. They realise that capital cannot grow out of fiction and that their labour, which is a material reality, is the fuel that the capital is dependent upon, in this region in this specific space and time.

Freedom from statelessness is experienced but within the limits of state's inability to convince them of their ability to provide for welfare and the Gonds' movements in and out of their villages which some would argue is a form of desperate measure to get by the people living at the margins. However, as Robinson and Tormey (2012) observe on other similar indigenous battles against formal territorialisation and limited and controlled mobility, the ethnographic accounts is to not judge these movements as being a solution to state control or state authority but it is to capture the anarchy as it happens in action which in the case of the Gonds of *majoori* and striving for dignified wages amongst insecure, temporary and irregular forms of work. This kind of existence, according to Robinson and Tormey, is referred to as "actually existing anarchy" (2012, p. 115). In this chapter, I describe contemporary life and political economy of the region. I describe the everyday lives of the town people and their relations with the Gonds, the relations of the Gonds with the forests, and how through labouring Gonds have acquired their social reputation and negotiate the ebbs and flows of life in Panna. In this chapter, I build upon the logistics of body, gender and labour which continues in the form of case studies in Chapters 4–6 later in this book. Even though my case studies are grounded in "social realism" and Marxist analysis of late capitalism and its impact on social transformation in rural India, I found that the Gonds are entrepreneurs and rely on their ability to "labour" for all their small and big needs. This made me realise that I needed a more versatile and flexible definition of labouring and how that was different from wage labourers that could connect not only how the Gonds sought autonomy to improve their living conditions but also what are the different normative shifts happening in gender relations as women's work is also associated with wage work that contributed equally towards household income. In this chapter, I further investigate from where do these virtues of choosing to labour for freedom and to remain autonomous come from? What does family represent for the Gonds and how does it help the Gonds to experience autonomy?

In that sense, how to conceive the concept of Universal Basic Income (UBI), a cash-based social welfare scheme that is expected to replace existing cash based within the Gonds' desire to be free and their embodiments of anarchy through labour? This chapter will also show how to conceive of labour beyond wages, secured forms of work and formal unions but in the form of Maussian social exchange of gift and reciprocity experienced from the informal economy and not from the state. Mauss is invoked here because Gonds conceive of precarious labour in terms of money and social aspiration to maintain status quo in their village which cannot be possible from local sources of livelihoods in the region.

3.2 Labouring Lives

The concept of *roji* (livelihood) for the Gonds goes beyond household needs. For earning *roji*, they do *majoori* (labouring). It is their main option to meet all their needs: be they immediate, non-immediate, short term, long term, emergency or non-emergency. The wider economic context of Panna makes Gonds in high demand for doing unskilled work. In the absence of any formal industries which require qualified, educated and skilled workers, Gonds are available to do any kind of work that others in the town would not because it would be below their educational levels and social status. Also, breaking and slicing of stones involves a lot of physical strength and toiling for 8 hours per day together under the sun. Very few in the town can sustain that harshness except for the Gonds which is also why the Gonds demand higher wages. Recently, there is a labour shortage in Panna district to work in stone quarries as Gonds have started to migrate, and there is no other community that can fill in these physically demanding jobs and to labour under the hot sun for almost eight hours a day. It was clear that labouring (doing *majoori*) was not just for money but a part of much wider ideology of life which not only encompasses their economy needs but also their physical and Builth needs. Labouring was an answer to everything from poverty to sickness to living economically less dependent on modern amenities like cooking gas and electricity. However, without the forest, the Gonds cannot achieve this holistic and wholesome life. They would not be able to cut cost on their living, cooking and heating. Forest is what subsidised their lives. As a result, their approach to formal state, formal work, secured job and a regular source of income is equated in terms of choosing to move away from the forests and depending upon the state. But the state institutions and its governing bodies and the bureaucracy behind it has made the Gonds highly suspicious of the state. The Gonds have achieved economic success only recently compared to other communities in the surrounding region, and this threatens the existing social hierarchy in the region. At the same time, the Gonds are important for the local economy which is based on manual labouring types of work including any household repairs of other communities. But being a "Gond" in Panna is to be in an inferior position and is associated with doing unskilled wage work, even though it may be an honest and dignified source of income. There are jealousy and animosity towards the Gonds because of the Gonds' ability to sustain labour-intensive work. What is inferior is not the precarious labour that Gonds perform, but being a "Gond," in and of itself, that has a negative light. It is this taboo of engaging in precarity that the Gonds challenge through their engagement with a wider and diverse range of livelihood activities.

That is why the Gonds have a lot of pride in their ability to labour hard despite harsh and hazardous working conditions, including spending time away from their families. The Gonds refuse any kind of charity unless it is done in the name of a religion. One evidence of this was when a new Hindu temple was inaugurated, there was a communal feast organised by the temple trustees and it was close to the village of Mahalapur. It was only at this time that I saw the Gonds participate in a free meal. They also refuse free help from their own close relations, unless they are very desperate as this offsets and compromises their social status. Maintaining their reputation is important socially, as they look favourably on people who work hard as a prerequisite for social advancement.

Gonds' labouring bodies have become the marker of their ability to have as much control over their means to make their living. Being able-bodied is a marker of family's social prestige: to remain debt-free through labouring. Thus, remaining free and independent from any debt results is a very important morality of labour and resilience for the Gonds. Men boast about how they can leave and start a new job or take long breaks before resuming work. The attitude of Gond men towards livelihoods is casual as compared to women whose attitude matches their deep concern about ensuring income. In fact, amongst men, livelihood symbolises their employment or occupational status—for example where they take pride in their ability to break stones or in terms of their bodily strength.

They compete in their ability to predict where good stones are found as against finding big boulders. The latter is less favourable because they cannot be sold in the commercial market.

While the Gonds have acquired a reputation for labour in the informal economy and do precarious forms of work, they have also acquired misconceptions which form the base of my ethnographic interest in the Gonds. One of the most common stereotypes on the Gonds is that they earn a lot of money because both men and women work. This stigma with money and gender is due to the fact that even though the area is dominated by Rajputised gender norms of preventing women to work outside of the household, the Gonds cannot afford to follow such norms as they need every single member of the household, including women, to work. However, the labouring ability and skill to do precarious work is hardly considered as noble by the locals. Besides, the Gonds have more egalitarian gender relations than the Rajput communities as women have always laboured with men especially collecting forest woods and having the knowledge of the different forest trees and fruits which is still considered valuable in such forest-dependent communities. So, even as the Gonds accommodate and adapted the Rajput influence due to coming in touch with the Rajput community more directly due to modernisation through infrastructure expansions such as the roads and transportation networks, the Gond women continued to labour. On the relation between misconceptions about the Gonds doing precarious work and labour that others in the village associate as being desperate (as described below), I would like to draw upon Ferguson's recent ethnography of social assistance in Namibia where he shows how modern state's various social assistance that primarily emphasise male independence and autonomy challenges private and domestic spaces of the very recipients of these schemes as in these cultures women are more autonomous and authoritative than the modern state would have expected them to be. He notes how

> ...non-market distribution in this what comes to be an inconsistent to a kind of gender owned, in which the very possibility of direct distribution threatens to emasculate the adult and return him to the humiliating dependencies of the intimate domain. Just how directly contemporary common-sense links programs of distribution with the domestic domain is revealed in the widely circulated image of the 'nanny state', in which the welfare state style is a grotesquely powerful nurturing woman while recipients of distribution are attributed a kind of humiliatingly inappropriate immaturity, helplessness, and childlike dependence. (2015, p. 43)

I would also argue, based on my ethnographic observations, that the Gonds's lack of democratic consent to various government social assistance is due to these social assistance being perceived as emasculating the Gond men, labelling them as wife beaters and drunkards (even though drinking alcohol is practiced amongst the very government officials who also engage in alcohol drinking in the region). As Ferguson (2015) observes, the social assistance assumes the household earner to almost always be a male person, and if, in postcolonial contexts, he doesn't consent and comply to state welfare, he is labelled as being less masculine. Thus, social assurance schemes meant to improve lives and alter the gender relations in intimate and domestic spaces. Similarly, the Gond men who do not adhere to welfare policies and instead choose to migrate and engage in the informal economy are not only labelled negatively by the welfare state but also by the rest of the town too, as if welfarism is the be-all end-all solution for everyone.

Another stereotype I found in the town about the Gonds is that they will spend Rs. 5000 a week which is also not true because they have medical bills considering that Gonds often fall sick. Their bodies are also overworked with disproportionate food intake and lack basic nutrition needed to boost their immunities. Throughout the duration of the fieldwork, the strain of exhausted labouring bodies without any rest, was apparent in the form of emaciated and undernourished bodies. One is immediately struck by how hard working the Gond people are and much thinner and leaner compared to other communities in Panna town. This is because they take pride in the fact that they earn dignified wages and always have disposable income and never take out debts as they want to avoid the shame it will bring to their families. The very act of breaking stone in Panna is considered to be an act of desperation and misfortune that everyone will avoid in town even if it means high wages. To understand the Gonds's plight and constant battle with poverty is to know how they have been failed by the state and the society and not the local stereotypes which put the blame on the Gonds. According to Wood, poverty is a lack of resource including money or skills which could be exchanged in the local economy (1998).

For the majority, life proceeds on a day-to-day basis with the knowledge that the removal of the last stone from the quarry will signal the end of income from this pursuit. The Gonds constantly labour to keep cash coming in for self-sustenance either through subsistence farming, leasing their farms, or from other labour and land arrangements with immediate family members or with neighbours and other social networks. The men trek away from Mahalapur for two weeks to a month to work in stone quarries, where they earn up to Rs. 15,000–20,000 per month. Upon returning to Mahalapur, they rest their overworked and exhausted bodies while their wives keep cash flowing through the collection and selling of wood from the forest. The money from the wood supports the purchase of weekly groceries, and the money from the quarries and migration is saved for children's weddings. Gond women, whether married or widowed, fetch wood on a daily basis. This livelihood is becoming increasingly difficult due to access restrictions by the forest department on the collection of wood for household purposes.

At the same time, the Gond women support and in some cases even run the household as there were a significant proportion of female-headed households. The women will daily walk up to 10 km from Mahalapur to Panna town to sell 50 kg worth of forest wood carried on their heads. The money from forest woods supports buying weekly groceries which can be a minimum of Rs. 700 for one family. The money earned from forest woods lasts for up to a week, and the money from the quarries is being saved for their children's weddings which can cost up to Rs. 60,000 per wedding.[1] While Gond women do labour as men and earn for the household women despite Rajputised norms of gender relations, the Gonds trek about 60 km away from Mahalapur for two weeks to a month to work in stone quarries and only then will they earn up to Rs. 15,000–20,000. Upon returning to Mahalapur, they will rest for up to a month before beginning new work, and all the cash will be spent on alcohol and savings on celebrations for marriages and birth.

3.3 Gonds as Subsistence Farmers-Patriarchy and Kinship Norms

Even though the Gonds are a tribal community, they continue to maintain their subsistence farming life. They supplement their forest-based traditional form of livelihood through selling forest woods by maintaining their food self-sufficiently and constantly keep avoiding starvation which is a real threat considering their family sizes are growing and there not enough agricultural yield from their farming activities. Mahalapur

---

[1] There are at least 10–20 weddings every year in Mahalapur, and they take place during the harvest time after April.

is largely comprised of marginal, subsistence and landless farmers. In agricultural work, the household members divide the labour amongst themselves, which means that there is no need to hire anyone from outside. Alternatively, some do not cultivate their own land, or cultivate only a part of it, and rent out their farmland to some other Gond families in the same village or a neighbouring village. Some households engage in reciprocal agricultural arrangements where each spends some time working on the others land and will get a yield in return for their labour. Such examples are described in Chapters 4 and 5. Households that depend on mining and migration will often not have the time to cultivate their farms, and so they will make arrangements with other non-migrating households to cultivate, taking a portion of the agricultural output as their rent. While this is, formally speaking, a form of sharecropping, it is evidently quite different from the traditional form involving large landowners.

The Gonds combine both farm and non-farm work to get by. There are different generational occupations/labouring patterns. The older generation has only worked in stone quarries. The younger generation (above 12 years of age) has recently started to work in road construction after awareness of a deadly disease—silicosis—that Gonds of their parent's generation contracted while working in the quarries.

Farm-work-based labour arrangements are usually between those related along the agnatic line in Mahalapur. Such households will usually have a male household head. The female widows who have not yet claimed their property rights to their deceased husband's share of the land will not be able to engage in any agricultural arrangement—like Leela Bai (discussed in detail in Chapter 4) who, instead, will work on someone else's land outside the village of Mahalapur as a sharecropper.[2] She will not get any share from the family's land because it is barely enough for her three married brother-in-laws and their families. Also, she is not the wife of their blood brother. Her dead husband's family had moved to Mahalapur from a different village. She is the wife of their brother whose father was the brother of the other married three brother-in-laws. As a result, her residential status is the same village as that of her dead husband originally had belonged to but she never lived there.

---

[2] Sharecropping here is not the same as in the past, working on large farms under big *zamindars* (*landlords*). Sharecropping can be practised on another Gond's farm or any other household who has a farm not larger than two or three acres.

Such female headed households will be the most invisible by the state and the most vulnerable and desperate as they will have to labour all their lives as they cannot qualify for the various social schemes until they provide proof of their domicile status which in the case of Leela would be different than Mahalapur. Domicile status records are held by the state as they conduct regular household surveys for elections and vote cards are distributed according to what the state accepts as proof of domicile. The local authorities know the procedure on how people like Leela can claim domicile status but will not help her unless she first goes to them for help.

3.4 Landholdings, Ownership and Land Grabbing

Landholding amongst the Gonds is complicated by a number of factors. Gond social and legal norms mean that typically the younger Gond generations automatically inherit land in a collective form but, in terms of use, the land gets divided into plots for individual siblings, which usually means four or five in number. So taking an acre as a starting point, the five acres granted to some landless Gonds in the 1970s during Indira Gandhi's time, translated into only an acre per sibling by now. For Gonds who have land today, it is because their ancestors practised slash and burn to clear forest and convert to a farm. This practice has now been officially banned since 1985 and after 2008 under the Forest Rights Act,[3] the government (rural administration) officially transferred this land to the tribal communities on the grounds that they are natural owners after centuries of being attached to the land. However, during my fieldwork, I found that there was a lot of commotion about who owns how much land as it is very easy to prove that they don't own land instead of proving otherwise. The government produces satellite images of the boundaries of the person's landholding but says that without the red line boundary of where one land ends and another begins, the status remains unclear. People sell and buy land bypassing the government procedures and influence the state authorities to manipulate the boundaries of the land. Recently, Malay Singh, an unpopular stone quarry owner amongst the Gonds, forced a Gond from Mahalapur to sell his small patch of land for Rs. 10,000 and started quarrying the land and never

---

[3] Scheduled Tribes and Other Traditional Forest Dwellers (Recognition of Forest Rights) Act passed December 2006 and came into force January 2008.

gave him the full amount of Rs. 1000. There are many such incidents throughout the district where due to lack of economic opportunities, people eventually are forced into selling their lands to big money lenders who immediately start quarry work. Aditya says that this practice of losing land through forcible land grabbing by elites and the state is making the Gonds even more vulnerable especially in Mahalapur as it is very close to the expressway. The location makes it financially lucrative prospect for potential buyers. According to the *panchayat* secretary, people like Malay Singh take advantage of the Gonds' vulnerabilities due to current forest policies and their attraction for alcohol. He grabs their land by forcing them to sign off their lands by getting them drunk.

Mining and farm work are a common source of livelihood even for those who are landless. While the Gonds with some land in the village, will migrate only when there is an urgent need to raise money, the landless will often migrate but some family members will farm by renting land from those who have, and meet their food security. Some will take over the farming completely and take a portion of the total yield as part of their reciprocal exchange to labour the farm. This arrangement works for both the households as those households that depend on mining and migration will often not have the time to cultivate their farms even if they have land. Instead, they will make arrangements with other non-migrating households to cultivate these households' lands, in exchange for a portion of the agricultural output. In Mahalapur, farm work-based labour arrangements are usually between Gonds who are agnatically linked.

3.4.1 Types of Farming

There are two types of farming in Mahalapur—rainfed and irrigated. The rainfed farming is done in the monsoon. The costs of rainfed farming are half for those for irrigated farming. The crops grown in irrigated farming are wheat, mustard and bajra, and in rainfed rice, lentils and soya bean. The total cost of irrigated farming is approximately Rs. 4500 per acre of land, of which Rs. 2500 goes for buying seeds and ploughing and Rs. 1500 for buying the fertiliser. The cost of watering the field is Rs. 500 per acre. Some households save the seeds from their previous year if the yield was good. If it was not a good year, they either buy seeds in the market or borrow from others, giving a share of the yield in return. Cultivation and planting are performed by tractors.

These tractors are hired from other communities mostly from *Bengalis* and Yadavs. Each hour of use of the tractors costs up to Rs. 125. The ploughing season starts in the months after the monsoon, and the Gonds will start putting thin woods fences around the crops to protect them from animal damage during the seedling period. As a task, the job of putting up a fence operates on virtually a year-round cycle, starting with the collection of forest wood for the fences and ending with full protective fences around the entire crop. The larger the fields, the longer it will take for fencing. An acre of land can yield up to 10 quintals of grain. This yield from the farm is in addition to the government's subsidised rate of buying grains on rationing/control using farmers' Below Poverty Line (BPL) ration cards as I will discuss in Chapter 6 on the state. The excess yield from the farm is sold back on the market. The ploughing and planting goes on for the first twenty days of the agricultural cycle. The crop is guarded by Gond household members until the harvest season. The chopping and stacking, too, is done by household members. The most important crop for the Gonds is wheat, which is the source of carbohydrates, and *chana dal* (legumes), which are a source of protein. Beans are also a source of fibre, as prior to producing seed, beans produce leaves which are eaten as a local relish. From September until the harvest season in March, all of the Gonds who own land will be extremely busy taking care of their farms.

There is no difference between the quantity of food available for men and women. If men consume more, this may result from the physical demands of their work, or such consumption may be recommended by doctors because of sickness. Gonds try hard not to be dependent on their extended families for their basic and daily consumption needs as dependence would compromise their social standing. Consumption patterns are also important for demonstrating that they are self-sufficient and self-reliant in the matter of food security. However, recently, with the closure of the mines and growing restrictions on forest access, the situation of the Gonds in relation to land has become increasingly uncertain and the Gonds are forced to combine farm and non-farm work, including migration, to meet their basic everyday needs. Because of illiteracy and poverty, their tenure as landowners is becoming even more precarious as the Gonds incur debts that they are unable to service except through land sales to rich, predatory and landed elites.

3.5 Stone Quarries

Work in stone quarries is still undertaken by the older generation. However, while it remains the most reliable choice of livelihood for older Gonds, it is not popular among the younger generation because of their growing awareness of health risks, e.g. tuberculosis (nowadays, it is diagnosed to be silicosis). With the younger generation, migration to work on road construction, either within the state of Madhya Pradesh or outside is replacing work in stone quarries as the preferred livelihood. First, the debris is cleared. Depending upon the size of the site, the debris amounts will vary. It can take up to three truckloads of dump (debris) to be removed before a stone is dug out. Depending on the quarry owner, the debris will either be removed manually (which involves child labour as well as women with wages ranging from Rs. 60 to 125) or it will be removed using a heavy utility machine called a hydraulic evacuator. This machine costs up to Rs. 50 lakhs and is operated by a trained operator who is on a salary of Rs. 10,000 per month plus daily petty expenses. Machines are used in large stone quarries of approximately ten acres of land.

Once the stone is dug out, after removing 12–15 feet of debris (earth), it is drilled (using the smaller sized hammer) with holes to remove pressure. The smallest size of the stone is 4 by 2 foot, and it takes four *maistries* to slice that size into 300 chips over three months. With a small hammer, it is broken down into smaller blocks. Then, with a big hammer (about 12–15 kg heavy), these smaller blocks are sliced into thin chips and then shaped around the edges. In Panna, the stone quarries produce sandstone (by slicing the stone chips). The sandstone is of two types: red and white. The red ones are used for local/rural houses as floors, and there is a good market for that all over the country. The traders come to Panna to purchase these chips directly from the stone quarry owner. The white sandstone is exported to European and American markets, where it is used as paving in gardens and backyards. The agents for the foreign market come from Delhi to Rajasthan. Working in stone quarries is the most popular and the most reliable source of cash for the Gonds and it is for accumulative reasons. The pay is better than most other sources of livelihood. Finding work in legal stone quarries is difficult due to increasing encroachments by the forest department. As a result, many

Gonds end up working in stone quarries in and around Panna district. For this, they usually have to trek for about two or three weeks or months from Mahalapur, depending upon the contractual arrangement with the quarry owner. Only men trek to nearby districts to work in stone quarries. Gonds who work in the quarries are fairly stable and secure in terms of land and food and work in the quarries only to raise money for marriage purposes. All Gond men break big boulders of stones using primitive implements like a hammer and a nail. They study the boulder carefully and identify the spot on the boulder which will instantly break it into several pieces without much effort. These kinds of men will also bear the cuts and signs of small and major injuries on their hands. They sustain such injuries as they work without any protection or gloves and have no health insurance which is why they demand a higher wage or else will not accept the contract which is not even written as and is oral in nature. They are aware that none in the district will do such a work and the contractors and employers will come with work to the Gonds. And they never work alone. They will only work with other Gonds who are if possible from their own village so that they can retain a higher bargaining power with their employer. Thus, they are certainly organised. In the evening, their wives and children will be seen giving such men a massage or some will drink alcohol to nullify the aches and pain.

But this tradition is being replaced by the younger generation who trek to nearby places to work in road construction instead due to their awareness of contracting silicosis, a toxin released from working with stones which has a high health risk. Also, with the threat of stone quarry closure, migration is a lucrative option for savings in harsher and vulnerable times as I will discuss in Chapter 5. Some child labourers and women who work in quarries just outside of Mahalapur are often involved in the crushing of big blocks of stones for which they get paid based on a number of *tasla* (a unit of load of stones crushed and measured in terms of small bucket full of crushed stones). One *tasla* fetches up to Rs. 25. On an average, one person does not crush more than 4 or 5 *taslas* of crushed stones. Usually, it is women and children who crush stones and men slice and cut rocks. These crushed stones are then converted into cement used in both home and road construction.

3.6 Working on a Piece-Rate Basis in Stone Mines/Contractual Work

This is the most common form of work in stone quarries for the Gonds in Mahalapur. *Thekedaari* is also a form of *majoori* for the Gonds but the difference is that the labourer has the freedom to leave and start the work as per his capacity even in the middle of a contract. This form of labouring arrangement assures maximum bargaining power for better wages but also at the cost of working in riskier conditions or being jailed if caught by the forest department. In any case, the contracts are more flexible because he can choose to work as much as or as little he wants to be based on his need. It is not permanent which means they can do other work while also doing contractual work. Contractual work is mostly found in the stone quarry sector and is done by highly skilled stone cutters. When the employer or the labour contractor comes to collect the *majdoors* (labourers) in the village, he first has to explain the work to them. Then, the Gonds decide whether they are capable of doing that type of work. Contractual work is also a form of casualisation. If the labourer feels that he can finish the task faster than the time the employer has set, then he prefers to take a contract (a type of lease arrangement) because it is more profitable and he can take up another task while working on the existing one. So it is flexible for the labourer and does not have to worry about completing the work as per the employer's time. In a contract, the labourer will select a patch at the site of the mine of his own choice and mine it as per his own time and convenience (see the case of Nandu below). The completion of the task depends on the Gonds. The value of the work arrangement will be fixed between him and the employers' accountant (*munshi*). For men working as *maistries* (professional stone miner), the wages are up to Rs. 250 per day based on piece rates. It is only Rs. 150 per day if they opt to work on a long-term non-theka basis. The rates are fixed after the Gonds determine how many days they can commit and the probability of finding a good quality stone. However, there is no guarantee that once everything about the contract is discussed that the Gonds will finish the work. Sometimes they might decide to change that job if they find quarry work at another site where the possibility of good quality stone is higher and he knows he can make more profit. Sometimes, they will leave the work unfinished to attend social events like festivals and marriages and return back to work. The Gonds usually do not leave the work unfinished but sometimes, it so happens that the land is not of good quality and so they come back to Mahalapur. The advance is then adjusted when the Gonds begin to work on a new quarry with the same Gonds taking an advance from their employers to be used as emergency money for their family needs. This advance system is a risk to both the labourer and the mine owner (Guérin et al. 2013) and they both have to plan to protect their wages and advance money, respectively.

The Gonds are able to buy essentials like kerosene and grains on their BPL ration cards. However, considering the size of their families, it is never enough, especially kerosene, because the poor can only buy up to 3 litres per month. A kerosene-burned fire is the most common form of night light source affordable to households. In addition, low level of agricultural productivity and costs means that any immediate expenses, such as medical bills, jeopardises basic food need. Wedding celebrations, usually this is paid for by taking on additional work like employment in stone quarries which nowadays, due to forest restrictions, involves trekking about 80 km and living away from family for a week to a month. Gond households devise livelihood strategies mainly for food security, thus, work to have a stable agricultural production. They practice subsistence farming and wood collection as a fallback livelihood (Froerer 2011) as mentioned at the beginning. According to my household surveys, more than half of the households in the village own no land (see the tables in Chapter 2, p. 43). They have to balance the basic needs of their household alongside the altruistic and individual needs of each member. As per my household surveys in about 12 villages covering over 500 households so far in Panna block, the livelihood portfolios of the Gonds are seasonal, but some could be more consistent with only one source and some could be just a random combination of many sources. The variation is more from household to household and less from village to village as the alchemy of the livelihoods produced depends on the labouring ability and to take up risks depending on the physical abilities of each household member. This ideology of altruism and individual needs is always a matter of constant negotiation in a Gond household. This occurs as they experience economic and social shifts which combine both farm work and non-farm work. At the same time, they try to fulfil their obligations towards their kin.

3.7 The Labour Contractor

I wanted to know why they depend so much on labour contractors when they can directly approach the rural administration and the mining authorities for work. Aditya told me that it's possible if they all co-operate with each other. However, it's not that easy to always directly find work because they feel that they are not politically organised as the other communities are in Panna. In the past, Aditya had got work for road construction and made Rs. 3000 in only 3 days! He did the legwork required for the documentation and arranged money, labour, and raw materials needed for the construction a road of about 20 km. If he wants, he can again do the same but then he will have to miss his lectures at college and be marked as absent which will go negatively for him in the future. He has his heart set on a career as a teacher.

Some like Ramcharan Lal, a young Gond working on quarries locally, "think very lowly of labour contractors." He breaks down the terminology for me. "The" = thug, "daar" = alcoholic, "ri" = womaniser. Of course, this was said in a joking way. The main reasons why the Gonds cannot on their own become labour contractors because they do not have extra money lying around. Most of the labour contractors will use their own money or jewellery to pay the labourer when there is a delay in the money to arrive from the market.

I was approached by another contractor/owner who is well known to the Gonds and has quite a few from Mahalapur working for him. He told me that owning a stone mine is not at all profitable these days. Even if he does make more money than the Gonds, he still thinks that it's a net loss. A mine is now only supporting households for basic needs. I noticed that he didn't even have a motorbike unlike other contractors and instead was using the local NMDC run buses. This shows that income levels from stone quarry are not as significant even for the contractors.

3.8 Death by TB

The problem of TB is affecting mostly male members and of all age groups. There is a lot of awareness through the widespread death due to TB but not enough active steps to control it. Everybody seems to have an idea of how it's caused. Some say that it's mostly the mistake of the miner. It sounded mostly like he was blaming the villagers for not looking after their own health by over drinking and not eating enough. There are about 5 or 6 older Gonds above 60 who also suffer from TB despite not working in the mines.

This aspect is very interesting. I felt that Brijesh Singh would speak in a way that would be more sympathetic. Rather, he spoke more in a criticising way that the Gonds in the village were drinking to their own death. He was referring to more physical exertion and working under very hot sun as the main cause of TB. However, for miners like Sukhram, the problem of TB is described differently. He would say that TB is caused to those who do not care for their bodies. There is no doubt that TB is caused by both drinking as well as over physical exertion and not eating enough and on time after working under the sun. However, there were those who had TB and had not worked in a stone mine. The alcohols are not very expensive. They are priced conveniently to suit their pockets and are easily available. The money spent on drinking is not much but it varies depending on the financial capacity of the person. The minimum is Rs. 30 for about 250 ml. The Gonds say that the drinking problem was alien to them up until the *Bengalis* arrived. They say that the *Bengalis* add a kind of a tablet that contains a spirit which makes them addicted to drinking. Before this kind of alcohol, they were drinking homemade liquors out of the *Mahua* flower. The trees of these flowers are found all over the village.

3.9 NMDC AND ITS RELATION WITH THE VILLAGES IN THE TIGER RESERVE

One of the major benefits for the villages from the NMDC is the buses that they run between the Tiger Reserve and Panna town. They are meant to run for free for the villagers residing inside the reserve. People from all age groups and walks of life like women returning from the town after selling woods, school kids, shoppers ride on these buses. However, recently, NMDC has given the buses on hire to private contractors. These contractors have started to charge Rs. 5 to women who return from the town after selling the woods. My informal conversation about this practice with the younger Gonds reveals that the bus fare is not charged to everybody. Even when I ride in these buses, I have never been asked to pay. I have been told that only certain targeted groups who are very dependent on the buses are charged especially in the morning buses up to the time of mid-day. These are people who are very dependent upon these buses, and the bus staffs keep a watch on these targeted people. The younger male Gonds like Jitendra, who don't depend on these buses, say,

> We don't care that they charge a fare because most of us don't use the buses.

However, my interactions with some of the women who go to sell the woods in Panna town on foot daily, and return by bus, complain that they have to pay Rs. 5. Some like Aditya's mother, Usha Bai, say that they don't mind paying this fare because she sympathises with the staff who do not get that well paid. There are also some Gond women who have beaten the staff who keep pestering them to pay. Aditya too was once asked to pay the fare. However, his case is different because he does not use it regularly and has his own bicycle. When he was asked to pay the fare, he threatened the contractor saying that if he demands the money again, he will make sure the bus contract from the NMDC is over for him! The Gonds know that the bus is primarily meant for them to travel freely to the markets and town as part of the corporate social responsibility of the NMDC but they still can sometimes get charged by the bus operators.

Aditya knows about the need for NMDC to serve the community residing in the reserve. He knows that if the company gets into trouble with the higher authorities, then they will need to show to the government that they have been doing community work out of the profit made out of the diamonds mined by them. Aditya knows it because the community officer of the mining company is close to him and has shown concern about improving the village life if possible. However, the favours from the company are not much and unpredictable and unreliable, except the bus services.

Aditya told me that if the situation gets worst in the future regarding the bus fares, then the entire village is prepared to block the buses from coming inside the reserve. Ramcharan Lal says that a lot of time villagers have badly beaten the bus staff members who demand money from them. The Sunday trip to the markets is done separately on a paid van that the villagers have arranged for themselves from Panna. They have given a contract to a local school bus driver who drives a small van during the rest of the week and on Sunday drives them from Mahalapur village to the town for their marketing. They all pay Rs. 5 for coming and going to the market.

3.10 The Case of India's Universal Basic Income

In addition to NREGA, India's major cash-based scheme paid in return to do labour for government projects in their own villages, there are additionally other several schemes already in place such as Make in India, Adarsh *Gram* Yojana, Pradhan Mantri Awas Yojana, Mudra Bank and Garib Kalyan schemes. In Panna, ash-based assistance was also in the form of senior citizen and widowed households. However, the current government consideration of the UBI Scheme might do away within existing cash-based social assistance completely. The amount is slated to be Rs. 12,000 per person per year. However, critiques of the UBI scheme already worked s existing cash based scheme were not successful due to lack of infrastructures. Usually in places like Panna, where there are even fewer basic infrastructures than rest of the country, the implementation would require a lot of careful planning to make sure that the intended beneficiaries receive these cash transfers. Currently, NREGA was not popular amongst the Gonds because it was paid after the work was done and it required the approval in the form of a signature from the village head. And then the Gonds were expected to trek to the banks to receive this money. However, the UBI schemes are much needed in for the Gonds especially on moral grounds as is the case in Norway as demonstrated by Ferguson (2015). He shows how communities have been compensated by corporations who are profiting from Norway's natural resource base. Similar arguments in the case of the Gonds who are being displaced and evicted from their forests due to a Tiger Reserve is missing.

In the west, the production of citizenship and entitlement to state welfare and universal credit are interdependent. The European counterpart of the Indian citizen is entitled to basic income from the country's mineral wealth, like mining in the case of Norway as observed by Ferguson (2015), which is commercialised for the global wealth production.

In this light of global experiences of citizenship with respect to resources, wildlife and labour are vital in the discussions of policies of basic income. The region of Panna, as is in most parts of Central India, is abundant in terms of forests and mineral wealth, and I would also add the Gond's ability to labour in precarious forms of work is a vital asset mainly that of breaking stones. It will be very vital to conceive basic income in Indian context in global wealth distribution and contribution and whether the Indian welfare state can democratically assure a compensation in the form of basic income and universal credit or if there is another alternative. The self-determination and the sovereignty of the postcolonial Indian state have complicated the very democratic process in which such communities which are marginalised can be rightfully compensated either for rights to forest and for economic growth. In that case, basic income in the face of a burgeoning and ever pervasive informal economy can be counter-productive to the very principle of both welfare states and basic income. This book will address these moral problems through individual case studies and in the concluding chapter.

In a developing world like India, which is richer in resources and minerals than most Western countries, the targeted recipients of the social assistance, the Gonds, are expected to be scarified for the economic ambitions of the country and in the process of the production of the modern welfare state without any comparable compensation as will be shown in this book. The basic rights of Gonds remain suspended until they are resettled and compensated. Also, what rights will the Gonds have if they permanently face migration as a permanent form of livelihood and continue to bypass the welfare state. The autocratic forest institutions produce and act like states and are even more powerful than the state, as is the case in Panna. Here, the forest department is a global conglomerate of environmentalists, and the forest department has been given presidential powers to declare an emergency over the state where it operates. Several studies on the state of India point to such contradictions and tensions between the conception and actualisation of the state effect in India where there are various units of the state that are more powerful than the state. Similarly, the accounts of the Gonds' experience with the welfare state shows the growing tension as they become aware that the state is weakened by the autocratic forest department.

3.11 Alcoholism

With migration out of Panna and moving of other Gonds into their village, both alcohol and gambling have become a big social problem leading often to domestic violence within the households. The Gonds blame the neighbouring *Bengalis* for an increase in their consumption. The Bengali are originally Hindu refugees from Bangladesh. They were resettled in the region as refugees during the India–Pakistan war in the early 1970s by Indira Gandhi. For the *Bengalis*, the alcohol, made out of the *Mahua* plant, is another source of income. Studying similar alcohol consumption practice amongst low-income boatmen in Banaras, Doron (2010) examines the ways in which alcohol is intermeshed with issues of cast, class, gender, and occupation and to uncover the many facets of alcohol use and their implications for the construction of identities, moral discourse and power relations. The drinking practice of boatmen were viewed locally as a pathological characteristic associated with lower castes (historically, low-caste and poverty status have overlapped in India) (p. 283). Drinking alcohol amongst the Gonds too was treated as a regenerative agent: a means for relieving bodily aches, fatigue and the burdens of the working class (ibid.). Doron further calls to reconceptualise the drinking of alcohol within the wider power structures, cultural sensibilities, embodied practices and economic realities within which alcohol consumption occurs. Further, Doron adds that "drinking sits comfortably alongside other deficiencies characteristic of their class like sexual promiscuity, disorderly, violent and criminal behaviour in public spaces and lack of value placed on hard work and education"(p. 290). Furthermore, the poor are described as passive victims unable to recognise the ill effects of alcohol due to their backwardness and ignorance.

3.12 Spirit Possession, Shamans, and Indigenous Healing

As mentioned earlier, there were no major hospitals in the region and the nearest one was not until two hours by road on a bus. As a result, for most common ailments, the Gonds still use indigenous medicines but they also have their own moralities of judging serious and long-term illnesses which they think is caused by spirit possession indicating a moral and ethical dilemma faced by the village or the household. When sick, the Gonds often will first go to a *guniya* (a local shaman), believing that the sickness has been caused by spirit possession. They will sacrifice hens or goats and go to the hospital when these rituals fail to rid them of their bodily pain. Sometimes, they start with hospital treatment first and, should that fail, they seek relief in shaman practice. According to shaman ritual, the Gonds believe that their enemy has sent a spirit to trouble them and that only a sacrifice to that spirit will pacify them to leave. There are believed to be at least four such spirits roaming the village of Mahalapur, but not everyone has seen them and they are thought to be immortal.

Some from the older generation say that they have seen these spirits, but none from the younger generation has. Up to Rs. 2000 can be spent for the ritual of removing these spirits. The belief is so strong that every year, just before Diwali in early November, there is a festival for their communal goddess (*Kher mata*) who sits in their village at that time. People offer sacrifices in the form of hens or goats, and do communal feasting, to remove these spirits from their village. Every three years, the village is made sacred by sprinkling alcohol made out of *Mahua* at the boundaries of the village. Some Gonds say they have seen bad spirits running away from Mahalapur through the boundaries. Another instance of the importance of spirits for the Gonds was more recent. Aditya's wedding in March 2012 provided another example of the importance of spirits for the Gonds. His family forgot to cook the sacred food offerings to their gods before serving the guests. The most important food in the marriage is made out of deep-fried wheat ball called adda. This is a holy food and must be offered first to their goddess before the guests begin eating the wedding feasts. Aditya's family reversed this order. The goddess apparently got so angry that she punished everyone by making them tremble and collapse, relieving them of this condition only when they asked for forgiveness. More recently, Aditya said, his elder sister too was possessed by a spirit, one sent by her in-laws from her first marriage. His family believed that they set this spirit on her because she had left their son for another man. According to Aditya's family, the in-law's son was angry. Initially, the woman's family tried medicine from Panna hospital. When that did not work, they tried remedies from another hospital in Jabalpur about sixty kilometres from Mahalapur. Even that failed. Then someone mentioned a shaman in another village and only after being treated by him did she feel better.

3.13 Conclusion

The Gonds are surrounded by severe economic gloom which is not caused by them. However, a rapid rural survey of the households revealed that remarkably none of the Gond households complained of bondage or were in debt. As a result, instead of focusing on the "economic" reasons behind the plights of the Gonds, I instead focused on the subjective experiences of living and managing poverty and performing various kinds of precarious kinds of work. I discovered, as is the main aim of this book, stories of resilience, dignity and agency of labourers with no material assets and very little literacy, a remarkable ability to do temporary, insecure and precarious forms of work which challenged the stereotypes of the Gonds as described above by the locals of Panna. The aspirations of the Gonds should be accepted with the caveat that diversifying is neither a permanent strategy nor to be deemed to create stability or certainty about the Gonds' future. This book does not claim to be in the kind of anarchist writing but it does support its principle of showing support and solidarity with the Gonds's everyday struggle, though subversive, against the autocratic forest department and a weak welfare state. It shares the Mauss's approach of life where social contracts can be fulfilled by mutually and informally agreed notions of exchange rather than overwhelmed by monetised terms of exchange between individuals, institutions, social groups and societies based on solidarity and reciprocity. Strangely, the Maussian aspects of exchange are experienced by the Gonds in the book but not by engaging with the state, but with the informal labour markets, thus throwing a new spin on our understanding of how markets and societies are integrated into everyday lives of people in rural India. Also, it is important to note how to evaluate citizenships of tribal populations such as the Gonds whose displacement itself will produce wealth that can be used as compensation money in the form of UBI.

References

Doron, A. (2010). Caste Away? Subaltern Engagement with the Modern Indian State. *Modern Asian Studies, 44*(4), 753–783.
Ferguson, J. (2015). *Give a Man a Fish: Reflections on the New Politics of Distribution.* Duke University Press.
Froerer, P. (2011). Education, Inequality and Social Mobility in Central India. *European Journal of Development Research, 23*(5), 695–711.
Guérin, I., D'Espallier, B., & Venkatasubramanian, G. (2013). Debt in Rural South India: Fragmentation, Social Regulation and Discrimination. *The Journal of Development Studies, 49*(9), 1155–1171.
Robinson, A., & Tormey, S. (2012). Beyond the State: Anthropology and 'Actually-Existing-Anarchism'. *Critique of Anthropology, 32*(2), 143–157.
Wood, G. D. (1998, January 14–18). *Investing in Networks: Livelihoods and Social Capital in Dhaka Slums.* Paper Presented at The National Workshop on Urban Livelihoods, Institute of Development Policy Analysis and Advocacy (Idpaa), Dhaka.

CHAPTER 4

Family and Kinship: The False Binary of the Subjective and Empirical Definition of a Household

My understanding after a year amongst the Gonds suggests that the growing forest restrictions are also rapidly changing marriage, household units, household division of labour and kinship relations and thus the meaning of a household as well as family. I tried to understand the Gonds' meanings of a household and a family and found that for them the difference laid in terms of size and sharing of resources and that the family (*parivaar*) was "bigger" than the household (a smaller scale of *parivaar* meaning only married couple). A *parivaar* usually means joint family system with more than one generation. In that sense, a *parivaar* (a household) is also a family for the Gonds. In this chapter, I primarily focus on the household organisation, the coordination between different members to make a living and give the full picture of the social relations and family systems around sharing and generating livelihoods to maximise gain with minimal means. I begin by describing the lineage and kinship systems, the homestead separation as a response to growing family needs and the growing ambiguity between Gond households from a family as they experience newer economic opportunities.

4.1 Lineage and Family Systems of the Gonds

The Gond joint families are linked lineally and reside in clusters in the forms of single rooms which can be either large or small. The number of such "private-rooms" varies depending upon the number of married sons and their children. A *parivaar* means one married couple with their children. Presently, barring a few neolocal (new occupants) families, almost all the *parivaars* are descendants of the first six settlers, and the second-generation villagers are largely agnatically descended from the first generation. There are only two main gods and goddesses whom everyone respects and worships on all social occasions—*Bada Dev and Kher Mata*.

Different clans have come together to form the village of Mahalapur. They are not genetically linked but, the different homesteads are linked collaterally. The Gond homesteads (parivaars) are clustered around different generations depending upon the number of male members who are married. Newly wedded couples will continue to help with the parent's household cost, agricultural cost and in return share the cooking hearth until they have an independent source of finance. The base of kinship amongst the collateral Gond households in Mahalapur is agnatic, as is the case in most of north India. These agnatic lineal relations show solidarity with each other during times of grief and celebration. For instance, if a member of the lineal family dies, then all the agnates of the lineal collateral family will show solidarity by shaving their heads. These forms of participation are also called "lineage of cooperation" for those agnates who attend each other's social functions and "lineage of recognition," which is based simply on recognition of a previous agnatic link (Mayer 1960, p. 169). Such social gatherings in typical north Indian society require participation of male members, and the female members are usually involved in cooking meals on such occasions (Parry 1979). In Mahalapur, there is not much of a gap between the eldest generation and the successor generation, as the latter marry and bear children at an early age. The households restructure and reorganise depending upon marriages and reproduction which also influences their livelihood strategies.

4.2   *Nyaarpanna* (Separation of the Cooking Hearth)

A household development cycle varies as per marriage, widowhood and birth of children. Most widows will continue to stay in the same house as they had already separated from the main homestead once they had their own children and have their own cooking hearth. The Gond household and kinship relations within a Gond household were flexible and changed with respect to household development cycles involving new births and recent deaths. Gonds separate from their parivaar due to a combination of many factors depending upon their circumstances.

For some, it is due to an increase in the number of children and for some, if they can afford it, privacy is preferred.

The separate houses would be marked with a heavy wooden log in Mahalapur. This kind of separation is termed as *nyaarpanna* amongst the Gonds. It means coexisting separately within a shared courtyard and having an independent cooking hearth for the young family of the sons, depending upon the birth order, but still maintaining the kinship ties. *Nyaarpanna* lessens the burden on wives, who will not have to cook for all the members of the household. It also avoids domestic conflicts between different daughters-in-law over sharing kitchen resources such as oil, sugar, wheat and other essentials. Some married sons separate to avoid conflicts between their wives, as also observed by Fortes (1949) and Parry (1979) in their village studies in north India.

As far as caring for the parents is concerned, the youngest son has to perform the duties, as he will usually continue to stay in the parents' home, while the eldest son will have moved due to an increase in his family size. Even after separation from the parental homes, such elder sons continue to look after the parents and the younger unmarried siblings or even contribute towards their sister's marriage costs and other financial needs of the households. On the other hand, there is also a bilateral advantage in continuing to maintain ties for both the parents and their sons after separation. As observed by Fortes (1949) and Parry (1979) in their respective works on the structural function of kinship, the process of household separation is very complex. For them, these structural changes involved the division of both material and non-material assets. There is material advantage for the married sons to inherit land from their parents. The emotional advantage for their parents is that the sons will care for them until they die and their dead bodies will receive proper funeral rites based on the Hindu belief system. The final death rites are performed only by a male family member. Below, I discuss the household of Sukhram to give a full picture of how *nyaarpanna* depends on the type of household and kinship organisation and what co-existence means to these households.

For instance in Sukhram's house, he is the household head and lives with his wife and two sons and one daughter. Aditya, the eldest son, got married in 2011 and has a private room built for him in courtyard of his parents' house but he continues to share the cooking hearth as he is not yet financially independent. Once, Aditya's children are born, he will start to gradually separate from the homestead and make way for his younger brother (*nyaarpanna*), Manoj, who will occupy the room vacated by Aditya in the courtyard and look after his parents. So there is no *nyaarpanna* in Sukhram's house as long as Aditya shares his parent's cooking area until he becomes financially independent. Aditya's paternal uncles will not share that homestead. They will have their own households clustered around their married sons away from Sukhram's house.

For women who move into Mahalapur after marrying men of Mahalapur, the households are not as cramped and there are others in the house, such as sisters-in-law and mothers-in-law, who help with raising the children and also with doing domestic chores. Most widowed households cannot afford their children to be sent to school except if the number of children is more than three or four, then that at least one of them attends school. For widows, the problem is not so much about space but about making sure that the older children look after younger siblings, cook food and, if possible, see that the younger ones are attending school. The situation may be different, however, for less stable households where there is only one earning member with many mouths to feed, as in the case of widowed households. If the widowed household has only two children, then all their time is occupied with wood collection, filling water and cooking, and if they are a bit older, they will start doing independent work, such as young men working on road construction. Such households have to send their children to work to meet the household needs. On average, a typical Gond household will be composed of at eight or nine members with a mother, a father, grandparents and up to four or five kids. However, some households are unusually large, like Siddhi's, who has nine children, with eight being girls. The entire village mocks them for being large enough to have their own cricket team. Their weekly requirement is at least Rs. 700 for groceries. Thus, the Gond household cycle is determined by the ability of the family members to pool their resources to survive structural change, risks and vulnerabilities (Breman 2007).

4.3 The Dichotomies of "Household" and "Family"

In their pursuit of livelihood, I found the Gond household contradicting the bureaucratic meaning of a "household," by the state which is to access social benefits by the households and a voting unit to get the current political power to get re-elected. Both family and a household appeared to be indistinguishable. The social institutions of family and kinship help families cope and move out of poverty. My data revealed how and why the household was more dependable and reliable for the Gonds than the state. For the Gonds, both empirical (with an emphasis on resources, strategies and assets) and normative (kinship and patriarchy, and cooking hearth) definitions of a household are important for understanding agrarian households and how they restructured and reorganised through divisions of homestead or separation and nuclearisation.

Livelihoods perspective offers us a more normative understanding of a household. A household is a "co-residential unit, usually family based in some at, which takes care of resource management and primary needs of it's members" (Rudie 1995, p. 228). It emphasises assets, resources and strategies. Households undergo both nuclearisation and division but the sense of privacy is also becoming more and more compromised as there is not sufficient space to accommodate all households.

However, in Mahalapur there are also uxorilocal households like that of Neelam and Shilpa who might not share the same courtyard as their parent's house but will not stay too far and so their children will be seen playing in these courtyards and sometimes looking after farm work like guarding and putting fences around the farms and, sometimes, will also sleep in the grandparent's house. This is not *nyaarpanna* as this kind of household separation (arrangement) happens between brothers. Neelam and her husband live adjoining her parents' house with five children. The space is very cramped. It is a bit different for the same situation for Shilpa, Kesar Bai's eldest daughter, who has moved to her natal place with her four children and husband. The newly built house is too cramped for six family members and, often, some of the children stay with Kesar Bai and help out with domestic chores in return. She and her husband live adjoining her parents' house with five children who are small and need to be looked after. The children spend the entire day playing with other kids in the village, and the very youngest one, who is about two years old, is under the constant care of Shilpa who will take her baby to the forests while collecting woods. It is common situation, and both their parents and Kesar Bai go to work and return in the evening. The household development cycle is shaped by the wider social context (Gardner 1995). There is no typical or ideal household development cycle (in this case also involves *nyaarpanna*) amongst the Gonds mainly because variations in: (1) landownership and power relations between fathers and sons in the household, (2) the abilities and strategies of each household to meet their basic needs through outside income and (3) the chances of inheritance for the household male member from the living parent based on their personal relations between father and son (Parry 1979).

Birthing, nursing and caring for the younger ones are an entirely female domain. The gap between each child is usually two years, but it can be less, as in the case of Uma,[1] for whom Mahalapur is her in-laws' home and had two children in successive years. Even if the preference is to separate from the main household after children are born, there are very few households that enjoy complete privacy, as separation means only an additional room being built within the same courtyard or, if there is any available space, somewhere in the village that has not been claimed by someone else.

There were many subtle social norms in Gond culture which I interpreted as Hinduisation.[2] For example, women, whether widowed or married, always wear the veil when leaving the house unless Mahalapur is their natal home. Covering her face with the end of her *saree* is the signifier of her social status in the village as that of a daughter-in-law. For the elderly men too of the household, there are cultural norms in place. It is considered inappropriate to be in the vicinity of the younger daughter-in-law. They have to stand outside the door and shout the name of their brother or son if they want to see him.

This suggests based on the discussion of *nyaarpanna* above that both empirical and normative definitions of a household are important. As noted by many anthropologists in South Asian (e.g., Gardner 1995; Parry 1979), agrarian households in villages are increasingly experiencing both social and economic changes due to industrialisation and urbanisation (Gardner 1995). As Gardner noted in her study of the village of Talukpur in Bangladesh,

> ... unlike academics, local people do not think, or operate, in terms of narrow sociological categories, and boundaries around households,

---

[1] The second Uma is different from Neelam introduced earlier. Unlike her, Mahalapur is the in-laws' place for this Neelam.

[2] Social mobility of the Gonds by experiencing newer forms of wealth is Hinduisation but is partial form of Hinduisation as there is a wider acceptance of the labour work participation of the Gond women unlike the traditional norm that prevents women of higher caste communities to be seen doing unskilled wage work which I saw in the case of widows, older women and elderly married women.

homesteads, and individuals, are far more blurred than most accounts suggest. (1995, p. 100)

Gond households, too, are undergoing change due to factors such as (1) closure of stone quarries, (2) restricted access to the forests, (3) migration and (4) recent infrastructural development such as expressways and bus routes that connect their village to nearby cities and other states of India. Ahmed Ali (2005), in his research on food security and livelihood strategies in rural Bangladesh, found that "households are not static entities but restructure over time due to internal and external factors" (p. 42). Further, Pennartz and Niehof (1999) referred to this restructuring as "household life changing course" and showed that restructuring is a coping strategy to deal with internal and external factors. Internal factors included birth, death, marriage, marital conflicts such as separation, divorce or abandonment, and the need for childcare or care for the elderly. External factors included housing problems, lack of income, education, healthcare opportunities and security (ibid.). I am aware that as anthropologists, we have to contextualise "resources," "assets" and "strategies" as there are hidden power inequalities and not every member will have access to all the assets and resource in an equitable manner.

Gond Households are changing but sense of privacy is also becoming more and more compromised as there is not sufficient space to accommodate all households. Further, Niehof (2004) shows how migrating households need to be treated differently than those which are non-migrating because migration member does not directly participate in daily activities but will in the form of remittance (p. 323). A Gond household in terms of its composition, size and the development cycle shapes the strategies and agency of the household's members. The Gond household member's agency arises from kinship structure, household members' marital status, education, asset holding, experience and the ability to access financial sources.

4.4 Marriage

Marriage is prominent social institution of the Gonds. Marriages are exogamous and so the brides have to be from outside of Mahalapur. Recently, weddings are also an arena of conspicuous consumption for the Gonds. Even though, compared to the past, the duration of marriage in terms of celebration has reduced, the expense has added up.

Preparation for marriage begins during the winter season and is consummated just after the harvest season which is also when all the migrants start to return from circular migration. Early marriage is preferred as there are other siblings getting ready for marriage. Another reason for early marriage is social prestige. The age of the bride is about 14 at the time and 16 for the boys at time of the marriage.

For a girl, most of the time before puberty is spent learning domestic chores. By the time she reaches puberty, her parents will start looking for a groom. Sexual intercourse is prohibited between the couples during the first three months of the marriage. The bride, instead, stays in her natal home and continues to visit her in-laws. After three months, the groom will finally bring her to his home. After making this transition, the bride will not visit her natal home more than once a year unless there is sickness or an emergency that might require her to visit.

Unlike the common Hindu practice in India of matching horoscopes, the marriage alliance of the Gonds is a practical arrangement, and usually the bride is destined to spend the rest of her life with her husband. Such women will experience a weakening of ties with their natal homes, especially after children are born and responsibilities increase. On festive occasions and when she gets pregnant or is ill, her natal sisters or someone from the natal side will visit. She will also be allowed to visit someone on her natal side who is unwell. Overall, her travelling to the natal village will reduce gradually. However, recently, those the de facto female-headed household like widows and are sole earners are experiencing increasing ties with their natal homes because it helps to lessen their kinship obligations with their in-laws' house and instead depend on their natal family.

4.4.1 Stages of Marriage

There are three stages involved in a marriage ceremony: *lagan* (engagement), *tilak* (marriage) and *bidaayi* (farewell to the bride). Although they do not follow all the customs and caste-based hierarchy of being a Hindu, the Gonds do consult a pandit (priest) in times of marriage to know the auspicious date for the marital alliance. These pandits, however, are not consulted to match the horoscopes of the bride and groom, as they are in other Hindu/Rajput households. The meaning of marriage is different for the Gonds than for the dominant Hindu society. For the Gonds, marriage is a practical alliance and there are fewer complex norms to regulate the addition of the new bride as household member, provided she can cook and clean. In recent times, a pattern has been observed where the new bride is not expected to go to the forest to collect firewood. This work is performed by the younger girls, mothers or grandmothers of the household.

The main expectation is that the bride will do household chores. The marriage alliance between the two families is expected to be life-long, with very few complications in terms of interference in their married lives from the daughter-in-law's family. Another difference between the Gonds' marriage and Hindu marriage is that there are not many elaborate rituals performed during the Gond wedding. In contrast, Hindus believe that marriage is a seven-life-term commitment between the bride and the groom, and the couples must sit in front of a holy fire to commit seven lives to the matrimony alliance.

4.4.2 Sharing the costs of the Wedding Ceremony

For the bride's family, there is no exceptionally great demand, except to keep the cost of wedding feast down. In terms of sharing the wedding costs, usually, the groom's family will pay for feeding the guests. It is not uncommon for daughters to marry a man who might not be financially stable or independent, but if the groom is educated and employed, then the marriage will be more expensive as the groom's family will demand a dowry but that is very rare. Currently, educational background does not figure significantly into the cost of a marriage, as education itself is still considered luxury.

In a year, it's common in Mahalapur that up to eight to ten children get married. A dowry is not mandatory as both the groom's and the bride's families are poor, another distinguishing difference between Gonds and non-Gonds marriage norms. Says Hari Ram,

> In our community, the wedding expense are low if the families involved in the wedding are poor. They state it clear that they cannot afford to feed the entire village and so only the elderly men will attend the wedding. If the families can afford it, then the entire village including children and women will be invited to the wedding feast. (Fieldnotes 2012)

For poorer families in Mahalapur, the total wedding cost will from Rs. 2000 to 4000 and it will be equally divided between the bride and the groom's family. For slightly well-to-do Gond family, the dowry will be up to Rs. 10,000. For instance, Brijesh, a wealthier Gond in Mahalapur due to his large landholding, found a wife for his son who was more educated than him. As a result, there was no demand of dowry by Brijesh under the understanding that she will seek a formal employment and he even paid for her to finish her graduation and her computer coaching due to which, today she works as a teaching apprentice hoping that it will lead to a more permanent job. She also has cleared her entrance examinations to become a teacher but Brijesh could not raise the "bribe" to buy her a job as a teacher which is very much sought after in places like Panna. Brijesh, due to his well-to-do status, has managed to experience social mobility through his daughter-in-law's education because he had contacts with influential and rural elites who inform him about how to access government jobs and schemes for the marginalised. The desire to do non-wage work associated with women members is important marker of social prestige.

However, Gonds also try to avoid dowry because then they will also have to give dowry in their daughter's wedding. Says Rajesh, Brijesh's son who get married to a more educated, college-going girl,

> I received marriage offers from other families as well but they wanted to offer dowry. We did not accept otherwise who will marry my sister. If we accept dowry then everybody in the village will know as in our community. The dowry is exchanged in front of village elderly men who witness this transaction and the marital alliance. In the future, if my sister gets married, then we too will have to pay the dowry. So I married a different girl whose family was ready to give their daughter without the dowry. (Fieldnotes 2012)

The practice of giving dowry is public because that serves to help the girl in case there is dispute between the two families or if the couples do not get along and cannot be resolved, the marriage can be dissolved legitimately using these witnesses. This practice too is not a traditional Hindu practice of dowry-giving where the amount is not fully revealed but displayed through materials like cars, a house, scooters, etc.

The number of days of marriage is now only one day. This is because, unlike in the past when the guest would walk on foot 20–30 km to attend weddings from distant villages, nowadays, they come by buses and their transportation cost is covered by the grooms and bride's families together. This transportation costs put a strain on their budget and they cannot arrange for their accommodation. So guests are invited to stay only one night and the next morning, they are expected to leave. However, Pritam, a local school teacher in Mahalapur, says that, in the past, the Rajput influence of marriage practice amongst the Gonds was absent. Instead, he says there used to be a Gandharv style of weddings where young Gond men and women would self-select each other and the ceremony used to be plain and simple, unlike the current practice of Rajput-style weddings, where brides and grooms do not see each other until the wedding and where a priest performs the wedding ceremony.

There is another reason why bride's family hunts for the grooms these days which is the growing practice of dowry amongst the Gonds. Previously, money was never a part of marriage unlike now, when there is a probability that the groom's family will demand some money. To minimise the risk due to financial cost of extra money spent on wedding, the girl's parents will themselves hunt for a boy who is either of their social and financial standing or lower than them so the expectation of a grand wedding and huge dowry is minimised.

4.5 Types of Gond Women in Mahalapur

In the following sections, I discuss the three types of Gond women that I encountered, viz. married women for whom Mahalapur is their natal village, widows and married women for whom Mahalapur is the home of their in-laws. I discuss each type with respect to resistance to kinship obligations, inheritance of property, work and economic freedom. I analyse in terms of gendered forms of creating social protection and security by de facto (Niehof 2004) female-headed households as widows who are sole earners (Lewis 1993; Arun 2012) as women meet their household needs and cope with seasonalities and calamities of rural livelihoods (Agarwal 1990).

4.5.1 *Women Married into Mahalapur*

Inheritance and land rights amongst married Gond women nowadays follow the Hindu/South Asia (Kapadia 1996) norms. Parry (1979) discussed inheritance of property in India in the context of the Hindu Code Bill of 1955. According to this bill, the household head has the power to renounce his son's inheritance if their relations are strained.

In Mahalapur, children make sure they maintain good relations with their parents so that their right to inherit land is not denied. During my time in Mahalapur, I observed that married sons separate from but still continue to maintain and perform their duties towards their lineal family as a way to maintain cordial relations with their parents. This kind of relationship increases the male's chances of inheriting land from his living parents. If both the parents are deceased, then the land is equally divided amongst the male siblings by default. All they need do is to produce the death certificates to the *patwari* (the land gazetteer) at the rural land record office.

Parry (1979) discussed the practice amongst Hindu women of renouncing their inheritance rights from their natal side. According to Hindu customs, there is an unwritten norm of non-material assistance from her brothers, such as moral and emotional support in case of conflicts with her in-laws. In a typical Hindu household, there are other advantages of her giving up her inheritance rights in the natal home. She is assured a share of agricultural cash crop from her natal home as in the case of Ratna, who was married to Ramcharan, in the village of Mahalapur. This marriage is hypo-gamous because Ramcharan's wife is wealthier than him. Their food security is taken care of, as they receive up to sixteen quintals of wheat from her natal side each agricultural year. This gives them elevated status in the wider household. Women also give up inheritance rights because there is nowhere else to go but back to their natal family if she separates from the husband or if she falls out from their in-laws after her husband's death. However, being married allows Gond women to have property rights in her husband's share of the farm after his death. Usually, this norm is practised in Mahalapur and the land rights are transferred to the wife without her having to contest them.

The household role of cooking and looking after the children is a huge burden that prevents most newly married women from socialising with each other. Even during festivals, women will go out only with the other women who are part of their extended kinship networks. In such a social context, it is rare that women will discuss their intimate lives out of fear of the men finding out either at work or from relatives. On the other hand, women in a particular household find little support from other women, like their sisters-in-law or mothers-in-law. Thus, young married women fear that they will be alone if they share their feelings about work and social life as brides or women who are married into Mahalapur.

Neelam, for whom Mahalapur is her in-laws' home, was heavily pregnant with her fifth child and was only 24, looked extremely pale and sick. When I asked her mother-in-law, she seemed unconcerned and instead said that she did not know why she looked like that every time she became pregnant. I told them that perhaps she needs to see a doctor or get some medication. The response was, "Why are you adding more financial burden on us?"

In their 1994 study in rural Rajasthan, Raheja and Gold showed that Ghatiyali women internalise submissiveness. However, they also argued that these women used folklore and oral traditions to create spaces of protest and resistance in their everyday experience of male domination, both sexually and non-sexually. Women, in their study, only partially internalised submission. This is an irony considering women goddesses like *Durga* are revered by Gond men as in most north Indian Hindu societies. Women are sources of positive images through weddings, festivals, songs and other rituals. *Durga*, a Hindu goddess, is revered and feared by all including men who will pray and fast for the goddess to seek her blessing for a good harvest. *Durga* is a symbol of fertility for most peasant communities in rural north India. In their own households, however, men fear such power and sexual acceptance for their wives and, in fact, make a distinction in their minds between their wives and goddesses. On the other hand, for the women, the husband is a *swami* (a lord), just like the Hindu male gods Shiva and Vishnu. Gond widows were reduced to only economic unit and were expected to be asexual and apolitical within the wider north Indian ideologies of kinship and patriarchy. Sexuality is related only to fertility. Women like Uma show how they totally internalise submission to the in-laws.

The only time women (married and widowed) feel free to speak their minds is when they go to their natal homes or if somebody from their natal home comes to visit them. When Uma's father paid her a visit, her body language seemed very relaxed. Another way for women to overcome the pressures of household chores and deal with their in-laws is having a supportive husband who can intercede. The politics of socialising with other women unrelated through her in-laws' kinship is strictly frowned upon as there are certain family secrets concerning how a household is run that families want to protect. Most of these "secrets" concern their consumption practices and social habits.

Kandiyoti (1988) coined the term patriarchal bargain. According to Kandiyoti, it also influences specific forms of "women's active or passive resistance in the face of their oppression" (ibid.). Further, she noted that the patriarchal bargain is influenced by local historical and social contexts, and that it changes over time but undergoes transformation for renegotiation of relations between genders (p. 277). The patriarchal bargain is a strategy used by women in traditional and conservative families to exert their influence in balancing gender relations in a family (p. 285). These strategies are identifiable as they are implicit within

> ... the culture, class-specific, and temporal concreteness and reveal how men and women resist, accommodate, adapt, and conflict with each other over resources, rights, and responsibilities. (pp. 285–286)

In Mahalapur, the women who marry men of Mahalapur experience this kind of bargaining by bearing a male child and engaging in farm work as well as wood collection at a later stage when children have grown in or when there is nobody helping in getting woods from the forest or they are landless. Gond women contribute equally to the household income and thus, patriarchal ideologies are not as rigid as in other households where women's labour is not accepted for household consumption. At the same time, they are also predisposed to being attacked on their way to the forests and to minimise this risk, they never go alone. This is another reason why children's schooling suffers as they accompany such women to the forests.

4.5.2 Uxorilocal Women

Gond women for whom Mahalapur is their natal village will remain in Mahalapur with their husbands after marriage and receive all the initial support that is needed to start their married lives. This is because Panna district is well connected by bus routes all the way to Delhi from where Gonds can take buses to various cities where work can be found. Mahalapur appeals to newly married males who are looking to start a family, build homes and escape bondage-type situations in their own village. According to the village secretary, the number of such uxorilocal households has swelled in recent years. I find this interesting considering that Gonds from Mahalapur are migrating for work outside and the economic sources are dwindling. *Gharjamayees* are husbands of daughters from Mahalapur who have taken residence (uxorilocality) in Mahalapur but are not part of the extended family (thus their separation of the household is not considered as *nyaarpanna*). This is because, according to Hindu norms, the daughter has been married into a different lineage with different sets of ancestors. This changes her social, economic and moral status in the village. A case in point is Neelam, a Gond woman who was born in Mahalapur but continues to stay in Mahalapur even after marriage. Even though Neelam's house is only a wall away from her parent's house, she will not share the same courtyard as her parents as that is the space for her brother, who is married. Even so, her children will be found playing and sometimes eating at her parents' house if they are very small and left alone while she and her husband are at work. Neelam will make sure that when she goes into her parents' house, her sister-in-law is not around. Otherwise, such a visit could be quite offensive for the sister-in-law whose natal space Neelam is occupying and giving the appearance that she does not respect her sister-in-law's privacy. Married couples prefer to separate from their parental home for privacy, but few can afford it. For such uxorilocal households, the access to her parent's farm until they share the agricultural cost and get some share of the yield. Such women who stay back into their natal village after the marriage do not enjoy the same amount of autonomy and freedom as the widows discussed below unless they decided to move to their husband's village where they can live off the land that belongs to him. In fact, many told me that Mahalapur is better off than most villages where bondage-type relations still exist and are very isolated from any modernity. Men coming from such villages find Mahalapur to be quite secure, as they can access different sources of livelihood, which also explains the increasing number of uxorilocal household.

4.5.3 Widows

In Mahalapur, many male members of the eldest generation have died leaving their wives behind to raise the children. I use Niehof's (2004) description of calling such widows as de facto female-headed households. Mortality for the Gond men often results from contracting silicosis by breathing the silica produced by the cutting of stone. Female widows in Mahalapur have to adopt different strategies in order to meet their household needs as well as perform the social obligation of being a daughter-in-law of the husband's family as a mark of obeisance.

A widow's share of the land is usually respected if all the paperwork involved is met with the help of the village *panchayat* secretary.

These women depend entirely on their children for assistance. This usually strains the fulfilment of their children's educational needs, as often the women are at work and cannot make sure the children go to school. Typical is Leela Bai, herself not older than 35, with the eldest daughter already married off and the next eldest at 15 years of age and about to be married. There are also four other younger children in the home, the oldest amongst them being about 8 years old, who takes over domestic household chores since both adult females of the house go out to earn. Leela Bai had to force her second daughter, Preeti, into the world of daily wages to meet household needs that had got out of hand because of the wedding of Leela Bai's other elder daughter. In 2011, Preeti would accompany her mother to the brick kilns nearby to earn and to save up for her own wedding to a groom. She got married last year in 2013. Another widowed household is that of Gori Bai, who was the most vulnerable household. Every time I visited her house, she always appeared to be sick herself or was looking after someone who was sick in her house. The strain on her body due to wood collection and selling to Panna was clearly reflected in her features.

It is not common for women to demand their share of the land that they have inherited from their husband's death due to kinship obligations, even if she is independent and taking care of her children. Social norms prevent her from alienating the rest of the extended family, even if she is considered to be a new household, has her own voter card, and also receives widow's compensation. Due to illiteracy and lack of any other form of secure social protection other than family and kinship support, the Gond women settle for submission without contesting their rights. Also, they fear that they will not receive full support from their natal home if they are financially more vulnerable than her in-laws' house and already constrained.

Such women in rural household find their time spent on caring, and income-generating activities compromise their leisure time (Folbre 1984; Kabeer 1994) which also has psychological consequences and compromise the nutrition of their children (Ali 2005).

The Gond women, especially as sole earners, widows or women who did not bear a male child, will correct these many social disadvantages by investing in their children, by building them homes and by helping them raise their grandchildren in the hope of receiving familial care in their old age. These are challenging situations for poor women as they seek social protection and care from their children in their old age. Palriwala (1998) noted that even though women were able to secure moral and symbolic support for their families in their roles as mothers and wives, their autonomy was still limited to meeting household needs first and foremost before her own. In the Gonds' case, too, women's individual aspirations and desires are often sacrificed for the household or the collective aspirations and desires of the household (1998).

The marital status of the Gond women determines their ability to remain independent, free and autonomous. Widows are financially more free but are more dependent upon their children to help in running their homes in comparison with married and uxorilocal women who have extended kin and husbands who will help with looking after their younger children. For lone earners, such extended help is available if the children are still small babies but, by and large, most widows observed have grown-up children who have started to help with running the household. Working and waging are grounded in their desire to seek social protection from their children when they grow old. Unnithan's (1997) study of Girasia tribal women's identity politics and agency explains the complex processes by which their decision to attain full freedom and autonomy is restrained despite having economic freedom and control over means of earning for the household. In Mahalapur, the landholding status is very crucial. Thus, there is less social control of the women's bodies for earning for their families amongst widows and older women. In contrast, newly married Gond women will not be allowed to even fetch wood from the forests or to be seen socialising with other women. Their movements within the courtyards too are regulated, as space is shared by men of the household and she cannot be seen in front of them.

Agarwal (1994) suggested that:

> ... women's subordination, given their vulnerable economic position, may be a long-term strategy to obtain secure positions for themselves within their households and communities. (p. 66)

Widowed Gond women as sole earners for the household protect and earn for their children's interests because, for them, their children were their investment in future and their hope for social protection when they aged. Thus, for the Gond widows, the ideology of social protection to provide a safety net through their children's future support is important.

4.6 Inter-generational Participation of Work in a Gond Household

Gond households, like any other farm-depended household, have more than one generation living in one household. They all help and share their labour to meet the household needs, which is largely around food security in the case of the Gonds, who are undergoing a transition in their livelihoods. Despite the rapid expansion of family size in a given household, the age of the grandparents or the eldest generation of most households is not more than fifty. Most of the eldest members of the household do not know their age. I had to guess their age by knowing the age of their grandchildren. Evidence of the age of the eldest generation was obtained through oral interviews. The grandparents still earn and continue to care for the other two generations unless they have a physical disability or are sick. They may also be physically fitter than the younger generations. In fact, in most households, farm work is done by the eldest generation. The women in the eldest generation still continue to gather wood from the forest as a daily routine to feed the whole family. Both parents' and grandparents' generations (eldest generation) have the same occupations which are agriculture, wood collection and stone quarrying, with women members doing wood collection and men working in stone quarries and the entire household helping with agriculture. However, the occupations of the eldest generation, such as stone mining, are increasingly becoming less popular with the youngest generation who instead prefer to migrate to work in homes and road construction. Awareness of silicosis due to working in stone quarries is high in the consciousness of the younger generation to switch into construction of roads.

4.7 Child Work Participation

Children play a vital role in the household management. Here, I explain in detail their important contribution to domestic chores, which makes them discontinue and ultimately stop schooling due to the amount of work that is expected from them. Parents encourage the labour of their children as there is always shortage of money in the house. Especially when an adult member falls sick or dies, family strategies come under stress and child labour become necessary until the household reorganises its strategies. If a household has more than three children, then the earnings of one of the children go towards the purchase of weekly groceries; the earnings of the other two are saved for unseen emergencies. However, it can also happen that the children might use their wages for their own personal use, especially the boys. While between 10 and 12 years of age, Gond children do light work like carrying small loads of forest wood (about 15 kg) or, more rarely, work in the stone mines, where they clear the debris. There are many other lighter tasks, such as transporting stones from one place to another, laying bricks in the tractors or arranging stones together. Whatever savings they keep will disappear during leaner days. Children's labour participation is part of most households' livelihood (Kambhampati 2009; Khanam and Ross 2011). Research has shown that child work participation almost doubles when children are not attending school, as parents trade their children's education for gainful employment (Gaur 2010). Kis-Katos's (2012) research in Uttar Pradesh, India, showed that most domestic work is gendered, and children's work participation towards the household economy is overlooked and unacknowledged. She attributed this to the fact that the poor households tend to distinguish between market work and domestic work. The decision as to whether to send children to school or work depends upon the parental assessment of which assignment—school or labour—will produce the best return for the household. Such assessments depend upon the households' consumption profile, asset ownership and the status of credit in terms of lending institutions (Kis-Katos 2012, pp. 494–495). If children decide to quit school for work, it is not judged against them by their parents. It is considered a noble thing to not depend on parents for conspicuous consumption, for example, new clothes, mobile phones, CD players or televisions. The Gond children are aware that the modern amenities are luxuries for their households and so will earn to buy them. According to Kabeer (2010, p. 206), such early contributions of children to both wage work and household work compromise their growth and these vital contributions are undervalued in the overall discussion of livelihoods.

The other job that young boys work is to clear debris in stone quarries, help in family farm work or some may accompany the elder migrants of the household by caring for the newborn babies of these migrants. These boys will start to behave autonomously at an early age and find very little use for education. Although child labour is illegal, it is rampant in the areas surrounding the town, and children can earn up to Rs. 60 per day if they do stone quarry wage work. The low interest in sending their children to school stems from the evidence of other unemployed Gond youths in Panna. Aditya is one such youth and he is a Gond. He recently graduated, but was doing *majoori* as he was still unemployed. For the most part, children start by doing *majoori*, to earn some money for the household. *Majoori* jobs are amply available for children and adults in the area. I show in Chapter 6 on the state about how schooling is traded for children's labouring and under what condition is this happening in Mahalapur by drawing upon Froerer's (2011) work in Chhattisgarh.

Child labouring in Mahalapur is a risky decision because financial independence at an early age makes them vulnerable to lose their childhood and by being exposed to the world of adult world too soon. Teenage boys who do "*majoori*," by the age of 10 onwards, start behaving like adults unlike those boys who do not. Some will remain within parental control, while some will start socialising like adults, using alcohol, smoking and sometimes gambling. Initially, they start to smoke or drink to impress older children. However, some become habituated to it. Adults in the household will give money to the children to buy alcohol for them, which provides children with a temptation. In 2012, I have witnessed such small boys who were smoking, drinking alcohol and trying to follow in the footsteps of elderly men of the village, and even sometimes beating up elder men of the village in addition to using foul language. However, a recent visit in 2014 revealed how the youth of the village have decided to discipline such children. They follow an ancient tradition of *panchnama* where five witnesses would testify in front of the village about anyone drinking or gambling. The teenage boys of the village took such measures in their village on board and have instituted a reformative measure where all adults who drink and gamble will have to pay a fine. This method has been in place since last year and has helped to bring down incidences of violence related to drinking and gambling. It has also discouraged the *Bengalis* from nearby villages and Panna town men from selling and making alcohol in Mahalapur or coming to pay to eat meat as meat is not consumed in most Hindu households in Panna town.

Household chores are performed according to gender and birth order. Domestic chores are done primarily by girls (Kingdon 1998) unless there are only boys in the family, in which case the eldest boy will cook and do other household chores. *Majoori* is combined between men and women and is also gendered. Forest wood collection is done only by women.

In Mahalapur, stone quarry work is done only by men. Women do not do any work in the quarries as there is always other forest-related work which keeps them busy throughout the day.

Almost all Gond households wish to have as many male children as possible and continue producing children until they have at least five in the hope of having at least one male child. Having a male child also helps to gain positive favour from their parents who own the household, as they are more likely to transfer their property to the married sons who bore them grandsons. The female children, especially the eldest one, are expected to do well in domestic chores and prepare for a married life. Only the younger girls in the household are fortunate enough to attend school on an uninterrupted basis, as elder sisters can manage most of the necessary household work.

Household chores and agricultural works are labour-intensive chores in the Gond household. No modern labour-saving devices, such as washing machines, gas cylinders or refrigerators, can be seen. As there is no refrigeration, meals are prepared and consumed on the same day. None of the households has a source of water at home. They fetch water from the communal hand pump to wash utensils of daily use. Carrying of water is the most labour-intensive task as buckets with a capacity of ten litres per fill are carried by young girls who carry them on top of their heads. Older girls will carry one on the top of their head and one little steel tumbler on their waist. They wear special head protectors called *kunthi*, made out of worn-out saris, that protects the skull and creates a cushioning effect to reduce the hardness felt on the head from the weight of the forehead-carried water-filled buckets.

A great deal of time is devoted to cooking bread (*roti*), starting from preparing the clay fire with wood and then directly roasting chapattis on the fire. Firewood is collected from the forests by women or girls daily and water, stored for daily consumption, is bought from the nearby hand pump. Domestic chores are essentially the domain of daughters in the family and are performed manually.

There is no class difference in the raising of Gond children. However, child rearing is gendered. Girls as young as six will start cooking *roti* on the hearth. They will learn how to collect and chop wood. Also, they will be taught to care for younger siblings. For most Gond children, family life is of crucial importance and there is usually not much time for friends, especially for the girls. Girls will never be allowed to venture out on their own, even if they are with other girls. There are fewer restrictions as to boys' movements in and out of Mahalapur. Girls are expected to be docile and submissive to the household needs, unlike boys, who have the freedom to choose between study and work and can start helping parents in running the households. Girls are expected to be "sincere" and boys can be "spoiled" (Da Costa 2010). However, eldest sons, or sons who have lost fathers, will experience less freedom as they must be available to help their mother in the care of the younger siblings. In a more stable household, where both parents work, younger children, especially the male children, will do very limited household chores, and most of their childhood is spent playing with other children in the village.

By the age of 10, the girls in this village start collecting woods from the forest. Girls from the age of 6 will start doing the household chores and taking care of the younger siblings. Kids above 8 will start doing hard labour, like selling wood in the town. As the girls are so involved in doing household chores from an early age, they become accustomed to this way of life and know only the domestic world until they get married. Marriage is a major life-changing event and brides can hope to have more freedom to assert themselves, depending on her husband. This is unlike the boys, who can assert their desires as soon as they start earning and are no longer expected to do household chores. Being a "girl" is short-lived as a female must become a "woman" in the form of a mother quite early in the course of life. This is unlike for boys, who can delay becoming a "man," as they are allowed to start earning or migrate for contributing to the household expenses. Boys who become men will start sharing their incomes with their wives, their children and their parental families. In Mahalapur, a boy becomes a man after marriage and starts his family irrespective of his age. Just like men, the women also leave home for work and return in the evening. For the Gond household, this is a vital contribution. Where heads of households are widows, the eldest sibling, too, will start to participate with the mother as an unskilled worker. The domestic responsibility of managing household chores then falls upon the eldest sibling, no matter how young and what is the gender. Thus, for young widows as de facto female-headed households, the constraints are more than married women and male-headed households.

4.8 Conclusion

Social relations for the Gonds are not only a resource within the household for its members but also amongst the other villagers seeking information about potential, new economic opportunities and work available outside Mahalapur. Gonds' strategies need to be contextualised in their desire for creating their own forms social protection, care, duty and security (mainly food security) and also fulfil their social obligations like marriages of their children. These diverse coping strategies are not isolated from the low impact of the state benefit programmes that do not reach them or reach very like education. Migrating and being absent from various development programmes, the Gonds seem to indirectly express these suspicions of why suddenly their "welfare" has become a concern and are conscious of their significance as vote banks to major national parties. We need a more robust and broader concept of inter-generational, temporal and historical perspective of Gond household formation is more appropriate for nurses dinghy diversity of coping strategies of the vulnerable households such as the Gonds as it captures a more dynamic and recent picture of the socio-economic transformation that the Gonds are undergoing.

References

Agarwal, B. (1990). Social Security and the Family: Coping with Seasonality and Calamity in Rural India.

Agarwal, B. (1994). The Gender and Environment Debate: Lessons from India. *Feminist studies, 18*(1), 119–158.

Ali, A. (2005). *Livelihood and Food Security in Rural Bangladesh: The Role of Social Capital*. Ph.D. Thesis, Wageningen University, the Netherlands, p. 203.

Arun, S. (2012). 'We Are Farmers Too': Agrarian Change and Gendered Livelihoods in Kerala, South India. *Journal of Gender Studies, 21*(3), 271–284.

Breman, J. (2007). *The Poverty Regime in Village India: Half a Century of Work and Life at the Bottom of the Rural Economy in South Gujarat*. New Delhi: Oxford University Press.

Da Costa, D. (2010). *Development Dramas: Reimagining Rural Political Action in Eastern India*. New Delhi: Routledge.

Folbre, N. (1984). Market Opportunities, Genetic Endowments, and Intrafamily Resource Distribution: Comment. *American Economic Review, 74*(3), 518–520.

Fortes, M. (1949). *The Web of Kinship Among the Tallensi: The Second Part of an Analysis of the Social Structure of a Trans-Volta Tribe*. London: Oxford University Press.

Froerer, P. (2011). Education, Inequality and Social Mobility in Central India. *European Journal of Development Research, 23*(5), 695–711.
Gardner, K. (1995). *Global Migrants, Local Lives: Travel and Transformation in Rural Bangladesh*. Oxford: Oxford University Press.
Gaur, A. K. (2010, August). Estimating Deprivation and Inequality in Human Well Beings: A Case Study of Indian States. In *31st General Conference of the International Association for Research in Income and Wealth August* (pp. 22–28).
Kabeer, N. (1994). *Reversed Realities: Gender Hierarchies in Development Thought*. London: Verso.
Kabeer, N. (2010). Women's Empowerment, Development Interventions and the Management of Information Flows. *ids Bulletin, 41*(6), 105–113.
Kambhampati, U. S. (2009). Child Schooling and Work Decisions in India: The Role of Household and Regional Gender Equity. *Feminist Economics, 15*(4), 77–112.
Kandiyoti, D. (1988). Bargaining with Patriarchy. *Gender and Society, 2*(3), 274–290.
Kapadia, K. (1996). Property and Proper Chastity: Women's Land Rights in South Asia Today. *Journal of Peasant Studies, 23*(4), 166–173.
Khanam, R., & Ross, R. (2011). Is Child Work a Deterrent to School Attendance and School Attainment? Evidence from Bangladesh. *International Journal of Social Economics, 38*(8), 692–713.
Kingdon, G. G. (1998). Does the Labour Market Explain Lower Female Schooling in India? *Journal of Development Studies, 35*(1), 39–65.
Kis-Katos, K. (2012). Gender Differences in Work-schooling Decisions in Rural North India. *Review of Economics of the Household, 10*(4), 491–519.
Lewis, D. J. (1993). Going It Alone: Female-Headed Households, Rights and Resources in Rural Bangladesh. *European Journal of Development Research, 5*(2), 23–42.
Mayer, A. C. (1960). *Caste and Kinship in Central India: A Village and Its Region*. London: Routledge and Kegan Paul.
Niehof, A. (2004). The Significance of Diversification for Rural Livelihood Systems. *Food Policy, 29*(4), 321–338.
Palriwala, R. (1998). *Changing Kinship, Family and Gender Relations in South Asia: Processes, Trends and Issues*. Leiden: Women and Autonomy Centre, Leiden University.
Parry, J. P. (1979). *Caste and Kinship in Kangra*. London: Routledge.
Pennartz, P., & Niehof, A. (1999). *The Domestic Domain: Chances, Choices and Strategies of Family Households*. Aldershot, Brookfield, USA, Singapore and Sydney: Ashgate Publishing Ltd.
Rudie, I. (1995). The Significance of 'Eating': Cooperation, Support and Reputation in Kelantan Malay Households. In W. J. Karim (Ed.), *'Male' and 'Female' in Developing Southeast Asia* (pp. 227–247). Oxford: Berg.
Unnithan-Kumar, M. (1997). *Identity, Gender and Poverty: New Perspectives on Caste and Tribe in Rajasthan*. Providence, RI and Oxford: Berghahn.

CHAPTER 5

Narratives of *Kamayee/Dhanda* (Income): Modes of Wages

5.1 Introduction

It was useful on several occasions to help them understand these programmes: help to fill in applications, to know about the ambiguity around buffer zones, or what happens to compensation money due to silicosis illness. The Gonds need to juggle multiple tasks, their insecurities and bureaucratic requirements, as well as illiteracy, which just adds to their vulnerability. My observations about the Gonds are a localised view of livelihoods, vulnerability and agency of the vulnerable households and thus cannot be generalised. I became curious about the livelihood world after the surveys which showed that the Gonds are making a living without three important forms of assistance which was state benefits, traditional patronage relations and lack of tangible and disposable assets. All they had was their able-bodies as well as ability to endure harsh and precarious working conditions. I could not overlook the fact that all kinds of precarious and risky works in the district are being done by the Gonds even though there are other unemployed and marginalised communities like the SCs and the OBCs. However, the difference was that the Gonds are the most vulnerable as they faced more constraints after the forest restrictions. This in addition to their inability to read and write prevented them from taking full advantage of state's social assistances targeted at them. The response from the rural authorities was, "we have all the information which the Gonds can benefit from but they have to come to know about them" without realising that even if the Gonds did come to the offices, it would not matter as the Gonds could not read or write as this was information written in documents and not verbalised. Later, I was even more confused when I was shown up to 50 odd scholarships that the government has announced for encouraging tribal people to continue schooling, an information that Sur Gonds could have benefited from had they known about it.

The majority of the Gonds live on a day-to-day basis by working in stone quarries which have a commodified structure of labour–capital relations. Most households comprise up to three generations with more than one sibling per generation which after marriage splits and starts another independent Gond household if the child is a son. In the past too, the Gonds had more children but they did not survive due to malnutrition or were stillborn and were cut off from society as they lived only in the forests and ate raw forest products. Nowadays, child mortality rates have decreased but the number of children has not because marriages still happen very early and by the time the mother is 23, households will continue to have more children; they have a male child. It's only then that women get operated from having no more children. After the age of 35, most Gonds get their children married who will by next year have their children. As a result, the concept of ageing is also very different in the community. It's measured in terms of the ability to fulfil social responsibilities and takes on initiatives to run the household tasks and needs roles rather than a numerical figure. In a very short span of time, the household head experiences several life-course events (marriages, deaths births) and similarly the household too matures quickly as household development cycle also simultaneously progresses at a very short space.

In this chapter, I describe these social ties as social capital for the Gonds. Social relations are very crucial for the Gonds to manage their household economy as well as participate in the precarious informal economy to stabilise their cash flows and agricultural production for survival, food security and fulfil social obligations. I focus on household patterns that I observed representing the diverse livelihood strategies by mapping the Gonds households profile with their livelihood portfolios. Within Mahalapur, different occupational patterns and livelihood strategies can be found according to household type and size. The older generation has only worked in stone quarries. The younger generation (above 12 years of age) has recently started to work in road construction in the region. This generation is also engaging in seasonal migration ever since becoming aware of a deadly disease—silicosis—that many of their parents' generation contracted while working in the quarries.

5.2 Brief Review of Diversification Livelihood Framework and Social Capital

The Gond households are undergoing household economy changes as they diversify, take up newer livelihoods for the younger generations, along with which come newer forms of aspirations, how they create their own forms of aspirations, their relation with the state and their own social protection. I discuss these key themes below engaging with the broader literature specific to my fieldwork amongst the Gonds of Mahalapur before proceeding to the case studies.

5.2.1 Livelihood Diversification, Vulnerability and Strategies

Livelihood diversification is mainly conceived by Ellis (2000) and Niehof and Price (2001) (as cited by Ali 2005, p. 42). However, even before diversification, the livelihood approach was dominated by household studies with the works like Schmink (1984) amongst others until the late 1980s. Although this trend ended with a pessimism that households are marginalised by wider economic and political contexts, the idea that households are not passive and atomistic in their coping strategy and that they have an agency which is exercised by acquiring, using and managing assets and resource done strategically (Niehof 2004, p. 323) took shape. According to Schmink (1984), the household is an economic unit where decisions of livelihood generation in the form of labour force participation, migration, consumption patterns are negotiated to cope with broader historical and structural processes (ibid., 87 as cited in de Haan and Zoomers 2005, p. 29). Later, this approach got replaced by livelihoods conceived in terms of capitals, asserts, resources, access and capabilities (Chambers and Conwoy 1992, pp. 9–12 as cited in de Haan and Zoomers 2005, p. 27) working at IDS in 1992 (inspired by Sen's work on entitlement explaining poverty and famine in India 1981). Since then, livelihoods framework in terms of these empirical units (beyond household economic analysis of livelihoods) took the shape of livelihood intensification, livelihood extensification and livelihood diversification

(Swift and Hamilton 2001 as cited in Ahmed Ali 2005, p. 54). The current modernist approach of livelihoods study is in the form of network analysis to understand how household members create both formal and informal networks to meet their livelihoods needs.

In all these frameworks of defining it, livelihoods is simply understood to be a way of making a living using resources, access to different capitals, assets, strategies and capabilities. Thus, Abrar and Seeley (2009) rightly points out that there is no such thing as the "livelihoods framework" and instead to directly analyse how people make a living given their constraints and coping strategies with their given assets, resources and capabilities. Concepts of gender and power have helped to understand how not everyone will have equal access to these resources and strategies and how certain forms of coping strategies are wielded and yielded by the households to meet their needs (De Haan and Zoomers 2005). Although, with the current political economy and its influence on the households, my study amongst the Gonds in Mahalapur shows that household should again be the focus of livelihoods approach considering that the formal institutions of state support (which I will discuss in Chapter 6 on the state) have failed them. So, the question that my book addresses is how are Gonds making a living? What informal institutions are the Gonds able to access and how do they manoeuvre and maximise their needs with minimal loss? What is the Gonds's bargaining power in the informal economy? Clearly, in the livelihoods approach, there are two schools of thoughts: one that looks at the households itself (like my own study on the Gonds) and the other which looks at how broader institutions beyond the households that influence their livelihood strategies. These two approaches can be divided into informal and formal study of livelihoods and my book is on the informal institutions accessible to the Gonds and how the Gonds make the maximum advantage of it why was is it so. I agree with Wood (2005) that of micro-level analysis of livelihood constraints and strategies helps to gain the link between the resources of the poor within the broader political economy in the form of social capital deployable to the vulnerable households.

Diversification is just one way in which rural people may respond to change. Hussein and Nelson (1998) and Scoones (1998) identified three main rural livelihood strategies: (1) diversification of income sources including, but not confined to, coping strategies, (2) agricultural intensification and extensification and (3) migration, whether local, national or international (Whitehead 2002, p. 577). However, especially in extreme

5 NARRATIVES OF *KAMAYEE/DHANDA* (INCOME): MODES OF WAGES 135

situations, such as drought, people may cope simply by adjusting consumption patterns (e.g. eating less as seen in some Gond households who took debt to raise money for wedding expenses). The purposes of these strategies are survival (based on stable subsistence), security (based on assets and rights) and self-respect (based on independence and choice) (Chambers 1989, drawing on Amartya Sen capabilities 1981). Furthermore, these strategies depend on the context of each household as well as are embedded historical practice (Carswell 2002). For the Gonds, the livelihood diversification is to combine farm and non-farm work such as stone quarrying while also practising subsistence farming and wood collection.

Neihof (2004) makes a distinction between coping and coping strategies for agrarian households who have to cope with both temporality and seasonality of agriculture but also for unseen economic shocks. Wood (2005) defines coping as an assessment of people's strengths as measure by access to these various forms of capital, which comprise their needs (p. 7). The former is a long-term response to crisis (ibid., p. 323). I use this idea of coping strategy to explain the Gonds's households livelihood diversification like migration strategy can be considered to be a coping strategy (short-term strategy) as compared to the long-term forms of livelihoods like wood collection and working on stone quarry, and more recently, is road construction which are means to cope. Thus, there is a combination of both short-term and long-term strategies of livelihoods which I discuss in Chapter 4 and this chapter.

On strategies, Thieme says,

> Livelihood strategies can be seen as a continuum that covers the range from a struggle to survive, security and growth. Livelihood outcomes are the achievements or outputs of livelihood strategies.... (2008, p. 54)

Further, she says that strategies are not rational choice but determined by sense of reality and are part of habitus (ibid., p. 61). Thieme combined her research on migrants in Kyrgyzstan to Russia with that of Nepalis to New Delhi between 2006 and 2009 and has applied Bourdieu's theory of practice to understand the Nepali migrants' livelihood and multilocal experiences through international migration. In my research, I treat the Gond household as a social field, as defined by Bourdieu (1977, 1986), and the household members as the agents. The social field is defined by the agents' capital and the agent's habitus, and agents position themselves and their interests based on whether they have access to this capital and why some have and some have not. For the Gonds, these strategies are deeply rooted in the sense of care and duty to their families and are influenced by the sociodemographic factors including but not limited to class, race, caste, ethnicity, migratory status, gender, age, marital status and physical ability (Vera-Sanso 2012, p. 326). These come in the form of kinship, social networks and social relations with labour arrangements with other Gond households and other influential people (Khan and Seeley 2005).

Livelihood strategies for the Gonds of Mahalapur are determined by the household head's age, gender and marital status as well as the landholding size. The agency, as the ability to access and produce resources within the households, determines these livelihood strategies—whether to collect wood, to migrate, to work in the quarries, to perform agricultural work or to work in road construction.

The possibility of diversifying may also be affected by social factors such as prejudice and cumulative social exclusion that may affect household members differentially or collectively. New labour opportunities, where positive, may be barred by gender or caste/tribe exclusions. For instance, in Panna district, the labour market is still in favour of male labourers who get paid more working in the stone quarries as compared to female work of collecting woods which is equally risky in terms of getting caught by the forest guards and protecting oneself from wildlife and other dangers to their personal security. Besides, children's work participation, especially girls, is also "unpaid" for and their agency is compromised for the household stability where they don't have a choice to opt out of. The Madhya Pradesh Human Development Report (MPHD Report) states that

> In order to increase wages in agriculture and to shift the workers to more productive areas, rural diversification is almost the only avenue open. (2002, p. 88)

Breman (1996) defines diversity of livelihoods "occupational multiplicity" as characteristic of the rural economy like those in village of Mahalapur. Such diversity questions the previously assumed boundaries between rural and urban, formal and informal, market and non-market (Whitehead 2002, 577), and agriculture and industry, and "the way people are interpreted as making complete transitions from one type of activity to another as development proceeds" (Ellis 1998, 1). Ellis (2000) specified that

> an individual has a diversified livelihood where s/he has multiple jobs or incomes, but a household can have multiple livelihoods, even though each member is in fact specialising in one activity. (as cited in Start and Johnson 2004, p. 1)

Breman and Mundle (1991) suggested that, for India, three important aspects have affected rural economies and led to an increase in diverse and multiple forms of rural livelihoods, namely (1) the decline of agriculture, (2) the rise in non-agricultural rural and urban employment and (3) the increased flexibility and insecurity of labour markets. For tribal peoples like the Gonds, there is the additional displacement from forest areas. For the most vulnerable groups, like the tribal communities, livelihood diversification implies a multiplicity of jobs, which includes badly paid work in exploitative conditions or being paid well below market rates. Much rural non-farm work is in the informal sector, lacking formal regulation. Lower castes are under-represented in better-paid non-farming work, according to Lanjouw and Shariff (2004). They conclude that there are constraints for the rural poor in accessing non-farm employment in rural India. In the postcolonial and liberalising economy of India, the impacts of livelihood diversification on households become critically important to explore.

For the study of the Gonds in Mahalapur, I use the livelihood diversification framework because it is flexible enough to capture the range and diversity of household livelihood resources, assets, and allows for accommodating the temporal perspective of the household life course and the household agency (Niehof 2004). I map the livelihood strategies with the different Gond households that I observed and describe in detail in Chapters 4–6 and show how these livelihood strategies change over different generations. I use the livelihood diversification framework, but with the caution of not overemphasising agencies of the people like Gonds as there are factors within the broader political economy that add to their already constrained livelihoods (Wood 2003; Staples 2007).

5.2.2 Social Capital, Social Networks and Social Protection

In Mahalapur, the Gonds are seen to use their kinship linkages and relations to access information for newer economic opportunities and to undergo various mutually equitable land and labour sharing arrangements with each other. Social networking either through the market in the form of their employers or in the form of natal support goes a long way towards ensuring the households especially the Gond widows' sustainability. There are a myriad of definitions of social capital but I am drawing upon those that closely to the case studies that I gathered in Mahalapur in terms of social relations and networks that might or might not work for some depending upon the household. I start this section by defining social capital as defined by Moser (1998), Adler and Kwon (1999), and Putnam (1995). Later, I will also engage with relevant critiques of social capital like Das (2004) and Cleaver (2005). These views are important because they help us to understand what resources the poor might draw upon and what strategies are employed to cope with constraints.

Social capital according to Moser is "reciprocity within communities and households based on trust derived from social ties" (Moser 1998, 10 as cited in Ali 2005). For Adler and Kwon (1999, p. 2), social capital is "a resource for individual and collective actors located in the network of their more or less durable relations" (as cited in Niehof 2004, p. 324). For Putnam (1995, p. 67) social capital is in the form of "features of social organization such as networks, norms, and social trust that facilitate coordination and cooperation for mutual benefit" (as cited in Ali 2005, 60). I have used the above definitions of social capital amongst several available as these emphasise on social relations and family ties available to vulnerable households like the Gonds who establish relations of trust and mutual benefits through labouring and land arrangements. I found that for the Gonds, social relations are more reliable and secured forms for making their living despite several constraints. Newer economic opportunities for the Gond households combined with the abolishment of all debts of the landless and subsistence farmers like the Gonds during Indira Gandhi's time have created a way for newer forms of solidarity between each other. These types of relations are done on a voluntary basis in the form of open exchange using labour and land sharing arrangements (Harriss-White and Garikipati 2008) as I will describe in Chapter 4. This is because both labour and capital for rural households create an economy which is entirely based on mutual trust, reciprocity and equitable relationship which is their resource and their coping strategy. This kind of voluntary networks Swift (1998) is horizontal between individuals based on trust and expectations.

Abrar and Seeley (2009), in their study of livelihoods of rural households in India and Bangladesh, showed that social networks may help the poor by providing work, financial support, justice and social security. According to them,

> A social network creates social capital for the poor, providing them with the means to survive in society by being part of a group. Such groups determine attitudes, behavior, values, identities, as well as access to and opportunities to gain resources. Networks are based on connections that can be strengthened by trust and personal bonds or ties. (2009, p. 95)

The Gonds build resilience to unforeseen and anticipated hardships that influence their livelihood decisions. Social protection is stretched beyond just immediate needs and hardships. Gonds compensate the low impact of state-led social welfare programmes through family and kinship relations as I will show in later chapters. Thus, the social protection of the Gonds needs to be contextualised within ideologies of duty and care (Gardner 2009). In particular for the women-headed households (de facto due to widowhood as described by Niehof 2004), the need for a constant flow of cash is more challenging as their options for work are more limited compared to men. Compared to women, the men have more dense and broad network to access work and can easily move around with fewer norms preventing them from doing so. In Mahalapur, the range of social networks is wide, but is not accessible to everyone equally. As Woods (2005) warns that these types of social relations like kinship, neighbours, community are institutional but are not organised and embedded in habits, customs, expectations and norms and subject to subtractability where a departure of one member might affect the quality of the networks (Wood 2005, p. 5). Thus, these networks can adversely effect disadvantaged members who cannot meet these expectations.

In that sense, social network is limited in terms of how wide and how intense (or how dense) one's the social capital is and it depends on what poor households can offer in return. Abrar and Seeley (2009) categorise these kinds of networks into horizontal (kinship, friends, homogenous) and vertical ties (poor and the influential, patron–client relationships).

According to them (ibid., p. 105), because these social networks are so diverse and uncertain, there are many problems with them for the rural poor and these problems can put their livelihoods at risk. Sometimes, the patrons are not available when they are truly needed, as in extreme emergencies or where high transactional expenses may be involved for the maintenance of one's social network. Female heads of households may be even more vulnerable for cultural reasons where seeking vertical networks or seeking external help outside of kinship and family structures might be considered a taboo. Thus, the vulnerable households prefer equitable exchange to avoid going into debts.

In another study on strategies of social protection of the older women labourers, Vera-Sanso (2012), in her study of older working women in the South Indian city of Chennai, has shown how poor families under-appreciate the economic contribution of the older women of the household and, in fact, treat them as a financial burden. Her study makes a valuable contribution to understanding the vulnerability faced by such women as vendors who earn for their families in the hope of receiving social protection in old age. In Mahalapur too, older but able-bodied women are found to work as casual migrant workers in construction, and almost all of them would fetch wood from the forest carrying the maximum allowed load of 40 kg on their heads and walking as many as 10 km to the town to sell it on daily basis. Vera-Sanso raised concern over the lack of an appropriate safety net for such women as a result of a lack of support from the state. This lack of support pressures poor families to postpone old-age care in favour of more urgent expenses (ibid.). It demonstrates how social protection, in this case for the elderly, is primarily located within their kin relationships due to the absence of the state in the lives of the elderly and because they continued to work for their families. My book too will pay closer attention to widowed households in Mahalapur who faced more constraints than male-headed households.

According to Gardner (2009, p. 11),

> social protection is any form of assistance given from one person or group to another that provides insurance against risks and shocks, 'safety nets' in times of crisis or social or economic resources in times of need.

According to Waddington, those persons, who often fall outside the social protection provided by the state, engage in a set of strategic behaviours to

...reduce risk, co-insure one another, and manage the investment and distribution of resources to ensure individual well-being in the present and foreseeable future. (2003, p. 15)

A study done on rural Tanzania by Cleaver showed how social capital as a resource in the form of social relations and bonding (Putnam 1995) did not result in favourable results for the poorer households. She was interested to know what happens to the agency of poor households in the sustainable management of the Usungu Wetlands Project and whether it is their social capital. She found that in conditions of severe poverty, the poorer households find their social networks contracted. The poorer households are disadvantaged due to a lack of material assets and, as a result, they could not participate in accessing and managing the wetland project with other more privileged households. As a direct result, these households remained chronically poor. Cleaver says that, for the poorer households,

...help secured was minimal, intermittent, and obtained through constant and costly reinvestments in uneven exchanges. (2005, 899)

Thus, Cleaver is critical of the understanding of social capital by Putnam (1995) and the World Bank (2003) that suggests poor households have each other to assist in dire economic circumstances in the form of bonding and networking. Further, she added,

the poorest people are disadvantaged both by the generalized norms and the personalized interactions implicit in collective action and are unable to negotiate such arrangements to their advantage. (Cleaver 2005, p. 899)

More importantly, through her study, she observed that the agency of poor people is critically dependent on three interlinked factors:

the able-bodiedness, their room for manoeuver within social relationships, and their ability to represent their interests accessible to them at low cost. (Cleaver 2005, p. 904)

Das (2004) too is critical about social capital as defined by Putnam (1995) in the form of social networks and resources between two poor people drawing upon his research on temporary migrants in Orissa. However, according to my work on the Gonds, I find that people who do not have any tangible or financial asset, still have their labour which can be used as a resource including social relations and linkages with extended kinships and other members of the village. These linkages and social relations help to seek jobs and sustain their livelihoods. On the other hand, I do find Cleaver (2005) criticism of social capital relevant because, for the Gonds, their fate has been turned against them after they lost their access to the forest which indicates the hidden power and inequality that creates a sense of injustice done to the Gonds. They have been reduced to their current economic plight because they had nothing to resist the forest loss except to diversify or more recently, migrate. Many during the fieldwork told me that they would rather not migrate because it is a huge strain to carry wives, children and grains in the form of grain to a new location. It is also risky and unpredictable no matter how good their relations are with the labour contractors and employers. In other words, social relationships are of no use in this context. Thus, Das's (2004) critique needs to be qualified, not in the least because, even for widows, any form of social networking and bonding either through the market in the form of their employers or in the form of natal support goes a long way towards ensuring the widows' sustainability. This is because in Panna all Gonds are members of the same class, ensuring everybody's bargaining powers have equal value whether labourer, employer, landless or landed. The creation of social hierarchy based on labourer–employer relationships is not as fixed, allowing enough room for unskilled workers like the Gonds to find a secure source of jobs. As a result, I would like to rethink Das's conclusions that social capital has no impact for the rural poor in India. However, we also need to know how poor use social capital under exploitative conditions of capitalism as was demonstrated by Raju Das (2004) and Cleaver (2005) in rural Tanzania. Both authors studied agrarian communities undergoing a capitalist transformation.

5.3 Brief Description of Different Sources of *Dhanda*. Sources of Income/Wage/Trade

5.3.1 *Forest-Related Activities*

Forest-based activities play an important part in the Gonds lives. Forests are used to collect firewood, keep cost of living low, for sustenance, and also for collecting Non-Timber Forest-based Products (NTFP).

5 NARRATIVES OF *KAMAYEE/DHANDA* (INCOME): MODES OF WAGES 143

In the case of Panna, the MPHD Report (2002) offers a case study of 53 households living on the outskirts of the Panna Reserve Forest. It revealed that the households earned a total annual income of around Rs. 3.23 lakhs through collection of *tendu* leaves, *mahua* products and firewood comment in how it is important for Gonds. While the 53 households also had other income sources, the income from forest produce accounted for 85% of the total income of 46 households. Each family earned Rs. 9450 on average a year from the forest (ibid.).

Another forest-based livelihood is wood which helps to keep their cost of living low. It is essential for cooking, making homes and making fences in their agricultural fields and for selling. Mostly it is woman's job to collect forest wood and then to sell it next day by walking 10 km to Panna town, carrying wood on their foreheads. Says Brijesh Singh, a middle-aged Gond:

> This is because it has become illegal to cut forests. So, the women are sent to do this work because it is easy to get away from the forest authorities when the women break the law because they say that they have families to feed. To impose a fine on a man seen inside a forest is easy because the guards say he will smoke and cause a fire in the forest. (Fieldnotes 2011)

It is a usual sight to see Gond women carrying wood and walking from Mahalapur to Panna town, about 10 km, to sell the wood. There are two kinds of wood—wet and dry. The wet wood is more environmentally significant. The Gonds cannot take this (according to the Forest Regulations) but they can pick up the dry wood. They collect wood clandestinely and, sometimes, their wood is seized by the forest department and therefore their journey may be wasted. A pile of wood will only earn Rs. 100 per day but it is immediate cash in hand. Even so, to earn so little, they spend an entire day making their way to the forest and then return home.

Money earned from selling forest wood helps in running the house during times when the man family member is waiting for another piece of contract work to come by. As a result, the women have acquired a lot of say in the way the household is run. However, younger brides are not meant to be seen in the public space and so will not do farming or collect wood. They will be mostly occupied in nursing children and doing domestic chores. Older women like Kesar Bai will continue to do both wood collection and work on farms with the help of remittance money to meet agricultural costs sent from her migrating children. If there is no other work and income coming to the household, then there is always wood collection work to do. If the forest department completely stops access to forests for the Gonds, then it will be a monumental loss of income to the Gond households.

5.3.2 Migration

Migration is to go to farm and non-farm wage work. It includes working in brick kilns (only in Panna), road construction, as well as stone quarries. Both men and women migrate, however, women migration is a recent phenomenon.

5.3.3 Road Construction

This is a new form of work available to the Gonds and is popular amongst younger generation of the Gonds. Similar to working in stone quarries, working and getting paid to build roads is done through contract that lasts up to two weeks per contract and the pay is up to Rs. 350 per day. As yet there are no known health hazards associated with this work.

Road construction jobs come through local contacts economy and labour contractors who also hire for other unskilled work in Panna town. There are two types of roads—the *Pradhan Mantri Sadak Yojna* which is for villages and the express roads for the main highways connecting different states. The wages are the same in both kinds, and work comes through those contractors who get the tender from the government. The wages range from Rs 300 to 350 per day and the length of the work depends on the length of the road. A 10 km length road takes 10 days. The work involves making the mixture (*masala*) and then laying it on the ground and making sure that it is of the right thickness. The village inroads are less thicker than the express/interstate roads and therefore the latter one takes longer as it is expected to be used by heavy trucks and other heavy vehicles and should be able to sustain the heavy load and in constant use whereas the village inroads can be less thick as only bicycles and motorbikes are expected to ride on them. In either case, the work itself is very strenuous and labour-intensive which is why Gonds demand such high wage. They have made a niche for themselves in such precarious and labour-intensive jobs requiring their bodies to be flexible and to be in squatting position at all times under the sun. I asked Manoj, Aditya's brother who does this job now and again as to why Gonds organise and make sure that there is permanent work available and demand better working conditions and he replies,

> oh madam, there are many such contractors who want to make us permanent, but we refuse because they won't give us the high wages. (Fieldnotes 2012)

Thus, by not bonding in a contract, the Gonds create their own form of organised wage security by putting themselves at high risk but also charging above market wages. They are aware about the politics behind permanent jobs which is less pay and repetitive work which Gonds avoid as there could be household emergencies and other seasonal fluctuations in farming as they are depended upon farming for food security.

5.4 Case Studies

In the following, I describe the different types of Gond households sustaining their livelihood throughout the year by doing farm and non-farm work. I map the various households to their livelihood strategies to survive, make a living, and to meet social obligations.

5.4.1 Leela Bai

Leela Bai is a young widow, aged 35. She lost her husband to TB about two years before I met her. She has five children to TB about two years before exploit them by making them do their labourer. Throughout the year, Bai and her daughter, aged 15, work at a brick kiln 10 km away from Mahalapur, where they load and unload red bricks onto and off of trucks with a handcart. They get Rs. 25 per trip and their daily earnings depend upon the number of trips they make per day. They have been doing this for the last two years. Before that, Bai sold wood, but since forest access was restricted she sought work at brick kilns. Pure milk is unaffordable for households like Leela Bai. Later, another Gond woman was arguing with her for not showing up for a work and was very keen on employing Leela Bai to join her. Such types of employers seem to target desperate households like Leela Bai who are lone earners and have about six children to feed. These kinds of households and de facto widows appear not to be in short of petty and urgent jobs.

During winter, Bai does additional agricultural work as a share cropper. The land is owned by a labour contractor who also hires her to work at his brick kiln. While she is paid cash for the brick kiln work, the terms of the agricultural arrangements are different as she is paid in kind by getting about a quarter of the total agricultural output of wheat. She does not have to pay for agricultural costs such as watering. She, together with her five children, do the labour-intensive parts of farm work such as ploughing, sowing seeds, putting fences up and guarding the farm in the winter for up to five months. This starts in November, just after Diwali and lasts until the harvest season in March. During this period, Bai moves out of Mahalapur with all her children and, together, they all guard the farm. The children guard during the day while Bai and her daughter work in the brick kiln. Then at night they all take turns. They return to their permanent home in Mahalapur around April.

There is no expectation from her in-laws that she will share her earnings with them, but would be expected to do so if she is living with them. In general, a Gond woman, both married and widowed, will continue to show obedience to her in-laws by following the norms as their daughter-in-law. But, Leela Bai has an independent income and this means that she is not required to give a justification to them as to how she manages to feed her family. In this sense, she enjoys complete freedom. While this does create a stir with her in-laws and other wives of the household, it does not result in hostile relationships.

Bai does not ask for help from her in-laws because this could entail an implicit reciprocity agreement with them, like doing cooking and cleaning her in-laws house. Instead, she relies on her eldest, married daughter who comes to help in extreme circumstances such as caring for a sick child in her home. Her brother will also help her from time-to-time. He checks on her family by visiting her on the site or her home in Mahalapur. Maintaining communication with her brother and married daughter has become possible with the use of mobile phones (see photo above). Being employed—even if it means multiple jobs—is a much better option for widowed households than depending on extended kinship.

Thus, lone earners and widows such as Bai would have to labour until she fulfils her parental role of raising money to support marrying-off her children. Money spent on marriage is earned by doing *majoori*, and being able to spend money on a marriage is a social marker of status.

Bai does not have a Below Poverty Line (BPL) ration card. This means that the only way she can meet her food security needs is through share-cropping. Having the card would potentially allow her to give up share-cropping. However, as discussed above, having a BPL card is connected to rural politics and only those who vote in favour of the local dominant political group have automatic access to such benefits. I asked her why she does not apply for the BPL card. She says that she did, but the *panchayat* asked her to pay money for it, which she does not have. There are many like her in the village who do not have a BPL card because they do not want to pay the bribe and get into a habit of paying money for everything. Instead, Bai prefers to work or wait or when the system becomes more transparent.

However, I discovered that those who have paid to obtain the BPL card say that it is not a bribe but a small fee so that the BPL card is posted to their homes directly. This is more convenient for them than needing to collect it from the rural administration headquarters in Panna, some distance away. However, most Gond households don't read and write and I also noticed that the households are not clearly demarcated to have full address that the administration can post to. Most Gonds are confused as to why they are being charged for the cards even when there may be a connection cost related to the cards being mailed directly to their homes. The only explanation that makes sense in my investigations is simply that it is not common amongst the Gonds to pay for the cards because of their suspicions that it might really be for bribery purposes, so it will take a while before they get used to this idea.

5.4.2 Nandlal Adivasi

Another case of vulnerable household is Nandlal Adivasi, aged 45. Nandlal maintains a migration-dependent household and he, too, is landless. His entire family including his wife and his three grown sons have migrated to Jammu for each of the last three years. They depend completely on migration for all their basic and major needs. In Jammu, they take irregular jobs such as building houses. They prefer to go there because it is an important place of pilgrimage and they can visit the goddess Vaishnoo Devi. Right now, there are two children of the three who are of marrying age and, so far, they have not had the time to seek a suitable bride. The estimated expense for two marriages is Rs. 60,000. Such funds are possible from the money they earn from migration and the work opportunities it brings. The whole family is involved in construction work, and they are all paid the same wages. They earn Rs. 170 per person per day, depending upon the type of work. Previously, Nandlal's family was totally dependent on stone quarrying. But over the last three years, the mines have been closed, forcing the family to migrate elsewhere to find work. All of Nandlal's wages are paid to him on time on the second day of every month. In addition, he and every adult member of his family receive an advance of Rs. 500 a month for personal expenses, which is deducted from the final monthly wages. He says that he is never sure where he will be next because he migrates to wherever he can find work. Because the work is unpredictable, Nandlal living arrangements are unpredictable.

The households of Leela Bai and Nandlal are similar in that they are both landless. But they are also dissimilar because Bai is the lone wage earner and is more vulnerable because she cannot expect much help from her in-laws. In Nandlal's situation, we see that he has the cooperation of his family. Because Nandlal's children are grown and, therefore, take care of their own needs, his situation is not as precarious as Bai's.

People migrate due to lack of jobs in Panna because not having land means that food security is always threatened. Whereas, for Leela Bai, except for the eldest daughter who is married, the rest of her five children depend upon her completely dependent upon her. In 2014, I discovered that her next eldest daughter too got last year in 2013 married; Bai and her daughter are in a position to labour, save and pay for the marriage. Thus, despite the fact that both families are landless, by the strategies of combining farm and non-farm work with strategic migration, both households are debt-free and relatively independent of their extended kin and can provide for their own, basic needs.

5.4.3 Multiple Earners and "Older Female Earners"

Here, I describe Kesar Bai and Sukhram's household where I found that all generations are involved in earning for the household.

I remember when I first met Kesar Bai, she was sorting, chopping and arranging the woods that she had collected earlier in the day. For some reason, I connected with her the way I could not with Leela Bai. I realised this was because Leela Bai's hands are full working and waging for the small children unlike Kesar Bai, whose children are grown and married and she had more time to spend with me. Later, I discovered that she also connected with me as she had lost one of her daughter who was raped and killed while going to the forest to fetch woods and that originally, the attack was targeted at her and since, then, that grief has never left her.

Kesar Bai relied mostly on forest work to raise her children by selling wood. She enabled three of her children to marry with the financial support she got from her slightly well-to-do natal family. She cultivates her own land as well as the land of her two eldest sons. Those lands are acquired when her husband died about five years ago. The *panchayat* will give them their share of land. Each son was given about 1.5 acres of land. As Kesar Bai was alone with five children to care for after her husband died, none of the children finished elementary school. From the beginning of their childhood, they had to help Kesar Bai to run the household. Many households in Mahalapur who are run by widows have similar story. Today, two of her sons, married, have migrated to Kashmir and have started working construction jobs, sending money back home to meet agricultural costs when they can. Kesar Bai does all the farm work on her own with some help from one of her grandchildren. The income earned by her sons from their ability to find work after migrating has helped stabilise the family's livelihood. Kesar Bai's youngest son works on road construction, either within the state of Madhya Pradesh or outside it. Such work has come to replace work in stone quarries common amongst the older generation as the preferred livelihood.

As observed by Vera-Sanso (2012) in her study of older women working as street vendors and earning for their son's families in Chennai, South India, older women are supporting themselves, their husbands, and support their younger relatives and help poor families in their fight against poverty by subsidising their incomes as well. Anyone who is a grandparent in Mahalapur, no matter what age, is automatically considered "old." Being elderly is not about age but a normative concept.

Kesar Bai is currently the head of the household. She decides who gets the land. She does the farm work that secures food for the household. In addition, she still collects and sells forest wood daily in Panna. She receives a widow pension every three months. At the moment, Utpal, her eldest son, with his wife and a new born son live in the courtyard of Kesar Bai's house. Although Kesar Bai is a widow, her general condition is quite stable because all her children are grown, married and take care of themselves. The household is run by a well-orchestrated and coordinated effort with the help of her sons. They help with the agricultural costs and, in turn, Kesar Bai guards their farms thereby stabilising her household. However, not everything is as stable as Kesar Bai and her son-in-law (Shilpa's husband) do not get along. Recent rumours of Kesar Bai having an affair with another male widow have upset Shilpa's husband who one day could not help raise his hands on her. Often, conflicts about sharing agricultural yield get expressed into interpersonal relations of the households.

5.4.4 Emergency and Unforeseen Hardships

The household of Sukhram (Aditya's father) is where all four livelihood options are practised: agriculture, forest wood collection, stone quarrying and road construction. Agriculture activities are practised by all household members. Wood collection is done strictly by Usha Bai, Sukhram's wife. Road construction is done by his sons while Sukhram himself works in stone quarries. Sukhram, aged 47, is a skilled stone miner. Usha Bai, his wife, is about 45 years old. They have two sons and three daughters. The household is mostly run on the incomes of Sukhram and his wife, whose regular income from selling wood sustains the family in terms of food. However, Sukhram has lost his land and so has been forced to enter into a contractual arrangement with his affinal cousin kin.

Sukhram looks after three acres of land and, in return, he gives back 4 quintals of the total grain output. He has made his name in stone mining and does not have to worry about getting work as a stone miner. Sukhram says that the reason he has managed to give his family a more stable living is because, unlike others working in the quarries, he never drinks. This is in contrast to some of the Gonds from Mahalapur who go away on a temporary work close by, earn their wages and then spend it immediately on drinking and gambling. Alcohol drinking amongst stone quarry workers is often reported even in the case study of Meher in Orissa (2009). He found that for the stone quarry workers, drinking alcohol was important to perform the laborious task of breaking stone as it helped to numb the body pain and continue to work. This relationship between alcohol consumption associated with precarious labouring needs more objective studying to know how it enables them to perform precarious work.

Sukhram farms his cousin's land and shares a part of the yield with him instead of money exchange. In return, he offers his labour for cultivating and meeting the agricultural cost of his cousin, Ramavse's farm. Although the entire household orchestrates themselves to keep the household assured of food security, the education of their other two children has been compromised as a result. Manoj, the younger brother of Aditya, does not have the same passion as Aditya to finish his education.[1] The increasing financial vulnerability of the household is always on Manoj's mind more than completing his education. Similarly, Kajal, Aditya's younger sister, stopped schooling after she finished eighth grade in Mahalapur village and has recently migrated to Rajasthan and made some money when I visited them in 2014. For Kajal, her constrain to continue beyond 8th grade is that she is the only one interested from her generation of girls and I asked her why don't they continue like her. She says,

Didi (sister), they go to forests instead.

Recently, the forest department has put restrictions on the amount of wood to collect from the forest and so a strategy by households is to recruit as many members to increase the wood in the house.

There are also conservative reasons that prevent young girls from finishing their education. These reasons are connected to the fear of outside influence caused by studying in towns within the northern patriarchal kinship systems (Kis-Katos 2012) like those in the Gonds community. In 2013, Aditya elder sister was seriously ill and the family had to pay Rs. 20,000 for her care. This exhausted all of their savings and left them with no money to farm. This compromised their food security for the next year (2014). To meet this sudden and unanticipated economic shock, Sukhram had to either borrow money or work in a stone quarry for three weeks to compensate. Thus, saving for unforeseen hardships and emergency keeps the situation amongst Gonds families very delicate and unstable.

Sukhram's family fear that soon the forest department, which seems to increase the control of movements into the forest each day, will severely affect their livelihood by limiting their opportunities to earn money. This is because most of stone mining is done inside the forest where high-quality stone is found. If this mining income is reduced, then Sukhram will be forced to migrate to Powai which is about 60 km from Panna.

---

[1] I discuss this more in Chapter 6 on the state about how schooling is valued amongst the marginalised population drawing upon Froerer (2011) ethnography amongst the Hindu Oraons in Chhattisgarh.

It is a place where illegal stone quarrying is known to take place and, it is a potential source of income but involves trekking and going away for 3–4 weeks at a stretch.

However, Sukhram is not too sure about this option because all of his children are now grown except for the youngest daughter. Kajal is about 14 years old. The eldest child is Aditya Gond. Aditya and the younger son, Manoj, do *majoori*, building roads, but only outside of Panna. Manoj, who is aged 16, wishes to finish his college course as it might give him non-labouring career options but Manoj is all too aware of the financial strain on the household and knows that he cannot be sitting idly by enjoying the luxury of going to college and studying like his elder brother, Aditya, while his parents labour for the household. He is considering other alternatives to education, as he remains unconvinced of its practical use since Aditya has yet to get a position as a teacher despite passing the teaching exam with distinction.

In the case of Sukhram and Kesar Bai, we see that the agricultural division of labour is along conjugal and inter-generational lines within Gond households while sharecropping (such as Sukhram's land arrangement with Ramavse) and seed exchanges occur along conjugal-affinal lines. More widely, such farm-based economic relationships are also formed along fictive-kin arrangements as all male members of the inhabitants of Mahalapur refer to each other as "bhai" (brother). Thus, sudden shocks can shake up long-term plans if households including education and that the forest remains a key source of income both in terms of wood and stone mining. Both Kajal and Manoj's are more keenly aware of the household's financial constrain and do not argue for furthering their interests in schooling even if they desire to. Says Manoj,

> If I also go to school like my brother, then who will help my parents in the farm and ensure there is food to eat?

5.4.5 Change in Household Development Cycle

Gond's livelihood practices are also influenced by the household development cycle, which changes with the needs of the household such as upcoming weddings like in the case of Brijesh Singh. He did not migrate for work until now when his two daughters are of marriageable age. He also has a widowed sister-in-law and there are other agnates of the family living in the same homestead who depend on that farm for food security.

Altogether there are about four families dependent upon the agricultural output from eight acres of land. Brijesh's wife collects wood from the forest and sells it. Both husband and wife work on the farm and sometimes the grown up children will help in guarding the fields at night.

Recently, he sold two acres because the burden of agricultural costs is too much for him. Brijesh was seriously ill with throat cancer and had also suffered a loss while trying to do commercialised farming. Ironically, his household does not have the BPL ration card because his political sympathies differ from those of the elected *Sarpanch* (village head) even though the *Sarpanch* is part of the same family lineage as him. I will explain this in Chapter 6 on the state but it's because he too does not want to bribe the *panchayat* as then it will be a habit as was seen in the case of Leela Bai.

Compared to other Gonds, Brijesh is relatively secure in terms of land holding size which allows him to work as a labour contractor recruiting Gonds from Mahalapur nearby villages. In the past, he worked for the forest department as a labour supplier for forest-related jobs like building roads inside the forests. He would pay the labourers from his own savings before receiving money from the forest department. As such, he was an important employer for the Mahalapur and received a small commission for very labourer that he provided.

Brijesh Singh has two young unmarried daughters: one about 9 and the other about 12 years of age. When his eldest married daughter migrated to Jammu, she took Brijesh's next eldest daughter, aged 12, with her to look after her infant child while she worked as a labourer in constructing apartment complexes. Brijesh also has one married son and his youngest child is also a son. While he is migrating to Jammu, his elder son looks after the farm work and works as a labour supplier for the forest department when they want labour. Migrating, for Brijesh Singh, is for larger life cycle events and a response to the depletion of more local labouring options increasing agricultural costs.

5.5 Inter-generational Change in Livelihoods

Here, I discuss how four younger households of Mahalapur earn a livelihood. All four of the individuals are born in the village of Mahalapur: Ramcharan, Nandu, Shilpa and Neelam. They are all married and living with their parents in the joint family system/household. Through their stories, I describe below recent inter-generational occupational changes observed amongst the Gonds in Mahalapur. Some households manage to escape working in quarries and how some have to continue with the older tradition of working in stone quarries based on their assessment of their household income needs.

5.5.1 *Ramcharan*

The livelihood profile of Ramcharan's household is very different from that of the rest of the village. Ramcharan, is aged 24, has never been outside Panna but, has some assets due to marrying into a better-off family which brings him food security. His father died at a very young age. His father married twice and after his death, the family was left to fend for themselves. Ramcharan recalls the days when his father was still alive as happier days because the family was well fed due to the father's earnings from the stone mines. But, since his father's death, the whole household had been forced to labour hard, by for example, selling and collecting wood.

Ramcharan works around doing all kinds of *majoori* except working in the stone quarry which killed his father and wood collection, which is usually the role of the female members of the household. However, unlike other men of his younger generation he does not choose the alternative of road construction. I never found him migrating, even to nearby districts for work. He says that he does not have to because work comes to him. I asked him how is that I see him in the village almost every day and he said he works but all his needs are met by the work that he can find in Panna itself. The other reason is that his household is not desperate, unlike most households in Mahalapur because his wife's family is well-to-do in terms of land and so most of their basic food supplies come from her family. I found out from others that Ramcharan had been good at studies like Aditya but after the death of his father to silicosis, he was forced to withdraw and do *majoori*. Thus, Ramcharan's earnings go into savings for the future.

5.5.2 *Nandu*

Another case is Nandu, age 24, a stone miner. His situation is the opposite of Ramcharan. Nandu works only on stone mining and is the only one from his young generation to do so. He is a young father of two infant children and lives with his wife and his parents. His mother still holds the ownership of three acres of land. He is one of the few entrepreneurial stone cutters in the village belonging to the younger generation. While I was there, I saw him twice turn down offers for work in road construction, even though it is very popular amongst his peers. Displaying the familiar preference for work flexibility, he does not like any permanent type of work and prefers to make money in one go and then take a break. He likes to choose his contractor and the mine owner carefully in order to avoid bondage. That way, Nandu is free, independent and also secures high wages.

5.5.3   Gharjamayees

By contrast, the *Gharjamayees* (households where husbands move into their wives' villages after marriage) are interesting because the women both they have "stayed back" after marriage (known as *rukjana*) in the village of Mahalapur. According to many that I spoke to, in this village, these types of households are increasing. I discuss two such cases—Neelam and Shilpa. As mentioned before in Chapter 4, both their houses are very small and cramped for them and their children; both households have at least four children.

Most of the time, the husbands are absent as they work away in stone mines, or have taken other long-term/permanent farm work outside Panna. The major reasons why men move into their wives' villages are because they might not have a landholding in their village of birth and might have lost their land due to family feuds or the land itself may be barren, or there is a water shortage in their village. In addition, it is worth observing that there are places around Panna where debt bondage is still practised. This still occurs in extremely remote areas like Powai and the Kalda districts, about 80 km from Mahalapur, where villages have no electricity. These places have a higher population of Gonds than around Panna town. Another reason why some men move away from their own village to Mahalapur is to escape starvation.

Such households in Mahalapur will not have any documentation to prove their residence in Mahalapur unless they show that their husbands, the *gharjamayees*, have removed their names from the voting list at their birth-village. If such uxorilocal households want to build a house in Mahalapur, then they can either buy land and building it or, if lucky, like Shilpa, their parents can settle them on land adjacent to their farms. Neelam's house is just built behind the courtyard of her parent's house.

Both Shilpa's and Neelam's households are totally dependent on farm and non-farm work and both women contribute equally towards their household needs. The question of whether they will get any output from their parents' farm is a sensitive subject because, after marriage, the "daughter" is no longer considered a member of her birth family and her family's survival is now a matter for her in-laws and husband. This is always a cause of strain between daughters and mothers. The mothers of daughters like Shilpa and Neelam will sometimes oblige by looking after their younger ones when they are very small but the preference is that such daughters should not expect their mothers' assistance in caring for their children. The whole time that I was there, I saw the *gharjamayees* only twice during the year when they came back to take a break from work. The main difference in uxorilocal households compared to other households is that men remain absent from home for a longer period of time.[2]

5.5.4 Gond Women, Work Participation and Hinduisation

Rural and agrarian India continues to depend on women for meeting household needs. However, the woman's reproductive contribution to the household is more highly valued than her contribution to household economic production.[3] According to a study on women's workforce participation[4] by Rahman and Rao (2004),

---

[2] *Uxorilocal Households in Mahalapur* In the village of Mahalapur, there are many (*gharjamayees*) move to their wives' natal village and raise families there. Such living arrangement is a common strategy for food security: although they are landless in Mahalapur, they might have some landholding in their original village. For food security, they contribute towards the agricultural cost and sometimes can also care for their wives' parents to reciprocate for the hospitality extended to build a house nearby the wives' parent's house.

[3] The normative shift in the social role of women in India due to their economic contribution is only restricted to highly industrialised and urbanised areas like Mumbai where economic differentiation of work has helped women's social roles to shift along class lines but not along gender or caste lines.

[4] Sanskritisation in urban households is also associated with Westernisation where households move from joint to a more nuclear family and women's work participation is allowed only in the formal economy and on farms sector. The practice of paying groom-price and veiling of the Gonds and other marginalised groups like tribal (ST) and Dalit (SC) women in India is a form of Sanskritisation.

North India tends to be more patriarchal and feudal than South India. Women in northern India have more restrictions placed on their behaviour, thereby restricting their access to work. Southern India tends to be more unrestricted, women have relatively more freedom, and they have a more prominent presence in society

They suggest that high female participation in the labour market has been seen in the low-caste category, especially for Schedule Castes and Schedule Tribes (ibid.). However, women's economic contribution, in these studies done in north India indicates that it has not helped them bargain for higher wages. In the process of economic reforms, agricultural labourers like rural women remain badly paid (Garikipati and Pfaffenzellar 2012).

Amongst the Gonds in Mahalapur, the earning ability of the women is seen as positive by her household members. This is unlike Hindu or non-ST households in the district where women's work is restricted to that within the household. Widowed women like Leela Bai start to experience more freedom and independence by moving out of their in-laws' home by raising their children on their own. Thus, an unintended consequence of becoming a widow is to become autonomous in the form of de facto female-headed household. However, north Indian social customs and norms in which I have found contrasts with most statistics on women's labour workforce and warn us not to generalise the diversification of livelihoods as I discuss in this section.

Married women in Mahalapur too earn for their households mainly through wood collection but they do not experience the same amount of autonomy and freedom as widows. On the other hand, there is no social transformation in the social status for such widows due to their economic contribution. While labouring to feed their families, women are expected to be head scarfed at all times or veiled if an elderly male member from her in-laws' house passes by. This norm is to honour the patriarchy. If the women who are widows continue to collect wood and do farm-related work, it is very hard to find any acknowledgement of their contribution even though both forms of work are labour intensive and are crucial to the survival and well-being of the Gond household. The dominance of Hindu culture on the women's bodies/appearance can be seen. For instance, Ratna, a young bride in Mahalapur who had gone to see her sick mother, shares her bitter experience.

Once, I did not veil while coming back to Mahalapur from my natal home and the neighbours complained about me to my husband. (Fieldnotes 2011)

said Ratna.

Veiling entails covering the face by the upper part of the sari. It is practised by Gond women who have come to Gond after marriage. Veiling continues even if they are widows. The women veil in the vicinity of elderly male members from her in-law, but in the vicinity of any another male member belonging to the same village they will head scarf. Such controls are strong for younger newly wedded brides but not so for widows, elderly women and young girls.

Working on the farm is extremely significant, especially for households of elderly widows like Kesar Bai, who have never done any non-farm work except for selling and collecting wood. Widows like Kesar Bai who engage in traditional forms of livelihoods do not experience the same form of freedom from their kinship and extended families as do those women like Leela Bai, who combines both farm and on-farm work and is a single earner. Kesar Bai, despite earning throughout the year for the family, is not a single earner as her children contribute towards meeting agricultural inputs and help raise money for their sibling's weddings. Thus, in Mahalapur, what gives women more autonomy is their ability to earn and run their home from their own earnings. Financial independence and control over household earnings gives such women more freedom, especially to widows for food security and wedding expenses for their children. Being economically insecure prevents Gonds from letting their women work to meet the household expenses. This is not to say that women from other poor communities like Yadavs, Sahus and *Bengalis* do not work—they do. The difference between the two types of women's work is that the wages the Gond women earn goes directly into household expenditure and, therefore, these households are dependent on the women's labour. In other communities, women's work, like collecting forest wood, is used more for household purposes. These women are not allowed to sell their labour in the markets or engage in economic activities that will earn cash for the household as that would mean being seen in a public space. These public spaces are highly controlled and regulated in male-dominated societies like Panna in ways that inhibit female participation belonging to non-ST communities in the labour market.

Neff et al. (2012) found that with increasing education in rural north Indian villages there seems to be a decline in the female labour workforce.

They pointed out that increasing educational opportunities notwithstanding, cultural constraints induce women to participate in farm work or to perform unpaid domestic work and the traditional roles of mothers and wives. This study also points out that this is common in places where there is very little industrialisation and urbanisation, and where the opportunity for non-farm work is minimal, as in small towns like Panna. In smaller towns, the social status is determined by the earning ability of the man heading the household. Traditionally, in India, a man is associated with providing for the family. It is observed that women's participation in paid work is restricted to lower castes, to tribes and to peasant societies, like the Gonds, where the landholding size of the farming households is not more than an acre.

5.6 Conclusion

The case studies of livelihood strategies reveal that Gond households have to be flexible and must adopt different types of livelihood portfolios in order to meet their most basic everyday needs of consumption and, more importantly, food security for their large households. The ethnographic study indicates, however, that not all households, especially the landed ones, are just "surviving" and "coping" with hardship. The cases of Brijesh Singh and Ramcharan due to their relatively better status of food security are stable households that are seeking to better their social position. Brijesh does this by supplementing his farm work by doing *majoori* in the town and migrating to Jammu. Ramcharan benefits from food security provided by his wife's family. Leela Bai earnings allow her to be free from kinship obligation to her in-laws, who might expect her to do their household chores in exchange for supporting her family financially. Gaining an independent livelihood is an emancipation process for single earners like de facto females-headed households as widows like Leela Bai by default. However, all households have to strategise their livelihoods to cope and survive and manage to hold up their heads in the village by providing for their children's weddings while also stabilising their food security. The case studies also show that in dealing with the economic hardships, it is the women who have to do the most laborious work and there is feminisation of agriculture as in the case of Leela Bai and Kesar Bai. Gonds are essentially a tribal society, and their ideologies regarding gender and work differ from the Hindu community as seen in Mahalapur. The Gond women participate equally as men in doing unskilled wage even though jobs remain highly gendered with women' access to the most lucrative jobs being still more constrained but they still accommodate north Indian Hindu norms such as veiling and head scarfing in front of elderly men of the household and the village. Temporality and spatiality of the seasonal livelihood strategies demand the Gonds to be flexible and also cope with unexpected household cycle events like deaths. In one respect, I find Corbridge and Shah (2013) observation that political clientelism by landed rural elites causes patronage-based patterns of development in rural north India. On the other hand, I believe it is not so simple to apply the same in Mahalapur without considering the local politics of the region which is not agrarian-based. Lerche et al. (2013) show, that forested states like Madhya Pradesh, unlike other less forested north Indian states have complex state–society relationships characterised by the balancing of tribal rights to forests alongside the need of the state to build schools, hospitals and provide jobs. This is difficult as land is scarce. The other crucial difference of Madhya Pradesh not being a typical north Indian state, is that it has a significant tribal population of approximately 20% (MPHD Report 2002) who historically are not integrated the same way as the Dalits population in Uttar Pradesh and Bihar.

REFERENCES

Abrar, C. R., & Seeley, J. (Eds.). (2009). *Social Protection and Livelihoods: Marginalised Migrant Workers of India and Bangladesh.* University Press.

Adler, P. S., & Kwon, S. (1999). *Social Capital: The Good, the Bad, and the Ugly.* Modified Version of a Paper Presented at the 1999 Academy of Management Meeting, Chicago, IL.

Alam Khan, I., & Seeley, J. (2005). *Making a Living: The Livelihoods of the Rural Poor in Bangladesh.* The University Press Limited.

Ali, A. (2005). *Livelihood and Food Security in Rural Bangladesh: The Role of Social Capital.* Ph.D. Thesis, Wageningen University, the Netherlands, p. 203.

Bourdieu, P. (1977). *Outline of a Theory of Practice* (Vol. 16). Cambridge: Cambridge University Press.

Bourdieu, P. (1986). The Forms of Capital. In J. Richardson (Ed.), *Handbook of Theory and Research for the Sociology of Education* (pp. 241–258). New York: Greenwood.

Breman, J. (1996). *Footloose Labour: Working in India's Informal Economy*. Cambridge: Cambridge University Press.
Breman, J., & Mundle, S. (Eds.). (1991). *Rural Transformation in India*. Oxford: Oxford University Press.
Carswell, G. (2002). Farmers and Fallowing: Agricultural Change in Kigezi District, Uganda. *The Geographical Journal, 168*(2), 130–140.
Chambers, R. (1989). Vulnerability, Coping and Policy. Institute of Development Studies, University of Sussex. *IDS Bulletin, 37*(4), 1–8.
Chambers, R., & Conway, G. (1992). *Sustainable Rural Livelihoods: Practical Concepts for the 21st Century* (IDS Discussion Paper 296). Brighton, UK: Institute of Development Studies, University of Sussex.
Cleaver, F. (2005). The Inequality of Social Capital and the Reproduction of Chronic Poverty. *World Development, 33*(6), 893–906.
Corbridge, S., & Shah, A. (2013). Introduction: The Underbelly of the Indian Boom. *Economy and Society, 42*(3), 335–347.
Das, R. J. (2004). Social Capital and Poverty of the Wage-Labour Class: Problems with the Social Capital Theory. *Transactions of the Institute of British Geographers, 29*(1), 27–45.
De Haan, L., & Zoomers, A. (2005). Exploring the Frontier of Livelihoods Research. *Development Change, 36*(1), 27–47.
Deshingkar, P. (2006). Internal Migration, Poverty and Development in Asia: Including the Excluded. *IDS Bulletin, 37*(3), 88–100.
Ellis, F. (1998). Household Strategies and Rural Livelihood Diversification. *Journal of Development Studies, 35*, 1–38.
Ellis, F. (2000). *Rural Livelihoods and Diversity in Developing Countries*. New York: Oxford University Press.
Froerer, P. (2011). Education, Inequality And Social Mobility In Central India. *European Journal of Development Research, 23*(5), 695–711.
Gardner, K. (2009). Lives in Motion: The Life-Course, Movement and Migration in Bangladesh. *Journal of South Asian Development, 4*(2), 229–251.
Garikipati, S., & Pfaffenzeller, S. (2012). The Gendered Burden of Liberalisation: The Impact of India's Economic Reforms on Its Female Agricultural Labour. *Journal of International Development, 24*(7), 841–864.
Hamilton, K., & Swift, J. (2001). Household Food Security. In S. Devereux & S. Maxwell (Eds.), *Food Security in Sub-Saharan Africa* (pp. 67–92). London: ITDG Publishing.
Harriss-White, B. & Garikipati, S. (2008). India's Semi-Arid Rural Economy: Livelihoods, Seasonal Migration And Gender. *European Journal of Development Research, 20*(4), 547–548.
Hussein, K., & Nelson, J. (1998). *Sustainable Livelihoods and Livelihood Diversification* (IDS Working Paper No. 69). Brighton, UK: Institute of Development Studies, University of Sussex.

Kis-Katos, K. (2012). Gender Differences in Work-Schooling Decisions in Rural North India. *Review of Economics of the Household, 10*(4), 491–519.

Lanjouw, P., & Shariff. A. (2004). *Rural Non-farm Employment in India: Access, Incomes and Poverty Impact* (Working Paper No. 81). New Delhi: National Centre for Applied Economic Work (NCAER).

Lerche, J., Shah, A., & Harriss-White, B. (2013). Introduction: Agrarian Questions and Left Politics in India. *Journal of Agrarian Change, 13*(3), 337–350.

Madhya Pradesh. (2002). Human Development Report. http://www.mp.gov.in/difmp/MPHDR2002.htm.

Meher, R. (2009). Globalization, Displacement and the Livelihood Issues of Tribal and Agriculture Dependent Poor People the Case of Mineral-Based Industries in India. *Journal of Developing Societies, 25*(4), 457–480.

Moser, C. O. N. (1998). The Asset Vulnerability Framework: Reassessing Urban Poverty Reduction Strategies. *World Development, 26*(1), 1–19.

Mosse, D., Gupta, S., Mehta, M., Shah, V., Rees, J. F., & Team, K. P. (2002). Brokered Livelihoods: Debt, Labour Migration and Development in Tribal Western India. *Journal of Development Studies, 38*(5), 59–88.

Neff, D. F., Sen, K., & Kling, V. (2012). The Puzzling Decline in Rural Women's Labor Force Participation in India: A Reexamination. *German Institute of Global and Area Studies* (Working Paper No. 196). Hamburg, Germany: GIGA.

Niehof, A. (2004). The Significance of Diversification for Rural Livelihood Systems. *Food Policy, 29*(4), 321–338.

Niehof, A., & Price, L. (2001). *Rural Livelihood Systems: A Conceptual Framework*. Wageningen-Upward Series and on *Rural Livelihoods No. 1*. Wageningen, the Netherlands: Wu-Upward.

Olsen, W. K., & Ramanamurthy, R. V. (2000). Contract Labour and Bondage in Andhra Pradesh (India). *Journal of Social and Political Thought, 1*(2). http://Www.Yorku.Ca/Jspot/2/Wkolsenrvramana.Htm.

Putnam, R. D. (1995). Bowling Alone: America's Declining Social Capital. *Journal of Democracy*, 65–78.

Rahman, L., & Rao, V. (2004). The Determinants of Gender Equity in India: Examining Dyson and Moore's Thesis with New Data. *Population and Development Review, 30*(2), 239–268.

Rogaly, B., Biswas, J., Coppard, D., Rafique, A., Rana, K., & Sengupta, A. (2001). Seasonal Migration, Social Change and Migrants' Rights: Lessons from West Bengal. Economic and Political Weekly, 4547–4559.

Schmink, M. (1984). Household Economic Strategies: Review and Research Agenda. *Latin American Research Review, 19*(3), 87–101.

Scoones, I. (1998). *Sustainable Rural Livelihoods: A Framework for Analysis* (Working Paper No. 72). Brighton, UK: Institute of Development Studies, University of Sussex.

Sen, A. (1981). *Poverty and Famines. An Essay on Entitlement and Deprivation.* Oxford: Oxford University Press.
Staples, J. (2007). *Livelihoods at the Margins: Surviving the City.* Walnut Creek, CA: Left Coast.
Start, D. & Johnson, C. (2004). *Livelihood Options? The Political Economy of Access, Opportunity and Diversification* (Working Paper No. 33). Overseas Development Institute.
Swift, J. (1998). Factors Influencing the Dynamics of Livelihood Diversification and Rural Non-Farm Employment in Space and Time. *Institute of Development Studies.*
Thieme, S. (2008). Sustaining Livelihoods in Multi-local Settings: Possible Theoretical Linkages Between Transnational Migration and Livelihood Studies. *Mobilities, 3*(1), 51–71.
Vera-Sanso, P. (2012). Gender, Poverty and Old Age, in Urban South India in an Era of Globalisation. *Oxford Development Studies, 40*(3), 324–340.
Whitehead, A. (2002). Tracking Livelihood Change: Theoretical, Methodological and Empirical Perspectives from North-East Ghana. *Journal of Southern African Studies, 28*(3), 575–598.
Wood, G. (2003). Staying Secure, Staying Poor: The 'Faustian Bargain'. *World Development, 31*(3), 455–471.
Wood, G. D. (2005). Poverty, Capabilities and Perverse Social Capital: The Antidote to Sen and Putnam. In J. Seeley & A. Khan (Eds.), *Making a Living: The Livelihoods of the Rural Poor in Bangladesh.* Dhaka: University Press Limited.
World Bank. (2003). *World Development Report 2002.* Washington DC: The World Bank.

CHAPTER 6

State (*Sarkar*) and Society (*Samaj*)

6.1 Introduction

In the previous chapters, I have shown how traditional forms of livelihoods for the Gonds such as dependence on working in stone quarries and on forests are dwindling fast. I have covered a range of diversity of livelihoods in the form of coping strategies by working in precarious conditions and demanding high wages. In this chapter, I describe the relation of the Gonds with the state through the various development programmes. I found it ironic that these programmes which are primarily aimed at the Gonds, as they are the poorest, do not reach out them and if it does, it reaches to only few and is delayed. Despite the state's efforts, why the Gonds were still marginalised and overlooked on by these services? Why are the Gonds independent of the state in meeting their needs? I discuss transparency accountability by the state and Sen's ideas of social transformation through schooling (1995). This was evident in all the Gond villages that I visited where the Gonds lived in poor living conditions but continue to work hard rather than complain about the state. This is a society that is poorly documented and very little is known about them. Thus, they are misunderstood by the state as being the same class and as other marginalised. These benefit programmes construct the Gonds as being passive due to their constrained lives which was not the case as per my fieldwork. In this chapter, I ask why are Gonds not availing of the state assistance which is targeted at them? How and why are Gonds' livelihood portfolios so diversified? To what extent are

© The Author(s) 2018
S. Yadav, *Precarious Labour and Informal Economy*,
https://doi.org/10.1007/978-3-319-77971-3_6

Gonds dependent on "brokers" (middlemen/*mukkadams*/contractors) for access to work or in order to sell their products, and is this associated with "neo-bondage" and/or poor working conditions/payment? What subjectivities are created by the Gonds by their performances of livelihoods?

In Mahalapur, these programmes are in the form of Senior Citizen Pension (Rs. 500 per month), Widow Pension (Rs. 250 per month) and *Samajik Sewa* (Social Welfare) (Rs. 150), Indira Awas Yojna, Din Dayal Swasthya Seva Yojana Card (for subsidised health care). While in paper form, the government programmes are understood by the Gonds, in reality they question government intent on the subject of social benefits and compensation.

Shah (2010) argues that poverty is to be understood within the context of social relations that produce poverty. This is more critical to understand within India's doubly marginalised forest fringe communities (2010, p. 96) who are the most vulnerable. Based on her ethnographic study on Munda's relations with the Jharkhand state's social benefits, the Mundas as the marginalised STs are suspicious of being seen by the state what does this mean. She finds that they feared the "dangerous" state and desired for a resurrection of their "sacral polity" embedded in the degrading moral environment in which these state benefit programmes are designed and implemented. According to her fieldwork in Tapu in the state of Jharkhand, Shah (2010) shows how Mundas associate lack of transparency and accountability in the implementation of development programs in the region as being immoral and unethical by the state representatives of district's blocks and *panchayats*.

Barbara Harris-White (2003, p. 77) in India Working observed how easy it is to rob the poor, like the Gonds, through the creation of a "shadow state comprising of the vast assemblage of bureaucrats, brokers, crooks, contractors and advisors that occasion the misuse of funds by the official state." This collection of persons and functions ensures that the system of programmes, rather than benefiting the poor, works on behalf of the private interests of a privileged who are either directly or indirectly connected to the "official state" and how the state sees its rural subjects (Chandokhe 2005). Corbridge et al. (2005) further showed in their study in Bihar and Jharkhand how "lower level bureaucrats," whom they also called "vernacular representatives," pretend that they know the local-level sociopolitical dynamics. Instead of helping, however, they tend to manipulate many programmes with their vernacular knowledge in favour of the few elites of the region. Corbridge et al. (2005, p.19) referred to the rural programmes introduced by the government as "war on poverty" Mahalapur. The authors conclude that, they find that it is through these social benefits programmes that the rural poor come in direct contact with the state as was also found in Mahalapur.

In my surveys, I came across many such cases where people were missing out on welfare programme benefits or were not listed in the right economic category because of the poor bureaucratic process. The poor find applying for the benefits to which they are entitled to very intimidating and daunting which Shah describes as a Kafkaesque's quality of the state (2010).

During my early days of village surveys, I interacted with the Gonds from other villages who told me that there are political leaders who pay them Rs. 1000 to vote for them. However, the benefits of such elections soon become a myth once the leader comes into power and forgets the Gonds until next time when a new leader appears and repeats the cycle. This appears to be the reason that the Gonds have lost trust in the state in issuing their below poverty line (BPL) and National Rural Employment Guarantee Act (NREGA). If the Gonds elect the opposition party member to power, then it is unlikely that the *panchayat* leader will help them to issue or renew new social benefit cards. My evidence from Mahalapur supports Shah's analysis of corruption in the mismanagement of money coming for rural programmes. However, the Gonds stay away from the state, not because they think their morality is superior to that of the state's superiority in terms of sacral ethics or morality, but because of their inability to understand the state's mechanisms and because they are absent from the village so cannot take full advantage of these programmes like literacy. Corruption in the form of development agents or intermediaries was because of the gap between the state and the rural populace who were unable to read and write. In that sense, Shah's (2010) analysis of corruption needs more comparative analysis and moving beyond just landed elites diverting these benefits for themselves. In Mahalapur, the literate marginalised were taking full advantage of the programmes and seemed to have all the cards. My research therefore shows that corruption and illiteracy need more ethnographic analysis.

One year of fieldwork in a district in Madhya Pradesh (MP) revealed a wide range of social welfare programmes for the poor in the form of housing, employment, education, food security and different forms of credits for small and landless peasants. What was also very interesting to note was that none of the programmes seem to address empowerment, legal rights, or how to complain about delayed payments through the NREGA or any other pension programmes where the Gonds experienced delays or did not receive them at all. Social welfare programmes are too bureaucratic and lengthy for the Gonds to waste time applying to them.

Aditya's family landholding status is ambiguous, and technically, they are landless even though his grandparents had acquired that land before 1985 through the slash and burn process. However, the land was located near the main highway MH-75 and according to my research, lands which are near the main road were not marked with proper boundaries in the records of the rural administration thus making such households vulnerable to the predatory practice of rural elites. The ambiguity persists because it is not clear where forest-owned land begins and where does the *Rajaswa* land end. Recently, a rural elite claimed Aditya's unclaimed land as his and bought it from the *Rajaswa* land. To claim their land back, Aditya will have to go to Bhopal, which is the capital of MP and is very far from Panna. Hence, Aditya has given up on fighting for their land (about 2.5 acres) for the time being. He feels lonely and intimidated by the formal process of legally claiming back his land from the state. Thus, this is an example of the world of bureaucracy and legal rights, which is a totally new experience for the Gonds which Shah (2010) describes as Kafkaesque effect.

6.2 Land vs. Social Benefits

Before beginning the discussion as to whether the state matters or not to the Gonds, it is equally important to answer how issues of social welfare like housing, schooling and employment programmes have replaced the agenda of land distribution in states like MP. How much does land matter to the Gonds? Why are issues of agrarian-capitalist relations and land reforms subservient to issues of education, housing and employment? This is especially crucial as land is still a main form of security for the Gonds and they are being made vulnerable because of their status and lack of education to bullying and predatory tactics which result in selling land to the landed elites.

As Lerche et al. (2013) suggest, these large-scale agrarian questions need to be understood with respect to their regional, ecological, local conditions. In her study amongst the Mundas, Shah (2010) observes that there is a difference between the hill people and the plains people and that the tribes and their relation to the landed elites in the tribal state of Jharkhand (Lerche et al. 2013) are not the same as in other north Indian states like Uttar Pradesh and Bihar. Agrarian-based capitalist transitions in rural north India have taken different trajectories based on their specific agrarian and ecological conditions which shape their association with the land. In the case of Panna district, mining is more lucrative as compared to agriculture even for the rural elite as there is a constant problem of water. Hence, class relations in places like MP are very different than those in Uttar Pradesh, Bihar and Punjab where agriculture is the mainstay of the economy (Pinto 2004). Based on these comparative and contrasting outcomes of capitalist transitions in rural India, it is clear that there is no state-wide landless farmers' association or union that can protect their interests because the agricultural seasons and practices are not the same, therefore making their vulnerabilities different from each other.

The only recourse is through the state and its various programmes. But the state is a reflection of the local, social relations. In Mahalapur and Panna, politics and politicians are made up of the same elite who are the landed elite and the initial beneficiaries of the agrarian reforms, especially in the northern states of India, like MP. The current Chief Minister of MP is from the landed class, and he owns many stone mine leases around the state. This directly shows how the state and society are embedded into one another.

Lerche et al. (2013) argue that even though the capitalist agricultural relations in rural India are in favour of the landed elites, the land reforms implemented in the early 1970s were another way to lift the poor (marginal and landless peasants, like Gonds of Mahalapur) out of poverty which never happened. However, recent research shows that almost 40% of the poor still remain landless (Rawal 2008, as cited in Lerche 2013, p. 342). The landless and marginalised have found employment in non-agricultural, waged work yet also continue to keep a "foothold in agriculture whenever possible."

6.3 Politics of the Cards

Patnaik (2007) raised the important question of how to locate the marginalised within the neoliberal discourse of participatory development and social change. They are highly pessimistic about various government surveys to study poverty in rural India in order to locate the poorest groups, especially in the tribal areas, and discover who are the most vulnerable and impoverished. Patnaik (2007) questions the poverty estimates followed by the Indian Planning Commission (2007). She finds the aggregate studies on poverty in India do not capture the increasing chronic poverty and food scarcity at the village levels. In contrast, individual economic and social indicators suggest that absolute poverty is high and that there has been an adverse impact of neoliberal policies on poverty alleviation through food. Drèze and Sen (2013) too concur that people fall in and out of poverty and that it is not a permanent condition contrary to the assumptions of the planning commission in India which sets poverty aggregate figures which remained unchanged for ten years or until the next census is conducted.

The socio-economic status of the Gonds is reflected in their ration card or the BPL. This ration card is offered on the basis of ranking households assets covering 52 questions. If the household answers in negative for the top 6 household assets, then they get the red card which is for the extremely poor households called the *Mahagaribi* card. If the household answers in negative for the next 14, then they get the yellow card which is for the below poverty category called the *garibi rekha* card. If the household answers more than 14 positively then they do not qualify for the BPL ration card as they are not considered to be poor. For the red one, the ration is available at Rs. 2 per quintal of wheat, and for the yellow card, the amount is about Rs. 3 per quintal. For those who do not have the BPL ration card, they have to buy the ration at the market rate. However, the ration card cannot help with buying vegetables, milk, fruit and meat. They can only buy *mitti ka tel* (kerosene), grains and sugar. The Gonds refer to this as *Galla Uthana* (collecting the essential supplies), and the rationing process is known as "buying from the essential." My survey (in Chapter 2) revealed that only 70% of the households in Mahalapur have the BPL card.

For instance, in 2011, Leela Bai had still not received her widow pension after her husband died three years earlier. Ashraf became her agent and filled out her application and did all the background work involved in getting her set-up onto the system. For this he charged her Rs. 3000. I asked Leela Bai how she felt about this and she replied that she does not mind because at least she does not have to do all the running around. Also, she cannot read or write, so she could not complete the application on her own. However, even of those like Aditya, who can read and write, their situation is no different than those Gonds who are unable to read and write.

The other cards that reflect the socio-economic status of the Gonds are the job card and the voter identification card. The voter card is important for the Gonds to get the BPL ration card as acquiring the BPL is subject to having a voter identity card. While these cards are meant to raise the Gonds out of poverty, they are misused by the politicians to secure votes. This entanglement of politics and economics is very well understood by the Gonds. Furthermore, because of migration for work outside of Mahalapur for eight months of the year, the Gonds are not around most of the year to participate in voting and other development programmes that the *panchayat* have for them. That makes them vulnerable to being ignored by the state as the Gonds are busy labouring in precarious economies to avoid their households falling into debt or starvation and have no time to participate in politics or engage in the bureaucracy for benefits. Those who stay behind tell me that they do not get to vote because at the time of the vote, they are working in quarries or on farms. Even for those Gonds, who might own more than an acre of land, which is more than the average household landholding of the Gonds in the village of Mahalapur, pessimism still persists. Brijesh Singh expresses his disappointment with the state as follows:

> I don't have a BPL card. I used to have one. These cards are changed every election year. If I don't vote for the incumbent candidate, then they will cut off my name from the list of issuing the BPL card, even though I qualify for it considering that I am poor. People who are rich and do not qualify are getting the BPL card made under their name. I don't want to make a BPL card by paying bribes which is what the *panchayat* is asking me to do. There is no point in paying money because then every time I will have to pay - every election year. I am better off like this without

paying anyone. I have two sons and 4 daughters. The youngest daughter is only 5 years going to the school. It is not that expensive to buy directly from the market. In the end, it all gets even.

Brijesh can afford to not have a BPL card only because his food security is met through his 8 acres of land unlike for majority of landless Gond households who genuinely need a BPL card.

This kind of disappointment in the state or the *panchayat* by the marginalised reveals their continued distrust and suspicion about the operations of the state. The discursive attitude towards the state is common amongst the vulnerable populations who deal with the state as little as possible as a coping strategy to limit their frustrations and focus on the stable ways to obtain income.

Shah (2010) questions the morality of such offices who knowingly prevent such "well-meaning" programmes for the doubly marginalised (marginalised both by the state and then by the rural elites) and forest fringe communities, like the Mundas, from getting benefits access, and that these ideas reach through such agents of change and development as there is a huge gap between the marginalised as the targeted population and these block offices where the money from the state is transferred into. For instance, in the rural employment discussion, I will show how the money is disbursed for the NREGA gets mismanaged even though the NREGA officer was confident that it is "fool proof." In fact, on the contrary, the middlemen still manage to make their "cuts" (profits) through the development programme resources.

6.4 Labelling and Accessing Social Benefits

The last names of most of the Gond families include "Gond" after their first names. The title "Gond" means they can qualify to obtain a caste certificate, called JatiPatra, from the *panchayat* which will allow them to apply for reservations in jobs and education meant for the Scheduled Tribes. It is this title/naming that allows the Gonds to be self-identified as being automatically poor because they are considered to be indigenous settlers. Some Raj Gonds, despite being landed, have registered as landless and have obtained the Below Poverty Ration Card.

Kapila notes how a north Indian pastoral group in her research took advantage of other ST quota when they belonged to the "open" category or the elite group. She says, "Scheduled Tribe" in 2002, which gave them "specific entitlements and rights with regard to aid, education, and jobs" (2008, p. 117). This shows how groups may take up the terms "tribe" or adivasi/indigenous because they find positive "internal" reasons to identify, for example, because it brings respect from others. Today, whichever be the reason this is called "identity politics" or "politics of recognition." Thus, in her ethnographic account of tribal activism in Jharkhand, Shah observes that it is useful to explore how particular groups position themselves as being indigenous (2010).

6.5 Understanding the Government Programmes in Mahalapur

I interviewed the village *panchayat* secretary, locally known as *Sachiv* (an emic term for secretary). To fully understand how these (programmes) reach the Gonds in Mahalapur and what effect they have had so far, I will briefly discuss the programmes available to the Gonds. After interviewing the secretary, I got to know the full historical and present economical context of migration amongst the Gonds and found out more about the reasons why the forests have become less accessible and linked it to the low impact of state benefits. The secretary says that the forests have been banned because *Bengalis* continue to fish and hunt for game and meat, and damage the sunflower buds which affect the entire forest ecosystem. These seeds, which *Bengalis* and other communities have commercially exploited, bring high returns in the market as it is used in cooking Indian dishes like rice pudding which is very important in this vegetarian-dominated place.

I asked about the practices by the *Bengalis* and other communities to the Gonds. The Gonds said that the *Bengalis* are not forest people and they do not know how much damage they are causing. The Gonds say the *Bengalis* do not listen when they try to reason with them. The other group that causes damage to the forests are the Yadavs. Yadavs let cattle graze inside the forests. Lastly, the Gonds damage the forests by picking up wet wood. Nowadays, the Gonds are only allowed to pick up dry wood, but Aditya says that even the collection of dry wood is restricted. To chop wet wood means to cut a new tree, unlike dry wood which has fallen on the ground.

Dhiraj,[1] a Gond in Mahalapur, who has never migrated, strongly expressed his feelings against the forest department as his whole family's survival depends upon the income coming from the forest. He says,

> Unlike others (Yadavs, Bengalis and other SCs), Gonds have no land. Our dhanda (enterprise) is forest and that is being restricted. The forests provide wood, mines, mahuwa, and food. Wood is used for cooking and keeping the house warm during winter. In extreme crisis, we will migrate wherever there is work so we can eat. Nobody helps us. For everything that we need, there is so much paper work involved, signatures involved, we do not understand all that much. (Fieldnotes 2011)

There are five villages under the *Sachiv's gram panchayat*. These five villages are made up of 3500 people approximately 900 households), of which 60% are Gonds, about 20% are *Bengalis*, and the rest are divided into Schedule Castes, Yadavs and Sahus. According to the *panchayat* secretary, the SC and ST communities work for NREGA only when they return from working outside of Panna. All *Bengalis* usually work for NREGA because they do not migrate. Currently, the *Sachiv* is getting Gonds from another village from his *panchayat* near Darera, which is the next Gond hamlet after Mahalapur. He says that even if he needs labour in Mahalapur, they are not around most of the year because they have migrated in order to rectify their drop in income. I asked him how he chooses labourers from so many households. He said that the procedure requires people to apply for a job under NREGA and within fifteen days a job has to be created by him. Nobody from Mahalapur applies because of illiteracy. So, sometimes, he will approach them to see if they are available to work. This is a proactive approach to finding workers. The Gonds told me that they get paid only after the *Sachiv* puts their name on a voucher and withdraws money on their behalf from the rural offices as most Gonds cannot sign the voucher for receiving the money.

I asked him how long the Gonds have migrated outside for work and he says that their pattern of migration outside of MP is recent. Previously, only the SC community from other villages were migrating

---

[1] Introduced in Chapter 1, page 20.

outside of MP. The SCs have been migrating for almost ten years more than the ST population because nobody in Panna would give them work due to their untouchability.[2] Earlier, the ban was only on hunting and fishing, but not on wood collection. The banning of wood collection is a direct blow to the livelihood of the Gonds as it means they do not have wood to cook and to eat so the Gonds also started to migrate with the SCs from around 2011. Earlier, the Gonds migrated only to Pardes, in the nearby towns (internal migration) to work in stone quarries. This type of inter-district migration has been going on for about 100 years according to Sukhram, Aditya's father.

6.5.1 Housing in Mahalapur

According to the village *panchayat* secretary, the Indira Awas Yojna (housing programmes) money comes out every year through a lottery system and there is a quota for tribal populations. This programme was aimed at providing social security for the poor in the form of housing. For example, if the government sanctions five households to receive the housing programmes, two of which will be reserved for ST people. This list is drawn from the list of those who are considered to live in *Kucca* (mud/manure) homes. In Mahalapur, so far only five households have constructed homes from this programme since it was introduced about thirty years ago (according to the *Sachiv*). Ram Kripal who built a house through this programme says that the money is less considering the cost of cement, labour and bricks. The rest of the money is raised through *majoori* or migrating for work.

Dhiraj, whom I had introduced in the beginning, shares his experience of applying for the rural housing programmes. He described it as being cumbersome which needs "*lekha padhi*" (literacy/numeracy) as nobody in Mahalapur can read and there is no help with filling in these applications. He was hoping that I would take a lead and help them in advocating for housing rights and other such benefits that require basic reading and writing skills. The situation in Mahalapur mirrors the common problems of rural housing which is understudied as compared to urban housing problems (Tripathi and Verma 2013).

---

[2] SCs are considered to belong to the polluting group of people in the caste hierarchy and nobody in Panna would give them jobs that would involve household repairs of the upper castes and so, the SCs.

6.5.2 Schooling of Gond Children

In Mahalapur, education is still seen as a luxury for the Gonds as they need their children to participate in the household chores while the parents are away earning a living. I noted that school time was the only time that Gond children were able to take a break from household chores. On the other hand, the state's promise of non-farm work through education is a mirage for the Gonds. Their current financial and household condition makes graduation an enormous challenge, all the more as it involves living temporarily in hostels in the town.

In this section, I discuss various reasons why schooling in Mahalapur is not continued after 8th grade and how it is valued over other forms of entitlements like labouring. I demonstrate the relation of the state with that of the Gonds and their understanding of the state's civilising mission and how it runs this project through a rural infrastructure and lack of motivation on behalf of the rural teachers. Currently, most Gond children in Mahalapur will at least try to finish until eighth grade, which is the maximum literacy level offered without having to go outside of the village. Sometimes, there are structural hindrances in the household development cycle in the form of parental death or severe illnesses to family members that can disrupt their basic schooling. Gond parents determine what level of schooling their children need to be educated, but the school facilities, even though free by the state, are very rudimentary and does not prepare the children to sit for competitive examinations that can help them to enter college education. The case of Gonds' social capital as a tribal community experiencing modernisation, can be compared to the differences as observed by Froerer (2011) in the case of Hindu Oraon and tribal Oraon in Chhatisgarh. I found out that the Gonds do not want to send their children to school after the eighth grade because there are no job prospects in Panna. Froerer's (2011) study was amongst the tribal groups—the Hindu tribes and the Christian Oraons in Chhattisgarh showed how education is perceived differently by two marginalised communities—Christian Oraons and the Hindu Oraons. She observes that for the latter, the civilising mission of education proposed by Sen was observed but not so amongst the Hindu Oraons. She explains this because unlike the Hindus, the Christians were not so much attached to the land, and did not hesitate to move out of the village and live a lonely life if it were necessary to escape poverty and marginalisation, whereas for the Hindu Oraons land was very important and leaving the family behind was a new experience. She uses Bourdieu's idea of cultural capital to explain why the Hindu Oraons group find the state's literacy and education programme dubious. She finds that under extremely poor conditions, the marginalised people value immediate material and economic gain over long-term transformative (drawing upon Sen 1999a) gain through education. Hindu Oraons want to know is how does it help to send their children to school if there is no employment gain. They considered literacy as de-skilling and also having far/reaching negative consequences like delayed marriage. While a bit of literacy is desired in a Hindu Oraon girl, too much is considered to be unmarriageable as she will not be able to find a husband who is less educated than her. In such marginalised groups, marriage is a more salient institution than literacy for the Hindu Oraons. Thus, Froerer concludes that, even though both Oraons share the same demography in the village in Chhattisgarh, their normative approaches to education are vastly different. For wage labourers like Christian Oraons, centuries of marginalisation have set a momentum in the form of education as social capital (Froerer drawing upon Corbett 2007, p. 11) with the Church playing a central role and helping them find employment and continuing to provide support even outside of the village. Working and waging have helped the Christian Oraons to accumulate cash that could be spent on children's schooling expenses as compared to the Hindu Oraons who did not have cash as they lived in an economy based on mutual exchange and some will run a shop, based on trust and reciprocity. Even amongst those, Hindu Oraon who completed 12th grade and could have secured employment outside of the village eventually returned to the village. The only Hindus who did non-farm and non-traditional work were because they were recruited by the Hindu right wing, the RSS, but soon found it a disillusionment with the religious ideology of modern change and of limited practical use. For them, there is a fallback employment through selling timber from the forests and other forms of rural small enterprises for the Hindu Oraons. Froerer concludes that even though

> ...there are countless of other civilising attributes that are linked to educational attainment, particularly in relation to the cultural capital and embodied distinctions associated with status confidence world, it is the concern with economic benefits (namely, employment) that is most commonly articulated.

Similarly, the Gond families in Mahalapur cite the example of Aditya, an educated Gond with a bachelor's degree, who is unemployed, and instead doing *majoori* alongside the rest of the Gonds who are illiterate.

So, the Gonds of Mahalapur have made up their minds that working for the household is more rewarding than going to school as it is time that they cannot afford to waste if they can work instead and earn some money for their families.

Individual household circumstances dictate whether the children can finish school. There is no parental pressure to do so. In the case of widowed households, it is very difficult to finish school, especially for females, as the mother is busy earning a living and the female children are doing domestic work. If both parents are working, then there is a higher probability that the female child may stay and finish their schooling or at least until the eighth grade. By that time, most girls have reached puberty and further schooling depends on her future in-laws and where she will be after marriage.

I agree with Da Costa (2010) that education must be grounded in the specific ones of peoples' felt responsibilities. In studies by both Lloyd (1994) and Desai (1993) (as cited by Kabeer 2000), it is pointed out that the demand for schooling is likely to be lowest in areas where poverty is endemic and where economic opportunities which require some minimum level of literacy to be realised are largely absent. Kabeer (2000) also shows that families who face major fluctuations in household income streams will seek to minimise risk in ways which impinge on children's educational opportunities.

According to the local school teacher, Pritam Singh, nearly 90% of the Gond children in Mahalapur will not go to school beyond the eighth grade, which is the maximum schooling in their own village. However, according to Aditya, the reason why many cannot finish schooling is because the school teachers in Mahalapur are very lax till eight grade and pass everyone, and so by the time they need to sit for higher examinations, the Gond children fail because their foundation is weak from the poor schooling standard in Mahalapur. Except for Aditya, the rest of his generation had to drop out and do *majoori*. In that light, it is remarkable that Aditya studied until graduation. Aditya got married recently and passed a state-level examination to become a primary school teacher with the hope of school employment. However, Aditya's parents were able to provide electricity and pay bills and so he could study for as long as he wanted especially during the examination times. Manoj and Kajal, his brother and sister, respectively, both aspire for college like Aditya, but household conditions have worsened since Aditya went to college and even as today he is contributing to the income doing *majoori*, it's not enough to meet household needs. Both Kajal and Manoj sacrifice and postpone their desire to finish schooling. Manoj will finish his schooling but not without interruptions as he has to take breaks and help his family doing farm work or work in road construction. Kajal will most likely unable to go all alone to the city to attend college unless there are other girls who can accompany her. The possibility of Sukhram allowing Kajal to live alone in the city is very low as there are negative perceptions about girls working, studying and living alone in citified. Also, education of girls is not encouraged beyond 8th grade at present in Mahalapur as Sukhram will have difficulty finding a more educated groom than her within their community. Even if he finds one, the problem of raising dowry for an educated groom could be additional challenge. This is unlike the case of Brijesh Singh who could find a more educated bride for his son who was a 10th grade dropout. He could do this as he had relations with other well-to-do Sur Gond families like him as he possesses 8 acres of land. Thus, vulnerable households like that of Sukhram have to carefully balance the needs and aspirations of their members and that also includes sacrificing the desires of some members for the larger good of the household. Schooling opportunities intersect with other opportunities such as employment, credit and questioning norms about providing family security (Da Costa 2010).

Many Gond households cannot afford their electricity bills and instead still use kerosene-lit lamps. Lack of electricity in such homes is another reason why children are unable to study as kerosene lamps strain the eyes if exposed for too long due to its overpowering smoke. The children, who start earning for their family, find schooling impractical. In addition, the infrastructure needed to motivate the young is totally absent. The school in Mahalapur is run by the rural administration, and the electricity and building infrastructure is provided by the NMDC. Formal schooling is a new experience for the Gonds. The school building is one big concrete rectangular block with no proper seating arrangement. Children are expected to sit on the floor. There are four teachers in the school. Not all four school teachers will be found teaching at the same time as one will be absent. The teachers also do not motivate the Gond children to remain in the school. Instead, the teachers just take it for granted that the "*adivasis*" are too poor to attend education. At the same time, many Gond parents have a very low opinion of the teachers. They think these teachers only work for their salaries. Instead of teaching, they are often found chatting with each other or taking an afternoon nap while the children play instead of studying. In Mahalapur, I have seen female teachers doing activities which are not related to teaching like knitting or other small household chores.

In addition to earning for the family, the influence of family-based soap operas and exposure to urbanisation through television and the life outside of Panna make the young feel that schooling has no practical value as everything around them is changing, except for Panna. From my interactions with the young of the village, this experience is due to the influence of leading a working life at an early age together with the influence of television which they consider as a more practical learning tool than going to school in the village. In my conversations with teenage boys, they have revealed to me that they view their parents as being less aware of the changing world than they are. This shows how difficult it is for the young Gonds to stay unaffected by the changes they see on the television.

From my interactions with the young of the village, this experience is due to children migrating. Work is a hindrance when they are exposed so early on to the adult world of work, and they lose interest in schooling. Some will continue schooling after returning from migration, but most lose interest again according to local school teachers. The local school teachers have complained to the authorities that attendance is low during the harvest season because the children are sent away to work in other villages nearby. Schooling is a recent experience for the Gonds' households; therefore, the children do not get much support from the parents if they need time to prepare for examinations. School supplies, like uniforms and books, are distributed freely by the local schools. Most children will start wearing these uniforms even at home so they get worn out very quickly. The secretary of the school, a Gond from the village, told me that this practice is very common and so there was a rule that children who come with "unclean" or "worn-out" uniforms cannot attend.

One day, a school inspector came for a surprise check. He came in a sports utility vehicle (SUV) van and was dressed formally. From the urgency and restlessness of the school teachers, it appeared that they had been forewarned that there would be a school inspection. The school inspector started to enquire about the school's day-to-day functioning, checked the attendance rolls, and enquired about problems connected to free food distribution.

Later, the inspector asked to speak to children in the class. Ganesh (Kesar Bai's grandson whom I discuss in detail below), aged 12, was chosen because he was bright. The inspector checked his homework book but did not ask him if he had anything to say about his experience in school and nor did the teachers tell the inspector that Ganesh, the eldest in his class, had skipped school twice because he had to help his family to earn money. Also, Ganesh has migrated to Jammu once to help his uncle with household chores while he and his wife worked in the construction of roads. The inspector never talked to any of the parents of the children even though they lived 50 yards from the school. In fact, judging by his behavioural language, it appeared that he did not even want to take the time to enquire at all.

Most of the migrant children cannot complete school. This is a more worrying situation as more and more Gond households are recruiting children to go to forests to increase the quantity of wood in the house after the quota of load has been reduced. While the local school master assures me that they hold special classes for such kids, most of the time the children rarely continue schooling upon returning to Mahalapur after migration. They prefer the world of work as they find very little encouragement from home to attend school. Instead, they help their families by attending the harvests and stacking up food for the rest of the year.

However, my own household interaction with the Gond parents tells a different story. Several of the households that I interviewed who have no children in school said that once there is a disruption to schooling due to working or earning for the home or just doing household chores, the local school will remove their names from the register. That seems to be the main reason why most children are not encouraged to go back. The Gond children feel there is no interest from the school teachers to get them back into school and in addition their parents are never around to speak with the teachers to negotiate and save their lost year. Taken altogether these children are not encouraged by either the school authorities or their parents to finish schooling.

Ganesh, aged 12, has done well at school. He also helps with the household chores and his grandmother, Kesar Bai, with agricultural work. She says that I should tell the school teacher to not sleep while teaching or do their domestic chores instead of teaching. Her comment is not an excuse for her grandson not to attend school but the anger is connected to a moral failure on the part of the state which offers everything free to encourage schooling amongst children but does not monitor the quality of education or question lackadaisical teachers. Children, like Ganesh, cannot take full advantage of schooling because there is so much to do in the house while the parents are away working. Parents who have not experienced schooling themselves cannot appreciate the returns of education of their own children (Homi 2012).

The school provides free meals. However, the major complaint that the children have is about the meal itself. The food is prepared by a "*Samooh*" which is a type of a cooperative. It is a self-help group and the people who cook are mostly women who get a small wage from the government. The food prepared is greasy and fried and the Gond children cannot eat that because they are mostly used to food prepared on firewood. The food is largely vegetarian with grains and pulses and overcooked vegetables in oil with a lot of salt and spices. The Gond children eat mostly vegetables, fish and Indian bread made on the firewood cooked with very little oil. The Gond parents have told me that children do not eat this food and instead it is fed to livestock. This also shows that even a free meal a day is not sufficient to encourage Gond parents to send their children to school which originally was why the programmes were started. The only thing that the Gond children could eat was "Halwa" an Indian sweet dish cooked in rarefied butter with lots of sugar. The fact that sugar is consumed by children shows that there is some connection between the nutritional needs of the child and the demanding school routine. Children need their sugar or high carbohydrates to study.

No doubt, the Gond children eat Indian chapattis every day, which meets their minimum carbohydrate requirement. However, most Gond children look underweight (malnourished) like their parents who are thin and skinny. Many studies in the Indian rural context indicate that school performance intersects with mothers' working in labour workforce, gender, caste and class that effect the overall motivations and performance of the children of the marginalised and other pre-existing social disadvantages. Such a complex affects their performance and motivation to continue schooling and pre-existing social disadvantages (Kingdon 2002 which is getting married; Kingdon 2002; Chambarbagwala 2008). I would also add nutritional status that hinders Gond children to study as their not taking enough calorific and nutritional food as they labour mostly collecting woods and other hard work.

Several parents told me about the case of Aditya who was one of three bright kids from the village but the only one who went on to finish a bachelor's degree. However today, he continues to do the same unskilled daily wage work as most others in the village. Aditya treks to nearby destinations where there are stone quarries or road construction work even though he has passed his village teacher examination. This is because the salary earned as a teacher is not big compared to what he makes working as an unskilled labourer. Besides, he is demoralised to find out that even after passing the written examination, he has to now "buy his job" as government jobs are very much sought especially after the recent Sixth Pay Commission hike in the salaries of government employees including rural school teachers. Pritam, who is the headmaster of the rural school in Mahalapur, earns Rs. 40,000 per month and his own son attends a private school outside of Panna with tuition fees of up to Rs. 10,000 per month. From local rumours, I gather that "buying government jobs" is a common practice for most in the region as government jobs are considered to be the most secure. This makes parents more sceptical about the future benefits of education for their children.

Many parents have told me that they would prefer their children to earn for the family or do household chores in the time that they would normally spend in the school. Another reason for not being able to finish school is the timing of examinations. They are held at the time when the Gonds are busy collecting and sorting Mahuwa (March till May). If children skip the examination, they fail and eventually their enrolment is cancelled. This happened to Ramcharan, Kotram and his brother, who are all Aditya's age but had to drop out as they lost their fathers to silicosis.

My study also points out that almost all of the female-headed households have children who are unable to attend school. According to Self (2011), the mothers' increased agricultural productivity and participation compromises the children's education as they assist her in agricultural work. Kambhampati (2009, p. 98) in her study in West Bengal shows that there is a negative relationship between women who wage in farm work and their children's schooling.

Naila Kabeer (2001) makes a valuable observation on why families such as the Gonds are losing out by not sending their children to school. This is common in households who do not have much to offer their children and are illiterate. Such parents will send their children to work with the purpose of receiving security and social care in their old age (ibid.). This happens because parents put a greater value on the immediate future of the household needs and cannot afford to think about the long-term security of their children except to continue with what they have been doing which is getting married, having a family and labouring (ibid.) especially for the widows who are de facto female household heads and have to recruit them to help making a living and surviving. As an educated tribal youth because Aditya is unemployed, he is not a positive motivator or role model to encourage the Gonds to send their children to school and instead parents find that it is more practical to send their children to do non-farm work. In their research on educated/uneducated and unemployed Muslims and Dalits in north India, Jeffery (2008) find that such families have very low expectations of the state being fair to these families for secured jobs and that it supports a dream for them. The failure of state schools in rural north India to maintain high numbers of school attendance indicates the failure of formal institutions like schools.

Da Costa (2010) drawing from her study in North East,

> Schooling is not simply a neutral thing to be acquired. It enters lives bathed in notions of a fire, promise, and profession. It is a mode of becoming and belonging to particular places, and times, within particular families and in relation to siblings, and a parents, with dreams for shared or competing duties. Our analysis of education must take into account to lend flesh and blood to stochastic projections, security, and empowerment. (Da Costa 2010, p. 178)

Aditya finds it frustrating that even though he has got his degree, he has to still pay a bribe to the officials to secure a job for which he is qualified. In the case of Aditya, his interests in education are economic and to improve his financial situation. Consequently, there is little purpose for the Gonds to encourage their children to pursue education if there is economic gain in the form of secured employment. For this reason, education for the rural poor does not derive non-economic benefits like an improved social status, and challenges the social and political atmosphere around them (although it could be an unintended consequence). Nevertheless, the Gonds are facing a severe livelihood threat by the forest department. This is similar to the observation by Chatterjee (1981) who found that the sweeper caste did not find any practical meaning in joining the movement which was to correct caste-based social equality in Benaras, but instead, joined the local labour and trade union to better their economic position.

6 STATE (*SARKAR*) AND SOCIETY (*SAMAJ*)

I also spent time trying to know how the village express their solidarity with each other. Kotram, who is very vocal amongst the younger generation and is also married, says that it's through kinship structure or through friendly relations with each other that they sort each other's problems like help through lending money. He says, "'We need money because it fulfills our needs and helps us to take a new direction. The older Gonds did not want money because at that time there was no need for education. Now, we need education to go ahead so nobody can take advantage of us like they did in the past'. The other reason why education is stressed in the Gonds households is because in the past, there were no schools! Jagdish, who is in his early 70's, says, "I am not literate because during my time there were no schools in the village."

Education is a tool for them to correct the wrong that has been done on them like stopping people like Malay Singh, who is a landed elite and has contacts with the rural government to shut down a local-run stone quarry because he is very influential. On the topic of starting a mining cooperative provision that allows the tribes to mine on their land—says Kotram, "We know that we can form a mining co-operative society, but we don't get a good quality of mine. All the good quality ones are now inside the Tiger Reserve. The remaining ones have lots of boulders and not enough high quality stone."

However, I later found out that it was not that Malay Singh had shut down the mine in their village. What happened was that a Yadav was doing illegal mining and transporting the stones from the land that belonged to Malay Singh. The later asked for a small profit as it was his land that was being used for transporting. Yadav refused to give him the money and so in revenge, Malay Singh complained to the forest department who completely shut down the mine.

In summary for the Gonds, education is still a distant and almost inaccessible form of human capital as they are too preoccupied in making ends meet and so cannot afford to miss any urgent single opportunity that would bring them additional income. The education system in rural India discriminates on account of class, caste, gender, tribal, religious or linguistic identity (Jeffery 2008; Jeffrey et al. 2004, 2005) (cf. Da Costa 2010, p. 177). I would also add that people who mostly reside in rural areas with low literacy levels. In that sense, geography does matter in contrast to Staples (2007). I return to this "categorical marginalisation" of being *Adivasis* (Mosse 2010) in the conclusion (Chapter 7).

6.5.3 The Rural Employment Guarantee Programme

The NREGA was launched in 2006 and is one of the largest development programmes in MP in terms of the scale and volume of resources, since independence. It was introduced by the Congress-led coalition government balanced economic growth with equality of opportunity in employment through NREGA. The NREGA was major initiatives on the rural infrastructure development under the Congress-led coalition government in 2006. The idea of employment guarantee is to enhance the livelihood and security of rural households by providing at least 100 days of guaranteed waged employment in a financial year to each household whose adult members volunteer to do unskilled manual work (Mishra et al. 2010). The aim is to increase lean-season wages in rural areas, to stop forced migration (Mehrotra 2008) and generally to benefit marginalised people belonging to SC and ST communities (Jha et al. 2009) (cited in Mishra et al. 2010, p. 458). Unfortunately, this policy began with noble intentions for the poor, promising a generation of more rural employment but eventually ended up being misused in many places by non-eligible beneficiaries, and those who are not "qualified" to be poor, or get siphoned off by bureaucrats, and rich farmers who are not the actual targets of these programmes. This was seen in the case of many of rural households in Panna. I found very few in Mahalapur working under NREGA, and the demand for such jobs is very low to none.

Mishra et al. note that the government policies under the label of "rural benefits" never undergo an impact assessment (2010) of their programmes. Furthermore, Drèze points out that the difficulties in the successful implementation of the NREGA also depend upon how the poor households are targeted and that poverty is not a "static" condition as people move in and move out of poverty (Drèze and Sen 2013). Jha et al. (2013) also point out the difficulty in rural India and especially in northern and Central Indian states as it targets the poorer households. There are so many households who work on unverifiable income records and their physical assets and in addition have large families. The reason why some of the states like Tamil Nadu have done well on the NREGA is due to the capable bureaucracy and the political will of the state to implement the programmes (Carswell and De Neve 2013a)

Mahalapur, in MP, is presented as a much larger challenge to the NREGA and includes illiteracy and the unavailability of the workers to be around during census time. As a result, the government's targeting needs to be scrutinised. But this is contradicted by Jha et al. (2013) who examine MP and Tamil Nadu to assess the success of the NREGA and found that the former state had done better at identifying the poorer households because of its use of the practice of self-targeting the poorer households. Self-targeting makes the NREGA programmes self-selecting as richer people stay away from work that involves working on the roadside. The NREGA does not target people living in small towns or urban areas as people are usually not available to do physically laborious work like road construction and building houses. Besides, the political intention is to appease the rural population whose votes help major political parties to get elected. Rural development programmes like the NREGA are replacing electricity, roads and education, which were previous election agendas.

6.5.3.1 Who Works for NREGA in Mahalapur

In Mahalapur, working for the NREGA is, in effect, a matter of age, and whether they are able-bodied or sick, and if they stay put because they are unable to migrate. Usually, people who stay behind, the elderly and those who are suffering from silicosis are available to work under the NREGA. In addition, those who are taking a break before beginning their next job may also be available. The last category of people is rare because the able-bodied are mostly resting before beginning new work. Elderly women are able-bodied and work on whatever jobs come their way under the NREGA but some may have started to migrate outside of Mahalapur. In the NREGA, the work involves improving the rural infrastructure in the form of wells, ponds or building a reservoir; if there is road building, then there will be work available as carriers of rocks and stone. According to my survey and my observation over a one year period, only fifteen people from Mahalapur were working under the NREGA at any time. The rest came from outside to work and were not Gonds but *Bengalis* from nearby villages. This shows that only those people who stay put in the village are available to work in the NREGA. The reason why *Bengalis* do not migrate like the Gonds is because they are not as vulnerable due to forest restrictions and stone quarry closures. They have enough land and some capital and a small family size compared to the Gonds and can meet their needs a bit more easily than the Gonds who find themselves migrating and not available for the NREGA work.

Most of them were not aware that they can claim unemployment benefit from the rural block office because they are very busy keeping up with different laws and rules of the NREGA. In Mahalapur, the job demands made by the Gonds are very few and those who do get work are because the *panchayat* secretary goes to fetch them if possible as most migrate and those who stay back are engaged in domestic chores, wood collection or other existing forms of livelihoods which are paid in cash. There is not enough demand for jobs under NREGA.

6.5.3.2 NREGA Officer of the District

After doing all my initial surveys on livelihood and found that there was increasing evidence of migration despite the government's efforts to contain migration in the region by ensuring 120 days of work per year. I was curious to learn more about the NREGA and its status in Panna and how it relates to poverty alleviation. The central aim is to guarantee the safety nets and statutory rights of poor. However, considering the number of villages and the size of the households in each village, I thought it was impossible to contain migration and to guarantee jobs for everyone because clearly there were no industries and formal means of employment around.

My general interactions with the people of Panna town gave me the impression that it is a very challenging situation for an average person in the town to maintain a minimum balance of Rs. 50 necessary for a current bank account. I shared my findings about the NREGA with local authorities at a workshop day later, its impact so far, and how the NREGA is inaccessible to almost all households that I have visited. The officials became defensive and said that my viewpoints so far have not been accurate and expressed his regrets that I have this negative view about Panna. They said they will try to change this image about Panna, and that instead of saying that the glass is half empty, I should think that the glass is half full. They explained to me how the budget for the NREGA is made. First, there is a *Panchayat* Action Plan that the local *panchayats* put together that are made up of 5 *Gram* Sabhas—the equivalent to 355 villages in the Panna district and then these Action Plans are submitted as demands. This could be for road construction, digging ponds, wells, schools buildings or other needs.

The NREGA is on an individual and not on a per household basis. Every household is given 100 days' worth of work both skilled and unskilled which is the responsibility of the *panchayat*. It does not matter who works in the household. Every job that they do through the *panchayat* is recorded on muster roll which is submitted to the NREGA office. The payment is made every two weeks and the labourers stand in a huge queue outside the block office and their names are called and the money is not handed in cash but instead, the labourers bring a voucher which is again signed by the *Sachiv*, and is deposited into their account.

The *panchayat* is responsible for creating jobs out of which it is compulsory that 60% should be unskilled labour and the rest skilled. The NREGA has to create about 30,000 man days of work for each village. If the *panchayat* cannot create jobs, then the households will get unemployment wages and that is paid monthly, quarterly or weekly. But the Gonds in Mahalapur did not claim such unemployment benefits due to illiteracy, lack of awareness and also because they have been absent from the village.

The local NREGA officials found the possibility of corruption difficult as nowadays the money gets deposited directly into banks and so it is foolproof. However, my surveys observed that almost nobody in Mahalapur had a bank account. Those who worked under the NREGA got paid by the *Sachiv* when he entered their names on a voucher to claim the wages. However, there are many villagers and other rural administrators within the NREGA who maintain that a lot of programmes and information that villagers are supposed to know never reaches them. An interview with a rural administrator who keeps a record of the NREGA wage distribution in the Panna district for the *panchayat* rural works says that even with the computerisation of the NREGA, there are ways to practise corruption and mismanagement of funds within the NREGA because he has done it on his computer. The rural administrator says it is very easy;

> You enter that you are paying wages for 10 people for 10 working days and you request money for that figure but in reality, you only pay 5 people working for 5 days and the rest you steal.

Every Tuesday, the NREGA office holds a public redress hearing from 11 to 1 p.m. in the central office of rural administration. The officer meets people regarding complaints from villagers about the NREGA-related payments while some come there to talk about the lack of work. Some NREGA officials noted that many times, the villagers abuse the system by making false complaints about not receiving wages. They mentioned an instance where about 15 villagers complained that they had been jobless in the last 6 months. When they went to sort out that complaint and contacted the complainant who made this complaint on behalf of those villagers, they found out that the household which the complainer had belonged to was already working through the NREGA; in fact, the complainant himself was working in Mumbai. This left me wondering how it benefits the villagers to file a false report.

After talking with them, it was clear to me that he spends more time in his office and less time in the field. It also seemed from his statements, that even if the NREGA were not reaching everybody in the village, at least as a department it was generating many jobs in rural administration and so keeping many people in Panna town employed. There is no doubt that the rural employment departments are probably closest to the rural areas than any other departments in rural development. The NREGA administrators and officers do not know much about other rural development programmes for the poor (like education and housing), and especially those that are targeted to a particular social group like the Gonds. Later, a NREGA official wanted to show off the NREGA website to me and told me how everything is explained in detail. The website has both Hindi and English versions. I am aware of this website and it is detailed in terms of tracking the application status of anything that villagers apply for, like ration cards, passports, job cards and job applications. I told him that I know that website is impressive. Unfortunately, the people for whom it is targeted for are not able to read it, and most of them do not even know what a computer is, let alone the Internet.

Later, I attended another NREGA workshop on how to create jobs under the NREGA. However, most of the people were more concerned about why there were delays in payments for the jobs already completed under the NREGA and the problem of payment after the work was done. The meeting was not representative of the village scenario that I covered during my fieldwork. This seemed to me to be suspicious considering that there was not much work visibly seen under the NREGA. Most of the "work" carried out in Mahalapur was stone quarrying and wood collection as part of daily-waged and year-round unskilled work. If there is so much absenteeism in the jobs provided by *panchayat*, this may be due to migration and the availability of other forms of work, so I wonder how the money is spent that comes to the region with the NREGA?

6 STATE (*SARKAR*) AND SOCIETY (*SAMAJ*) 191

The workshop was attended by all the *panchayat* heads (*Sarpanch*), Gram Panchayat secretaries (*Sachiv*) and the members of the Zilla *Panchayat* (the entire village committee) of the Panna district. The villagers, like Gonds, were represented by the village heads. This also included the local MLA who is from the Congress party, and he turned up at the information workshop to speak on behalf of the villagers. He seemed to be quite well aware of the problems they were facing, like delays in their payment for work done under the NREGA. The most interesting part of the meeting was seeing how the local officers and administrators involved in maintaining the NREGA were complaining to the village heads for not creating enough jobs in the village. According to the NREGA officers, the government has a lot of money for the NREGA but they will only release additional funds if the *panchayats* create jobs for the villagers and show proof that there is control of migration in and out of Panna district. Other money available from the NREGA for village infrastructures, too, will also be made available but only if previous jobs are completed. According to them, about 75% of work which is already funded by the NREGA is still incomplete.

The MLA was not present to condemn the NREGA but to help the villagers understand how it works and how they can benefit from it. The atmosphere at this meeting was congenial, and there were few complaints from the *panchayat*'s perspective. However, this meeting was not attended by the villagers who were working on farms or in quarries or who had migrated outside of the area. However, later, I met some Gonds who had trekked 20 km to attend this meeting. They were harassing the NREGA officials as they had not received job cards for the last five years.

It was worth pondering on how the payments are made if work is being registered officially and placed alongside the stance of NREGA officials who seem to be overly confident about the operational status of the NREGA. I also met with some village heads who told me that nobody in their village is available to work under the NREGA because the villagers need more regular, permanent work. Instead, the villagers prefer to migrate. The NREGA works only for 3 months and it is per household and not per member of the household. The 3 months (approx. 100 days) available gets divided between husband and wife within the household and so most of the time the villagers have no work. Besides, the wages are only Rs. 146 (as per my recent visit in 2014) through the NREGA when other sources of income such as mining and agriculture, or what the villagers call "*majoori*," are year-round and wages range between Rs. 200 and 350 per day. Thus, there is a lack of interest amongst the poor like the Gonds simply because there are plenty of much better paid jobs available to them. This contrasts what Carswell and De Neve (2013b) has found in his study of the NREGA in Tamil Nadu where only old and women work for the NREGA. Unlike the Gonds in Mahalapur, the people in Tamil Nadu do not have access to the forests and have to sustain themselves working for the NREGA even if the money does not arrive on time.

At times, according to another village head that I interacted with, he gets labour (villagers) from outside his village to complete rural infrastructure programmes in his village as there is migration of local villagers from his locale. If there is so much absenteeism in the *panchayat* jobs due to migration and the availability of other forms of work, I could not help but wonder what happens to the money spent that comes under the NREGA. Perhaps more money from the NREGA is spent on supporting officials than on the actual poor households that are expected to be the recipients of direct government help.

6.6 Hi-Tech Rural India and Its Paradoxes

In the workshop, there was a lot of talk about how the NREGA was getting more and more transparent with the help of its web-based Management Information System (MIS) which aims to keep track of the rural infrastructure progress in each village. The MIS records the number of households working and tracks the payment process to each member working on these projects. The software tracks the activities/actions of all the rural programmes within the rural infrastructure.

In Mahalapur, there is a delay in the payment which is also why the Gonds have very little interest as they are always in need of cash: a reflection of the fast-changing local economy of Panna. At the workshop, I met rural officials who told me that in the future, there will be the possibility of starting mobile banks in rural areas for villagers who do not have rural banks within five kilometres of their village. These bank accounts will be opened on the basis of fingerprints of the household head in order to make it foolproof from identity abuse by middlemen such as the *panchayat* secretary.

The software is a monitoring and evaluation tool to make sure the labourers are getting paid on time by the bank. In addition, the software also acts as a whistle-blower on any rural administrator and village head who is not sending information from his end. For instance, one rural administrator asked a village head about the names of people who had been given money to build homes through Indira Awas Yojna because it was found that there was something suspicious about who gets money to build houses and who does not. The reply from the village head was that it was the fault of the bank in which the money is deposited and that he has not received any notification from the bank. He does not know if those villagers have benefited from the housing programmes. The rural administrator seemed angry at most of the village heads for payment delays and for not creating enough jobs.

Rural authorities have now realised that they need the full cooperation of the *panchayat* to receive data to make sure works/households/banks receive additional funds from the central government. The Gonds family size is quite large, with at least average five members per household, which makes it difficult to live off the NREGA wages.

6.7 Conclusion

The Gonds in Mahalapur work with their most precious asset, their able-bodiedness for the whole day or migrate seasonally out of Mahalapur for nine months. Therefore, it is very easy for them to lose out on the state programmes described above. The major reason why the NREGA jobs are not in demand in such forest-dominated regions like Central India where Mahalapur too is located is because forest-based livelihoods are still more reliable and most of the households fetch wood from the forest, thus the demand side is low making high increase of mismanagement of NREGA funds. The wood secure immediate cash-in-hand unlike the NREGA jobs which come after two weeks.

The Gonds need to juggle multiple tasks, their insecurities and bureaucratic requirements, as well as illiteracy, which just adds to their vulnerability. It was useful on several occasions to help them understand these programmes, help to fill in applications, to know about the ambiguity around buffer zones or what happens to compensation money due to silicosis illness. In one respect, I find Corbridge and Shah (2013) observation that political clientelism by landed rural elites causes patronage-based patterns of development in rural north India. On the other hand, I believe it is not so simple to apply the same in Mahalapur without considering the local politics of the region which is not agrarian-based. Lerche et al. (2013) show, that forested states like MP, unlike other less forested north Indian states have complex state–society relationships characterised by the balancing of tribal rights to forests alongside the need of the state to build schools, hospitals and provide jobs. This is difficult as land is scarce. The other crucial difference of MP not being a typical north Indian state is that it has a significant tribal population of approximately 20% (MPHD Report 2002) who historically are not integrated the same way as the Dalits population in Uttar Pradesh and Bihar.

The Gonds are poor today but do not want to be treated like a poor and do not accept assistance from anybody including the state unless it comes to them. They have pride in their ability to work to meet all their needs despite several government programmes. This was evident in all the Gond villages that I visited where the Gonds lived in poor living conditions but continue to work hard rather than complaining about the state. This is a society that is poorly documented and very little is known about them. Thus, they are misunderstood by the state as being the same class and as other marginalised. These benefit programmes construct the Gonds as being passive due to their constrained lives which was not the case as per my fieldwork. As said in the introduction, if the Gonds complain at all, it is against the forest department. They do not ask for cars or a luxurious means of living. They want their forests back and they respect wildlife. Such a change would help the Gonds to be more content.

The critical evaluation of the state in its discriminatory treatment of the rural population in India needs more careful ethnographic consideration. The blurring division between the state and the society is less obvious in cities as compared to the villages where traditional forms of social inequality predisposes the marginalised and the vulnerable to being socially excluded from various development programmes. The poor, like the Gonds, witness dubious practices of the state through their own experiences of delayed payments for jobs. The blurring division between what state and society also raise suspicion of the state when they are allotted poor-quality land for starting their own stone quarry so they have an opportunity to become independent of their employers.

They are aware of the nexus/bond between the higher-caste bureaucrats and officials of the region. The Gonds find security in their family units and rely on their ability to work which gives them their pride, dignity and income. They want more secure forms of social and economic schemes/institutions that they can rely on and feel socially protected by. I also showed the meagre amount of money received as pensions and compensation makes one question the survey methods and assessments done by the Indian government on poverty estimates and it is worth investigating why there are two conflicting reports about the numbers. It raises concerns about whether the centralised governance is an appropriate source for rural and participatory development.

The lack of demand for *panchayat* work making the Gonds to migrate shows that the Gonds are very much aware of the politics of these jobs and how these payments getting delayed and how the funds are being mismanaged. As I showed earlier, their value being autonomous and will work instead of going into debt or be bonded to their labour contractors or the employers. Working for the state too is a form of bondage for them as they have to wait for up to two weeks for the money to be paid after the work is finished and the amount of bureaucracy to receive the payment like going through the *panchayat* to sign the vouchers and then stand in long queues for wages which they can make up by working in the informal precarious economies by taking risks. Their strategy in the informal economy is to attain bargaining power by working in groups outside, and it has worked for them in securing wages on time. NREGA jobs are just another job for them even though it comes at their doorstep, it does not meet their household needs they thus have to labour in precarious forms of work.

While there are many signs of changes happening with physical infrastructure connectivities and literacy, for the rural and illiterate populace like the Gonds, the burden of India's economic growth can be seen in the form of slow or no change at all. Only when they migrate to places outside of Panna, they realise not being illiterate is not a handicap. Back in Mahalapur, they feel how much literacy is valuable but, constraints to livelihoods prevent them to take full advantage of the government's free schooling. Instead, the Gonds create their sense of entitlement in the sense of Sen (1999a) but not through the education path but through employment by earning for their families and fulfil their sense of duty by keeping their families from going into debt.

References

Carswell, G., & De Neve, G. (2013a). Labouring for Global Markets: Conceptualising Labour Agency in Global Production Networks. *Geoforum, 44*, 62–70.

Carswell, G. M., & De Neve, G. (2013b). From Field to Factory: Tracing Bonded Labour in the Coimbatore Powerloom Industry, Tamil Nadu. *Economy and Society, 42*(3), 430–454.

Chamarbagwala, R. (2008). Regional Returns to Education, Child Labour and Schooling in India. *Journal of Development Studies, 44*(2), 233–257.

Chandhoke, N. (2005). How Global is Global Civil Society? *Journal of World-Systems Research, 11*(2), 355–371.

Corbett, M. (2007). *Learning to Leave: The Irony of Schooling in a Coastal Community*. Halifax, NS: Fernwood Publications.

Corbridge, S., Srivastava, M., Veron, R., & Williams, G. (Eds.). (2005). *Seeing the State: Governance and Governmentality in India*. Cambridge: Cambridge University Press.

Corbridge, S. and Shah, A. (2013). Introduction: The Underbelly of the Indian Boom. *Economy and Society, 42*(3), 335–347.

Da Costa, D. (2010). *Development Dramas: Reimagining Rural Political Action in Eastern India*. New Delhi: Routledge.

Desai, S. (1993). The Impact of Family Size on Children's Nutritional Status: Insights from a Comparative Perspective. In C. B. Lloyd (Ed.), *Fertility, Family Size and Structure: Consequences for Families and Children* (pp. 155–191). New York: Population Council.

Drèze, J., & Sen, A. (2013). *An Uncertain Glory: India and Its Contradictions*. Princeton, NJ: Princeton University Press.

Froerer, P. (2011). Education, Inequality and Social Mobility in Central India. *European Journal of Development Research, 23*(5), 695–711.

Harriss-White, B. (2003). *India Working: Essays on Society and Economy* (Vol. 8). Cambridge: Cambridge University Press.

Homi, K. (2012). Loss in Rural Incomes, Children's Education, and Child Labor Simulation Estimates with Indian Data. *Journal of Developing Societies, 28*(4), 403–417.

Jeffery, R., Jeffrey, C., & Jeffery, P. (2004). Degrees Without Freedom: The Impact of Formal Education on Dalit Young Men in North India. *Development and Change, 35*(5), 963–986.

Jeffery, P., Jeffery, R., & Jeffrey, C. (2005). When Schooling Fails: Young Men, Education and Low–Caste Politics in Rural North India. *Contributions to Indian Sociology, 39*(1), 1–38.

Jeffrey, C. (2008). *Degrees Without Freedom? Education, Masculinities and Unemployment in North India*. London and Stanford, CA: Stanford University Press, Eurospan Distributor.

Jha, R., Bhattacharyya, S., Gaiha, R., & Shankar, S. (2009). "Capture" of Anti-Poverty Programs: An Analysis of the National Rural Employment Guarantee Program in India. *Journal of Asian Economics, 20*(4), 456–464.

Kabeer, N. (2000). Inter-Generational Contracts, Demographic Transitions and the 'Quantity-Quality' Tradeoff: Parents, Children and Investing in the Future. *Journal of International Development, 12*(4), 463–482.

Kabeer, N. (2001). Resources, Agency, Achievements. Discussing Women's Empowerment. Conference Paper at 'Power, Resources And Culture in a Gender Perspective: Towards a Dialogue Between Gender Research and Development Practice', Arranged by *The Council for Development and Assistance Studies, Uppsala University, Sweden in Cooperation with Swedish International Development Agency*, October 2000, pp. 16–54. Downloaded 2014, http://www.sida.se/globalassets/publications/import/pdf/sv/discussing-womens-empowerment---theory-and-practice.pdf#page=19.

Kambhampati, U. S. (2009). Child Schooling and Work Decisions in India: The Role of Household and Regional Gender Equity. *Feminist Economics, 15*(4), 77–112.

Kapila, K. (2008). The Measure of a Tribe: The Cultural Politics of Constitutional Reclassification in North India. *Journal of the Royal Anthropological Institute, 14*(1), 117–134.

Kingdon, G. G. (2002). The Gender Gap in Educational Attainment in India: How Much Can Be Explained? *Journal of Development Studies, 39*(2), 25–53.

Lerche, J. (2013). The Agrarian Question in Neoliberal India: Agrarian Transition Bypassed? *Journal of Agrarian Change, 13*(3), 382–404.

Lerche, J., Shah, A., & Harriss-White, B. (2013). Introduction: Agrarian questions and left politics in India. *Journal of Agrarian Change, 13*(3), 337–350.

Lloyd, C. B. (1994). *Investing in the Next Generation: The Implications of High Fertility at the Level of the Family* (Research Division Papers No. 63). New York: Population Council.

Madhya Pradesh. (2002). Human Development Report. http://www.mp.gov.in/difmp/MPHDR2002.htm.

Mehrotra, S. (2008). Nrega Two Years on: Where Do We Go from Here? *Economic and Political Weekly*, August 2.

Mishra, P., Behera, B., & Nayak, N. C. (2010). A Development Delivery Institution for the Tribal Communities: Experience of the National Rural Employment Guarantee Scheme in India. *Development Policy Review, 28*(4), 457–479.

Mosse, D. (2010). A Relational Approach to Durable Poverty, Inequality and Power. *Journal of Development Studies, 46*(7), 1156–1178.

Patnaik, U. (2007). Neoliberalism and Rural Poverty in India. *Economic and Political Weekly, 42*(30),.

Pinto, S. (2004). Development Without Institutions: Ersatz Medicine and the Politics of Everyday Life in Rural North India. *Cultural Anthropology, 19*(3), 337–364.

Rawal, V. (2008). Ownership Holdings of Land in Rural India: Putting the Record Straight. *Economic and Political Weekly, 43*(10), 43–47.

Searle-Chatterjee, M. (1981). *Reversible Sex Roles: The Special Case of Benares Sweepers.* Oxford: Pergamon Press.

Self, S. (2011). Market and Non-market Child Labour in Rural India: The Role of the Mother's Participation in the Labour Force. *Oxford Development Studies, 39*(3), 315–338.

Sen, A. (1995). Gender Inequality and Theories of Justice. *Women, Culture and Development: A Study of Human Capabilities,* 259–273.

Sen, A. (1999a). *Development as Freedom.* Delhi, India and Oxford: Oxford University Press.

Shah, A. (2010). *Shadows of the State. Indigenous Politics, Environmentalism and Insurgency in Jharkhand.* Durham: Duke University Press.

Staples, J. (2007). *Livelihoods at the Margins: Surviving the City.* Walnut Creek, CA: Left Coast.

Tripathi, R. K., & Verma, M. K. (2013). Social Sustainable Rural Housing in India: An Urgent Need. *International Journal of Social Sustainability in Economic, Social and Cultural Context, 8*(3), 71–83.

CHAPTER 7

Conclusion

Focusing on Gond families/households and on institutions of kinship and family, I have tried to understand a complex set of logics of resource allocation, hierarchy, kinship, gender, division of labour, mode of production, and negotiating and contestations of patriarchy and economic consumption within the household. Tribal households arise from labouring for their families first, especially in the absence of state and markets. State and markets have been appropriated to meet the needs of the Gond household. This appropriation of wider changes is also observed when the Gonds integrate with the wider Hindu society and adapt Sanskrit names to mask their tribal identity as they seem to accept the changing times and realities. In societies and communities such as the Gonds, the traditional social institutions are of greater source of reliance, care, welfare and well-being for both their immediate needs and their future. The values the Gonds are creating through precarious work are in the hope and anticipation that their loved ones and their kin members will reciprocate in future if they fulfilled their duties and obligations of marriage and taking care of them by labouring now. The Gonds have made a conscious choice to labour instead of accepting and managing with whatever resources they have available locally. However, the Gonds have set such a high virtue to labouring even if it is precarious that it requires an anthropological study as economic, linear and rational models cannot explain even if there is a logic and rationality behind the Gonds' choices. Why do such precapitalist institutions hold such a powerful grip and how do they continue to be a source of security for the Gonds as against the market or the state? How do the Gonds use the family to remain stateless? What are the temporal and even existential factors that Gonds take into account in the choices of livelihoods?

Through my reading on the political and social lives of people like the Gonds, often referred to as workers/labourers working in the informal economy, I found that there are three approaches: (a) state-centric (Corbridge and Shah 2013; Shah 2010; Drèze and Sen 1999, 2013), (b) market-centric (Breman et al. 2009) and (c) combining both (Harriss-White and Garikipati 2003; Picherit 2012). My study shows that the last one is appropriate to give the full picture of the diversification patterns and mapping of the Gonds' livelihoods in Mahalapur. While, on the one hand, the tiger conservation project is creating constraints on their traditional forms of livelihood, the informal economy has opened up newer economic opportunities for the Gonds where they could escape bondage-type employee–employer relations, demand high wages and make the employer depend upon them as they are the only ones to engage in precarious work like stone quarrying and being exposed to silicosis, which is a risk that other communities in Panna are not taking. In addition, there is also a movement by the Gonds from other villages outside of Mahalapur moving into Mahalapur showing signs of work opportunities in the "precarious economy."

Households are not static but restructuring over time due to internal and external favours. Internal factors are birth, death, marriage and marital conflicts such as separation, divorce or abandonment and the need for childcare and care for the elderly. Pennartz and Niehof (1999) refer this as the household life course. External factors are housing problems, lack of income, education and healthcare opportunities and security. My evidence that I provide in Chapter 4 on the Gonds suggests that both empirical and normative definitions of a household are important for understanding agrarian households and how they restructured and recognised through divisions of homestead or separation and nuclearisation. I find these distinctions of household division, separation or nucléarisation as superficial distinctions in the study of Gonds' formation of households in their pursuit of livelihoods. Instead, a broader concept of inter-generational and historical perspective of Gond household formation is more appropriate as it captures a more dynamic and recent picture of the socio-economic transformation that the Gonds are undergoing. This perspective I suggest is important, because we cannot predict or take it for granted that conspicuous consumption practices and social mobility of the Gonds by experiencing newer forms of wealth are eroding their cultural identity. My understanding after a year amongst the Gonds suggests that even if the newer economic forces are making the integration of the Gonds into mainstream informal economy, the Gonds' practices and lifestyles are still rooted in their attachment to the forests.

A household is a "co-residential unit, usually family based in some at, which takes care of resource management and primary needs of it's members" (Rudie 1995, p. 228). It emphasises assets, resources and strategies, the evidence of which I provide in Chapter 4. Households are both nuclearisation and enjoining but sense of privacy is also becoming more and more compromised as there is no sufficient space to accommodate all households. Household refers to a collective identity of a group of individuals unified by commonly held endowments and one or more of the following: a common budget air sign from greater or lesser degree of income pooling, common cooking quarters and/or a common residence (Bryceson 1980, p. 5). Households restructure to avert vulnerability (Moser 1996). Households risk continuum sustainability (Niehof and Price 2001). Households still stick with traditional and also combining newer forms of economic opportunities. Maintenance of livelihood through a bundle of activities can be regarded as a livelihood portfolio (ibid.). Livelihood portfolios are maintained in organised ways by using assets and resources with certain skills (i.e. inputs) to generate livelihood security, referred to as livelihood strategies which include physical, financial, human resources social capital (Ali 2005). As defined by Chambers, "Vulnerabilities here refers to exposure to contingencies and stresses and difficulty in coping with them" (1989, p. 1). In a situation of loss of assets because of the flood, the ability to earn an income by selling labour still governs ways of maintaining livelihood portfolios. Older people are at a disadvantage in selling their labour compared to their younger generation (Ali 2005).

According to Rudolph (1992, p. 120), "The household and family provide the crucial point of linkage between the individual and society as a whole, the point of linkage between the activities of individuals (agency) and the levels of institutional and social structure with which the individual interacts." A homestead consists of four to five huts in a single courtyard. The residents of a homestead can be divided into household living in separate huts, belonging to the same patrilineal family and including affinal relatives (Chen 1990). Disintegration of homesteads into different households is a common strategy amongst poor households who have larger families with limited space. How the household effectively uses the assets and what strategies are adopted to cope with economic stresses are determined by household, intra-household, community factors. Moser (1996) warns that not to take a reductionist approach overlooks power embeddedness (Pennartz and Niehof 1999), or to avoid essentialist approach (Gardner 2006) as from her study of migration-based remittance in Bangladesh which supports agrarian households in Talukpur. Based on this and my own evidence of the Gonds, I suggest the use of livelihood decisions to not to be distinguished into economic or non-economic needs because the households are not just economic or non-economic units. The household is a collective identity and a resource for the household members for their sustenance, protection and mobility. The households use both their household assets (tangible and non-tangible) and social relations to either survive or better their positions depending upon how they decide to use these resources and for what purposes and which member of the household does what kind of work. While for the poor households like the Gonds there is clearly a gendered division of domestic chores, women also have to double their roles by being available to do work outside of the home.

The labour absorption in the rural economy is segmented (Lerche 2009[1]; Carswell and De Neve 2013). Several studies have shown that often the Dalits and the *adivasi* communities will labour at the bottom of the pyramid (Breman 2007, 2010) and are the worst off in terms of access to formal work as well as wages and working conditions. However, the Gonds have been still successful in negotiating their wages and working conditions as will be show later in terms of the monthly income experienced. The reason is that stone quarry work is still an extreme kind of work because of the risks such as silicosis and people only wage if they are paid higher than market wages

---

[1] Excellent discussion on unorganised labour unions in India by Jen Lerche.

and financialise their consumption habits back in their village. Also, some like the Gonds are being pushed into precarious work as the agricultural productivity has reduced due to depleting water levels in states like Madhya Pradesh, and most of the subsistence farming is based irrigated as rains are unpredictable. This in addition to forest conservation-based displacement is also pushing the Gonds out. Most crops need huge amounts of water and that is expensive which also why lot of tribal populations are migrating from Central India and absorbed into the informal economy. In that sense, tribal and lower caste populations in the north-east have not similarly experienced lower agricultural productivity and their relations with them are not the same as it is in Central India. According to Lerche (2013), it's because their agricultural practices have been easier for the state "influence" to regulate. Also, agricultural crops grown in north-east are suited for a very different climatic condition and depend on differential access to rains and very few grow cash crops like other north-western Indian states. As a result, *adivasis* (especially from Central India) are more preferred in the informal economy as they can be easily bonded and are the most vulnerable. As most *adivasis* who undergo bondage-type relations are found in the brick kilns industry. But very little is studied on the road construction, and housing industry is where bonds from Panna migrate to work in states like Jammu. Studies on how bondage-type relations vary with respect to regions, communities, and states is not sufficiently done and; further, how *adivasis* experience bondage differently than other communities such as dalits who are part of the Hindu caste sytem but the *adivasis* are not. None of the Gonds have migrated to work in brick kilns from Panna.

The Gonds in Mahalapur work with their most precious asset, their able-bodiedness for the whole day or migrate seasonally out of Mahalapur for nine months. Therefore, it is very easy for them to lose out on the state programmes described above. The major reason why the National Rural Employment Guarantee Act jobs are not in demand in such forest-dominated regions like Central India where Mahalapur too is located is because forest-based livelihoods are still more reliable and most of the households fetch wood from the forest; thus, the demand side is low making high increase in mismanagement of NREGA funds. The wood secures immediate cash-in-hand unlike the NREGA jobs which come after two weeks.

The underlying intention behind the *Panchayat* Raj Institution was civil society. However, scholars studying the Indian state wonder if that is ever likely to be achievable considering that there is no bourgeoisie in Indian society who can negotiate claims against the modern state for not respecting rule of law, protection of private property, freedom of contract and protection from the state itself (Chatterjee 1998). Along similar thought lines, Benei and Fuller (2009) draw anthropologically upon Mitchell (1990) and Abrams (1988) on the division of state and society in an/the Indian context.

> The state can and often appears to people in India as a sovereign entity set apart from society by an internal boundary that's seems to be real as its external boundary. A local administrative office, a government school, a police station: to enter any of these is to cross the internal boundary into the domain of the state, whose conceptual separation from society is perhaps most ubiquitously symbolised by all its special purpose buildings with their painted notice-boards outside which in most tribal areas hardly anyone can read. (p. 23)

While there are many signs of changes happening with physical infrastructure connectivities and literacy, for the rural and illiterate populace like the Gonds, the burden of India's economic growth can be seen in the form of slow or no change at all. Only when they migrate to places outside of Panna, they realise not being illiterate is not a handicap. Back in Mahalapur, they feel how much literacy is valuable but constraints to livelihoods prevent them to take full advantage of the government's free schooling. Instead, the Gonds create their sense of entitlement in the sense of Sen (1999a, b) but not through the education path but through employment by earning for their families and fulfil their sense of duty by keeping their families from going into debt.

Not convinced if the livelihood framework can address poverty, Staples (2007) suggests that at least the resources, assets and strategies of the poor tell us about their agency to make a difference in their lives. He is not convinced that poverty is by accident due to geographical location but rather it is a social phenomenon where certain people want certain people to remain poor constraining the choices of such people. He described this problem in terms of core and periphery around mode of production where people at the core do not want the people at the periphery to benefit from the wealth. My own fieldwork reveals that the livelihood framework is too theoretical and overcomplicates the linear process of marginalisation and vulnerability that Gonds are facing which is increasing forest restrictions, increasing cost of living and increasing agricultural costs. The mismatch between the state policies to reach them in time caused the Gonds to integrate with the cash economy as they faced displacement from their traditional forms of livelihoods coming from the forests. Thus, as Rigg (2006) too says, "inherited poverty" for people attached to the land which is happening all over in agrarian-dominated counties in Africa, Latin America and Asia forcing "sons of soil" to seek non-farm forms of livelihoods. Mosse (2010), on his study of the Bhill labour migrants in Maharashtra, describes such marginalisation as "categorical marginalisation" that effects only certain groups and communities of the society. He draws upon Tilly's (1988) ideas of durable social inequality to explain chronic poverty of marginalised populations which are mostly tribal. My own study of such categorical and selective marginalisation suggests that instead of studying the contexts, we should go back to studying these household ideologies of duty, care, kinship, and gender ideologies and their perceptions of the broader political economic changes taking place around them. As I stated at the outset, the Gonds are not the only marginalised in Panna. There are other communities as well, but the difference is that they are literate and that is why they are able to take full advantage of the government benefit programmes like the Raj Gonds who are also "buying" government jobs in the district. This makes me wonder if the Gonds' diverse coping strategies can be captured by the livelihood analysis of the other marginalised populations and they are particular only to the Gonds.

Instead, my study suggests that in the informal institutions like the informal precarious economies, there is no distinction and that the marginalised also can exploit their employers by demanding high wages and not committing for long-term work. Like the Bhills in Mosse's study (2007), the Gonds too could not retain a hold on their productive assets—further eroded by ecological change—and are pushed out of the village economy into the "reserve army of casual workers and into complex patterns of labour circulation" through the "barrios and favelas of the world system" (Breman 2003, p. 5; Bernstein 2003) (as cited in Mosse 2010, p. 1161). For chronic poverty amongst *adivasis*,

Mosse traces the root to colonial forest policies of commercial extraction of the forests under the colonial monopoly which continued in independent India (Gadgil and Guha 1992, 1995; cited in Mosse 2010, p. 1160). When such populations come as migrants come to cities or places of work and find themselves to be alone, mosses wonders who politically represents them and how do they voice their concerns in the absence of any institutional representation? (Gledhill 1994; cited in Mosse 2010, p. 1166). In my study amongst the Gonds, I show that the avenues of labouring and the bargaining strategies are the places where one should start understanding the lack of representation of the marginalised as it might tell us about their ideologies of remaining independent and free. Another important observation is how important the role of agroecological factors is in the class formation and politics of development in India. To consider all farm households and treat them the same as they remain unchanged both by the policy-makers and by the Indian state, made me realise that the Gond's daily struggle to cope with the constraints of precarious working conditions did not fit these frameworks. Additionally, more research is required around subjectivities of informal workers, namely through their consumption habits and changes in the ideologies of the household.

I have used the idea of social relations but with a caution that these are social relations and networking as not everyone in the village has the same assets and access to networking and which can hide power relations and inequality. This is also supported by ethnographic studies in rural Bangladesh by Abrar and Seeley (2009) and Gardner (2009, 2012). The sources of income and livelihood are disappearing around the mines and forests, forcing the Gonds to migrate; otherwise, they would starve as they would not have resources to buy inputs for agriculture. That said, the region is much cleaner, greener and more spacious than other Indian states. The various state programmes on social welfare like housing, employment and education, which I have discussed in Chapter 6, have still not made a significant difference as there is constant conflict on the one hand, and the tiger conservation project wants more land for the tigers' natural habitat, while the rural administration needs the same land for the social development of the poor.

However, research (Cleavers 2005) shows that these types of networks are not available to everyone, especially not to single or widowed female household heads. Widows and single female heads of the household are vulnerable to the social taboo of seeking assistance from outside of the kinship structure. In Mahalapur, too, Gonds will hesitate to seek assistance from each other unless it is mutually equitable. Thus, a range of land and labour sharing arrangements are common (Harriss-White and Garikipati 2008). The main observations that emerged from working with the Gonds are to realise how important it is to reconceptualise both "a household" and "a family" which I have described as dichotomous for the Gonds. The Gonds are engaging in the "precarious economy" (also referred to as the informal economy by Breman), and both family and the market are important for the Gonds to make their living. The need to live on precarious sources of incomes is an important source of dignity for the Gonds. The Gonds do not wait for the state to rescue them from their drudgery of unsafe, precarious, daily working conditions which goes a long way to meeting their basic needs. This is evidence of the improved conditions of living happening within the informal economy and a limited impact of state programmes on their social lives. These decisions are embedded in the household ideologies of duty, care, social protection, stability, constraints and vulnerability. The Gonds are aware of the politics of development and poverty as played out by the state.

While I agree with Wood (2003) not to overemphasise the social agency as there are wider political economies that are marginalising the agrarian and forest fringe communities, my fieldwork amongst the Gonds shows how the "livelihood framework" is in fact too "cold" and "silent" to the poor people's agency and the resilience of the poor people. The extent to which, at individual and household level, both agency and resilience can be created is demonstrated, and being able-bodied and having family ties with household members goes a long way to compensating for the many constraints and in this process producing a different kind of "individual" which is remarkably understudied. My work on the Gonds shows that poor people are "poor" due to being vulnerable to constraints but they find other ways to compensate these constraints which are opened up by the informal economy. The Gonds' households accommodate and accept newer earning members and make room for de facto female-headed households as widows and earn dignified source of income—from bondage to their employers and labour contractors using minimum assets and maximising the output with the help of their able-bodied. According to Mitchell (1990), the boundary between the state and economy is less blurry and elusive than the boundary between the state and society as this book has shown from the economic behaviour and decision-making of Gonds' household.

I also showed how agency might not be the same for the women in Gond but for those who are de facto female heads due to widowhood like Kesar Bai and Leela Bai but unlike Usha Bai whose agency was restricted as her husband, Sukhram and her grown-up sons are there to contribute and stabilise the household income. Even amongst the widows, there are gradations of this agency with Kesar Bai having limited (what?) because of her grown-up and married children who did not need to be looked after and are working to contribute towards agricultural costs. It is equally important to note that social capital will vary depending upon the cultural make-up of the rural communities and will manifest itself depending upon the moral and normative structures around inheritance, patriarchy, kinship and gender relations. I would also add the risk that such networking is also equally important for more vulnerable households. Kesar Bai was more privileged than Leela Bai because she had more material assets in the form of land and grown-up children to help her increase her household income. Leela Bai is landless and had to stabilise her household in more vulnerable and riskier conditions. Leela Bai was able to contest the traditional bonds without any material assets. This confirms that women demonstrate individual agency driven by both external and internal conditions. External is market conditions in which negotiation of wages and labouring are made, and internal is subjective to the existing ideologies of gender and work. Markets are making such households undergo ideological transformations at the household level and challenging the dominating and existing norms of gender and work. The combination of these two factors enables such households to live a viable life without losing their social status as daughter-in-laws in their permanent place of abode, in Mahalapur.

At the same time, vulnerability produces networks based on the social context in which the agency helps to cope and adapt to newer opportunities and is determined by the social matrices of inner-household dynamics as well as the external market and state institutions. As Breman observes, "Living at the bottom of the rural economy is characterised by occupational multiplicity" (2010, p. 43). However, Breman does not really elaborate this process of engaging in multiple livelihoods. This is not the same advance system as defined by Breman (2010) because the Gonds are not bonded to the employers and they cannot be chased to finish the work as in the case of labourers working in Tamil Nadu's sugar mills (Guérin et al. 2009) or farm work in Breman's study in Gujarat (2010). The main difference here is that in Mahalapur debt is related to short-term contracts and usually settled once the contract is completed and the remaining balance paid to the *maistries*. They can also make their employer depend upon them in specific economic contexts where forest domination affects everyone equally. I studied how the Gonds create social capital (using Moser 1998; Putnam 1995; Adler and Kwon 1999) and social protection through mutual assistance support, trust, reciprocity (Gardner 2009) and solidarity to cope with the sudden change in their traditional dependence on forests.

In the pursuit of their livelihoods, the Gonds aspire for social mobility and maintain their social status in the village. The widows who have suddenly become lone earners experience freedom from kinship obligation to their in-laws and are allowed to run their households as compared to those women who are newly married or the uxorilocal women and other married women. These decisions and norms influence the livelihood strategies. The household composition in terms of age, gender in the household, number of people, landholding size and access to financial means constitutes the agency of poor households and forms the basis of protecting against economic shocks, vulnerabilities and food insecurity. More broadly, my household-level interactions revealed the resilience and agency of the Gonds despite the constraints on forest access. According to Cleavers (2005, p. 209), this agency is "dependent on three interlinked factors: their able-bodiedness, their room for manoeuvre within social relationships, and their ability to represent their interests in for accessible to them at low cost."

How can then anthropology help to explain the values of freedom and agency of labour in contexts such as those of bondage and starvation and a weak state to meet their everyday social and material needs? Further, while reciprocity as a social exchange has been studied widely by anthropologist, more attention needs to be paid on how to conceive dignity, autonomy, agency and independence for the poorer households who choose to labour and avoid debts for them and their families? What is the role of anthropologists in such contexts where poor demonstrate resilience and entrepreneurship and anarchy through pure and genuine available forms of protest, their body, labour and ability to do precarious work? What is the politics of such resilience of the labourers to strive for freedom and what moral and ethical implications on anthropology of mode of production, division of labour and social institutions such as kinship, family and patriarchy? How to explain when evidence provides that such labourers might in fact experience dignity and welfare and well-being but not by protesting against the state but instead choosing to labour for it?

In heterogeneous rural communities like in India, this is very difficult to assure, and thus, many households continue to feel vulnerable and can instead suffer negative impacts of the social capital. In that sense, labouring and waging and creating their own forms of social protection are a much stronger alternative, and relying on close kinship networks is more reliable. Also, social capital should not be a substitute for legal and institutional protection and security from the government. Social capital can only work when the state is weak and cannot be there in most extreme cases and emergencies like vulnerabilities and shocks due to the loss of the household income earner as also pointed by Gardner (2013) in her fieldwork in Bangladesh amongst the mining-affected communities. Social relations emerged as a form of social protection from their rich patrons in Britain as the state's reach at the village household level was very low. As Ellis adds:

> individual and household livelihoods are shaped by local and distant institutions, social relations, and economic opportunities. (2000, p. 6)

My studies show that more research should be done on the ideologies behind these strategies of livelihood diversification embedded in duty, care and social protection due to the opening up of newer economic protection and the limited impact of the state programmes. The study on the Gonds shows the need to contextualise the livelihood strategies of the poor households with social capital, the individual agency's gender relations, intra-household interactions with market changes in the surrounding and the local ecological constraints. As Harriss-White and Garikipati (2008) pointed out, most of India's poor reside in semi-arid tropical regions with scanty and uncertain rainfall and the need for the household to seek out market opportunities to smooth their livelihood strategies involves the feminisation of agriculture and in my study, also women's participation in non-farm work as migrants and forest wood collectors, causing increasing concern for women's welfare and ideologies of work and gender as these poor households get by on a day-to-day basis.

For the Gonds, these decisions are embedded in the wider processes of rural transformation and class formation. The role of networking allows them the flexibility to participate in the labour market. Das (2004) sceptical of social capitalists at the World Bank privileges social capital over material inequalities and class; in short, it is impossible to "separate social capital from material circumstances" (Mohan and Mohan 2002, p. 206). He was also critical of Bebbington (2002), who said that social relationships, such as family, are a resource for the poor that can facilitate access to other resources (Das 2004, p. 41). Das warned that not all social relationships are necessarily or automatically a resource. For Das, the resources that social capitalists referred to as capital are often absent amongst poor wagers and are not always adequate to alleviate poverty (ibid.).

I have problematised the observations of both Das (2004) and Cleaver (2005) by emphasising the need to analyse the networking abilities as social capital of the poor even if it is on a micro-scale. The WB and DFID views on social capital do not tell us about the inability of the poor to mobilise under exploitative conditions of capitalism as demonstrated in the study of temporary wagers in rural Orissa by Raju Das (2004) or in communities with members/households owning disproportionate capital as shown by Cleavers (2005) in rural Tanzania. Both authors study agrarian communities undergoing capitalist transformation in rural areas.

Through descriptive accounts of these strategies in the village of Mahalapur, India, I showed that the household members balance their altruistic and individual agendas and hence, these strategies are not random. These livelihood strategies are shaped by the wider collateral familial networks in addition to the newer market opportunities created in the local economy. The Gond's everyday micro-agency is temporal, low-key, barely visible, but helpful for the poor like the Gonds to live a viable life (Rogaly 2009, p. 10). Similarly, Carswell and De Neve (2013) study the agency of garment workers in Tiruppur where agency is demonstrated by labourers for material and economic improvement but has a wider social and cultural impact on their lives with non-material social transformations. They argue for "a broad conceptualization of agency firmly embedded in reproductive and social relationships" (2013, p. 64). Further, they show that this agency of the marginalised "accounts for the wider impact on livelihoods, social reproduction, and relations of inequality and dependency" (ibid.).

I agree with Rogaly that the agency of such temporary unorganised workers who are constantly mobile and work on piece-rate wages is short-lived and occurs on a micro-scale (2009, p. 1975). My ethnographic study on the Gonds' relation with the informal economy and the state places more emphasis on understanding how certain communities deprived of physical and material assets make a significant change in their lives while also being aware that the non-material assets do not last too long and even if they do make a difference. The change felt is only temporary in nature and is not secured because such workers work under unwritten contracts and labour in poor and uninsured conditions.

People's bonding and networking abilities are a "black hole" in the existing literature of gender studies and economic development (D'Exelle and Holvoet 2011). Social capital for agrarian households is often less acknowledged than it should be considered that for the poor and the landless, this is the most important resource. At the same time, we cannot generalise these networks because they are not the same for every household as I have shown in my ethnographic observations in Mahalapur. Every household should be treated as a separate unit constantly balancing and adapting to newer economic changes while also maintaining social status, and concurrently coping with economic shocks and vulnerabilities. Whether these networks are dense, sparse, homogenous or heterogeneous, also matters (Khan and Seeley 2005) for the vulnerable households predisposed to adverse social capital (Wood 2003, 2005) as informal support that are unorganised and based on norms, customs, obligations and expectations.

Thus, "poverty" is not such an apolitical and ahistorical institution and that it functions to keep certain kinds of people at the periphery so certain kinds of people remain at the centre (Staples 2007). Poverty needs to be seen "in a relational context and understood through both the social relations that produce it and the ways in which some people have control over and fight marginalised less powerful others" (Shah 2010, p. 98), especially this "categorical marginalisation" (Mosse 2010) also known as " forest fringe" communities and "doubly marginalised communities" in India (Shah 2010). Further, studying poverty amongst the agrarian communities like the Gonds in Southeast Asian countries, it is observed that poverty should be contextualised as "a product of resource failures and inequalities, and central to this are the distribution and productivity of land. We can in such a context, conceptualise poverty being reproduced overtime through inequalities in access to resources (especially land) being passed from one generation to the next. Poverty, in this sense, is inherited as, of course, is wealth" (Rigg 2006, p. 190).

This book has discussed the various ways the Gonds are moving out of poverty amidst the recently growing restrictions to the forests from

7 CONCLUSION 213

where they derived traditional forms of livelihoods. I showed that these decisions are rational and that these are embedded in the household ideologies of duty, care, social protection, stability and vulnerability. The Gonds are aware of the politics of development and poverty as played out by the state. Despite the state's efforts, the Gonds are disenchanted and use their "agency" of working and labouring to make a difference to their lives. The Gonds' multiplicity and diversity of livelihoods show that when faced with constraints to the traditional forms of livelihoods, people rely on non-material assets and use their able-bodiedness to work.

The sources of income and livelihood are disappearing around the mines, forcing the Gonds to migrate or else they would starve as they would not have resources to buy inputs for agriculture. That said, the region is much cleaner, greener and more spacious than other Indian states. There are two things which are clear: (1) that there is a strong correlation between the local politics and reproduction of poverty and high illiteracy and (2) that local development and progress are not possible without the permission of the Tiger Reserve. The state is the main agent of development in the Panna district, and the prejudices and stereotypes that the majority of the population has against tribal population are also reflected in rural administration. For instance, the local officials label the Gonds as unclean, "*dehati*" (rural), "*majboors*" (desperate), "drunkards" and "gamblers." These terms are frequently used to refer to them as being inferior to the rest of the non-tribal population. I have covered diverse life stories of the Gonds' households as encountered in the field. The advantage of using a life-course angle is to "examine the interface between personal history and place-between intersections of gender, age, class, marital status, place and moment" (Hapke 2001, p. 232).

In my study, I have shown that there are many gradations of vulnerabilities amongst the Gonds depending upon their household size, landholding size, gender and age of the household head, and their positions in the joint/extended family systems. Clearly, my studies show that there is no general way of explaining these strategies. The livelihood experiences are more personalised and subjective to the people that I interacted with and through my categorisations. Even if there is a simpler way to divide these households, the subjective experiences of the household transition with respect to the agency of each member to contribute to the household needs and balance their individual and collective needs of the family are more complicated.

I have treated the Gonds' household as a structure within which a range of subjective changes are occurring. I had set out my fieldwork to understand how are Gonds facing up to new odds due to restricted forest access? The Gond world of livelihoods is to juggle both the secular and the non-secular ideologies of change. The former is in the form of various *yojnas* like rural employment and subsidised schooling, and the later is in the form of family and kinship relations. To understand the strategies themselves as an arena to know these ideologies of household resiliencies, it's useful to distinguish them as secular and non-secular discourse of strategies. For the Gonds, I have shown that both Bourdieu (1977, 1986), Putnam et al. (1994) and Putnam's (2000) approach of social capital is necessary in understanding the contemporary rural India. Labouring embodies not only their physical ability to earn a living but it goes beyond that as they understand their political place in the labour market. Through labouring as their social capital, they are able to "effectively mobilise" (Bourdieu 1986, p. 249) in the social network that comprises of the labour market like the labour brokers, labour suppliers and the labour contractors. Social capital, for instance in the form of "bonding" thus, is a resource that is connected with group membership and social networks and its volume depends on the size of the network of connections that an individual can effectively mobilise (ibid.). Bourdieu's ideas are important for us to understand the traditional symbolic meanings that are associated with the process of social change driven by the state to the agrarian social base as Gonds who are subsistence and marginal farmers (1986).

On the other hand, Putnam et al. (1994) and Putnam's (2000) idea of social capital is equally essential to understand the newer forms of social capital that are being created with the Gonds' integration to the unorganised labour market where they practise their "agency" and "resist" the power of their employers. Putnam et al. (1994) and Putnam's (2000) idea of association, network and trust amongst the different components of the society explains how even as Gonds' economic capital is weak, their ability to labour and networking through labour contractors, brokers and labour suppliers helps them to stave off livelihood risk and vulnerabilities. These associations occur between various heterogeneous and vertical actors and networks. This type of social capital is a reflection of how state-led market reforms have created newer opportunities that help the young to diversify into non-farm types of livelihoods.

At the same time, poor people define networks based on the social context in which agency is proudness and adaptation to newer opportunities is determined by the social matrices of these factors and variants as was seen in the case of Kesar Bai and Leela Bai. Kesar Bai was more privileged than Leela Bai because she had more material assets in the form of land and grown-up children to help her increase her household income. Leela Bai is landless and had to stabilise her household in more vulnerable and riskier conditions. Leela Bai was able to contest the traditional bonds without any material assets. This confirms that women demonstrate individual agency driven both by external and by internal conditions. External is market conditions in which negotiation of wages and labouring are made, and internal is subjective to the existing ideologies of gender and work. Markets are making such households undergo ideological transformations at the household level and challenging the dominating and existing norms of gender and work. The combination of these two factors enables such households to live a viable life without loosing their social status as a daughter-in-law in their bona fide residential status.

For the Gonds, these decisions are embedded in the wider processes of rural transformation and class formation. The role of networking allows them the flexibility to participate in the labour market more here. I have problematised the observations of both Das (2004) and Cleaver (2005) by emphasising the need to analyse the networking abilities as social capital of the poor even if it is at a micro-scale. The WB and DFID views on social capital do not tell us about the inability of the poor to mobilise under exploitative conditions of capitalism as demonstrated in the study of temporary wagers in rural Orissa by Raju Das (2004) or in communities with members/households owning disproportionate capitals as shown by Cleaver (2005) in rural Tanzania which was discussed in Chapter 5. Both authors study agrarian communities undergoing capitalist transformation in rural areas.

At the same time, I also support their conclusions that material assets are important in the discussion of poverty alleviation but that should not undermine the importance of social capital and networking abilities which are the preconditions for forging alliances and contractual arrangements for the poor which makes a significant difference in the lives of the poor like the landless. This group of people benefit by negotiating the gender and kinship hierarchies in the household units and help to break the traditional bonds of social relations which can impede in their agency and ability to labour. My ethnographic work on Gond women like Leela Bai and Kesar Bai supports the view that there is very little cross-fertilisation of ideas which has occurred between scholars of social capital (Adkins 2005; Bezanson 2006) and feminist economists (Folbre 1984; Kabeer 1994) (as cited in D'Exelle and Holvoet 2011).

Livelihood strategies are thought to be embedded in household assets ranging from social to physical for the poor households to help them cope and move out of poverty. However, not enough studies are done on the ideologies behind these strategies. My research shows the need to contextualise livelihood strategies of the poor households with social capital, individual agency's gender relations, intra-household interactions with market changes in the surrounding and the local ecological constraints. As Harriss-White (2008) pointed out, most of India's poor reside in semi-arid tropical region with scanty and uncertain rainfall and the need for household to seek out market opportunity to smoothen their livelihood strategies involves feminisation of agriculture and in my study, also women's participation in non-farm work as migrants and forest wood collectors, causing increasing concern to women's welfare and ideologies of work and gender as these poor households get by on a day-to-day basis.

Through descriptive accounts of these strategies in the village of Mahalapur, India, I show that the household members balance their altruistic and individual agendas, and hence, these strategies are not random but in fact well thought out and rational. These rationalities behind livelihood strategies are shaped by the wider collateral familial networks in addition to the newer market opportunities created in the local economy. Gond's everyday micro-agency is temporal, low-key, barely visible, but helpful for the poor like the Gonds to live a viable life (Rogaly 2009, p. 10). Similarly, Creswell and De Neve (2013) study the agency of garment workers in Tiruppur where agency is demonstrated by labourers for material and economic improvement but has wider social and cultural impact in their lives with non-material social transformations. They argue for "a broad conceptualization of agency firmly embedded in reproductive and social relationships" (2013, p. 64). Further, they show that this agency of the marginalised "accounts for the wider impact on livelihoods, social reproduction, and remains of inequality and dependency" (ibid.).

However, these observations of the Gonds' strategies and agencies cannot be isolated from the fact that this takes a physical and psychological toll on their bodies and minds. To assume that they don't want to send their children to school but rather to work would be a misjudgement considering that the schooling facilities and infrastructure are very basic and the quality of syllabus and teachers is questionable. I conclude by agreeing with Rogaly that the agency of such temporary unorganised workers who are constantly mobile and work on piece-rate wages is short-lived and occurs at micro-scale (2009, p. 1975). Further, there should be more emphasis laid on understanding how certain communities deprived of physical and materials assets make a significant change in their lives while also being aware that the non-material assets don't last too long and even as they do make a difference. The change felt is only temporary in nature and is not secured because such workers work under unwritten contracts and labour in indecent and uninsured conditions.

Not all poor households will have equal access to social capital. In that sense, social capital is a material resource and it has to have equitable exchange value in the community for it to work for the households. In heterogeneous rural communities like in India, this is very difficult to assure and thus many households continue to feel vulnerable and can instead suffer negative impacts of the social capital.

In that sense, labouring and waging and creating their own forms of social protection are a much stronger alternative and relying on close kinship networks is more reliable. Also, social capital should not be a substitute for legal and institutional protection and security from the government. Social capital can only work when the state is weak and cannot be there in most extreme cases and emergencies like vulnerabilities and shocks due to loss of household income earner. As Ellis adds: "individual and household livelihoods are shaped by local and distant institutions, social relations, and economic opportunities" (2000, p. 6).

In the case of Gond widows who suddenly household income earners, it is important to note that sociopolitical relations are gendered in rural communities and vary across life course, class, race-ethnicity and nationality (Katz 1993). This forms the ideological base of such income earners and their livelihood practices. It is equally important to note that social capital will vary depending upon the cultural make-up of the rural communities and will manifest itself depending upon the moral and normative structures present in the communities. I would also add the risk that such networking pose is also equally important for more vulnerable households.

There is a very high level of trust amongst the Gond households which help them to make different land sharing arrangements and meet their food security needs. They help each other in all kinds of vulnerabilities and shocks but will not tolerate if people do not work. Help or assistance is offered in only extreme and legible health and emergency conditions. With newer forms of wealth through labouring, the needs of the Gonds have multiplied and they need each other more than ever before to stay in touch with job opportunities, information about labour contractors and any new rural scheme or any update on forest laws. The Gonds are experiencing a very crucial phase of transition and need each other; thus, this leads to social capital in the form of networking, trust and obligations. As Vermaak (2009) pointed out, "some forms of social capital are not possessed by individuals but, as a result of the interaction between individuals, emerge in the form of trust, expectations, obligations, norms and shared information" (p. 401).

The fact that the Gonds prefer to have their freedom and independence over their ability to work indicates their great desire to not be tied down to one form of labouring and waging. This is one of the important normative ideologies associated with the Gonds towards work and what they expect out of it. They remain assertive and in control of the terms and conditions of the working even if the choices of work are no all desirable. Even though education is not their main priority, this is only because of the poor schooling facilities that are in place and lack of encouragement from schooling authorities to encourage children to go to school. Similarly, the accounts of the Gonds' experience with the welfare state show the growing tension as they become aware that the state is weakened by the autocratic forest department. At the same time, the book draws upon the struggles of the indigenous populations and voices of the marginalised as how they challenge the state in an anarchical sense.

In the meantime, as the welfare state attempts to improve the life experiences of its rural and tribal citizens, there is a growing influence of informal networks and institutions such as the informal economy and the family. These institutions still pervade above the rest of the dynamic phenomena of political economy of livelihoods. This challenges the welfare state's fluidity in all spheres of life, yet it struggles to hold on varied contexts, as identified by Trouillot (2001). The state can be conceptualised and actualised, according to him through atomisation, spatialisation, identification and legitimisation.

This labouring allows Gonds to experience maximum autonomy and dignity over their livelihoods, economic sustenance and lives. The bypassing of the state by those who cannot formally protest and hold the state accountable, as observed amongst the Gonds, is akin to Gramscian notion of the hegemonic state and Abram's notion of the elusion of the state where the state powers can be felt and experienced. Bypassing the state in the unorganised labour market is an act to remain invisible and immeasurable by the Gonds and to, instead, be self-governed on their own terms. This bypassing of the state by the Gonds, as an indigenous population, also makes it imperative to go back to the work done by anthropologists on the making of the nation-state.

The act of Gonds' limited interaction with the state is also a disagreement with this misrepresentation of the Gonds' cosmology and ideology of their social lives. Instead, by labouring and using their hands in every activity of their livelihoods, the Gonds reaffirm their faith in their ability and control over themselves. Thus, waging, which is measurable and observable, is a symbolic act for social mobility and to provide for their families.

REFERENCES

Abrams, P. (1988). Notes on the Difficulty of Studying the State (1977). *Journal of Historical Sociology*, 1(1), 58–89.

Abrar, C. R., & Seeley, J. (Eds.). (2009). *Social Protection and Livelihoods: Marginalised Migrant Workers of India and Bangladesh*. University Press.

Adkins, L. (2005). Social Capital: The Anatomy of a Troubled Concept. *Feminist Theory*, 6(2), 195–211.

Adler, P. S., & Kwon, S. (1999). *Social Capital: The Good, the Bad, and the Ugly Modified Version*. Paper Presented at the Academy of Management Meeting, Chicago, IL.

Ali, A. (2005). *Livelihood and Food Security in Rural Bangladesh: The Role of Social Capital*. Ph.D. Thesis, Wageningen University, the Netherlands, p. 203.

Bebbington, A. (2002). Movements, Modernizations, and Markets: Indigenous Organizations and Agrarian Strategies in Ecuador. In *Liberation Ecologies* (pp. 98–121). Routledge.
Bernstein, H. (2003). Land Reform in Southern Africa in World-Historical Perspective. *Review of African Political Economy, 30*(96), 203–226.
Bezanson, K. (2006). Gender and the Limits of Social Capital. *Canadian Review of Sociology/Revue canadienne de sociologie, 43*(4), 427–443.
Bourdieu, P. (1977). *Outline of a Theory of Practice* (Vol. 16). Cambridge University Press.
Bourdieu, P. (1986). The Forms of Capital. In *Handbook of Theory and Research for the Sociology of Education* (pp. 241–258). New York: Greenwood.
Breman, J. (2003). *The Labouring Poor in India: Patterns of Exploitation, Subordination and Exclusion*. Oxford: Oxford University Press.
Breman, J. (2007). *The Poverty Regime in Village India: Half a Century of Work and Life at the Bottom of the Rural Economy in South Gujarat*. New Delhi: Oxford University Press.
Breman, J. (2010). *Outcast Labour in Asia: Circulation and Informalization of the Workforce at the Bottom of the Economy*. Oxford University Press Catalogue.
Breman, J., Guérin, I., & Prakash, A. (Eds.). (2009). *India's Unfree Workforce*. New Delhi: Oxford University Press.
Bryceson, D. F. (1980). The Proletarianization of Women in Tanzania. *Review of African Political Economy, 7*(17), 4–27.
Carswell, G., & De Neve, G. (2013). Labouring for Global Markets: Conceptualising Labour Agency in Global Production Networks. *Geoforum, 44*, 62–70.
Chambers, R. (1989). Editorial Introduction: Vulnerability, Coping and Policy. *IDS Bulletin, 20*(2), 1–7.
Chatterjee, P. (Ed.). (1998). *Wages of Freedom: Fifty Years of the Indian Nation-State*. USA: Oxford University Press.
Chen, M. (1990). Poverty, Gender and Work in Bangladesh. In L. Dube & R. Palriwala (Eds.), *Structure and Strategies: Women, Work and Family* (pp. 201–221). New Delhi, New York and London: Sage Publication.
Cleaver, F. (2005). The Inequality of Social Capital and the Reproduction of Chronic Poverty. *World Development, 33*(6), 893–906.
Corbridge, S., & Shah, A. (2013). Introduction: The Underbelly of the Indian Boom. *Economy and Society, 42*(3), 335–347.
Das, R. J. (2004). Social Capital and Poverty of the Wage-Labour Class: Problems with the Social Capital Theory. *Transactions of the Institute of British Geographers, 29*(1), 27–45.
D'Exelle, B., & Holvoet, N. (2011). Gender and Network Formation in Rural Nicaragua: A Village Case Study. *Feminist Economics, 17*(2), 31–61. https://doi.org/10.1080/13545701.2011.573488.

Drèze, J., & Sen, A. (1999). *India: Economic Development and Social Opportunity.* Oxford University Press Catalogue.
Drèze, J., & Sen, A. (2013). *An Uncertain Glory: India and Its Contradictions.* Princeton, NJ: Princeton University Press.
Ellis, F. (2000). *Rural Livelihoods and Diversity in Developing Countries.* New York: Oxford University Press.
Folbre, N. R. (1984). Market Opportunities, Genetic Endowments, and Intrafamily Resource Distribution: Comment. *The American Economic Review, 74*(3), 518–520.
Gardner, K. (2006). The Transnational Work of Kinship and Caring: Bengali– British Marriages in Historical Perspective. *Global Networks, 6*(4), 373–387.
Gardner, K. (2009). Lives in Motion: The Life-Course, Movement and Migration in Bangladesh. *Journal of South Asian Development, 4*(2), 229–251.
Gardner, K. (2012). Transnational Migration and the Study of Children: An Introduction. *Journal of Ethnic and Migration Studies, 38*(6), 889–912.
Gardner, K. (2013). Global Migrants and Local Shrines: The Shifting Geography of Islam in Sylhet, Bangladesh. In *Muslim Diversity* (pp. 45–65). Routledge.
Guérin, I., Roesch, M., Kumar, S., Venkatasubramanian, G., & Sangare, M. (2009). *Microfinance and the Dynamics of Financial Vulnerability: Lessons from rural South India.*
Hapke, H. M. (2001). Gender, Work, and Household Survival in South Indian Fishing Communities: A Preliminary Analysis. *The Professional Geographer, 53*(3), 313–331.
Harriss-White, B. (2003). *India Working: Essays on Society and Economy* (Vol. 8). Cambridge: Cambridge University Press.
Harriss-White, B. (2008). 'India's Rainfed Agricultural Dystopia' in Special Issue. In B. Harriss-White & S. Garikipati (Eds.), *European Journal of Development Research, 20*(4), 549–561.
Harriss-White, B. & Garikipati, S. (2008). India's Semi-Arid Rural Economy: Livelihoods, Seasonal Migration And Gender. *European Journal of Development Research, 20*(4), 547–548.
Kabeer, N. (1994). *Reversed Realities: Gender Hierarchies in Development Thought.* London: Verso.
Katz, M. B. (1993). *The "Underclass" Debate: Views from History.* Princeton University Press.
Khan, I. A., & Seeley, J. (2005). *Making a Living: The Livelihoods of the Rural Poor in Bangladesh.* The University Press Limited.
Lerche, J. (2009). From 'Rural Labour' to 'Classes of Labour': Class Fragmentation, Caste and Class Struggle at the Bottom of the Indian Labour Hierarchy. In *The Comparative Political Economy of Development* (pp. 90–111). Routledge.

Lerche, J. (2013). The Agrarian Question in Neoliberal India: Agrarian Transition Bypassed? *Journal of Agrarian Change*, 13(3), 382–404.

Mitchell, T. (1990). Society, Economy, and the State Effect. In G. Steinmetz (Ed.), *State/Culture: State-Formation After the Cultural Turn*. Ithaca and London: Cornell University Press.

Mohan, G., & Mohan, J. (2002). Placing Social Capital. *Progress in Human Geography*, 26(2), 191–210.

Moser, C. O. N. (1996). Confronting Crisis: A Comparative Study of Household Responses to Poverty and Vulnerability in Four Poor Urban Communities. *Environmentally Sustainable Development Studies and Monographs Series No. 8*. Washington, DC: The World Bank.

Moser, C. O. N. (1998). The Asset Vulnerability Framework: Reassessing Urban Poverty Reduction Strategies. *World Development*, 26(1), 1–19.

Mosse, D. (2007). *Power and the Durability of Poverty: A Critical Exploration of the Links Between Culture, Marginality and Chronic Poverty* (Chronic Poverty Research Centre Working Paper No. 107). Manchester: CPRC.

Mosse, D. (2010). A Relational Approach to Durable Poverty, Inequality and Power. *The Journal of Development Studies*, 46(7), 1156–1178.

Niehof, A., & Price, L. (2001). *Rural Livelihood Systems: A Conceptual Framework*. Wageningen-Upward Series and on *Rural Livelihoods No. 1*. Wageningen, the Netherlands: Wu-Upward.

Pennartz, P., & Niehof, A. (1999). *The Domestic Domain: Chances, Choices and Strategies of Family Households*. Aldershot, Brookfield, USA, Singapore and Sydney: Ashgate Publishing Ltd.

Picherit, D. (2012). Migrant Labourers' Struggles Between Village and Urban Migration Sites: Labour Standards, Rural Development and Politics in South India. *Global Labour Journal*, 3(1), 143–162.

Putnam, R. D. (1995). Bowling Alone: America's Declining Social Capital. *Journal of Democracy*, 6, 65–78.

Putnam, R. D. (2000). Bowling Alone: America's Declining Social Capital. In *Culture and Politics* (pp. 223–234). New York: Palgrave Macmillan.

Putnam, R. D., Leonardi, R., & Nanetti, R. Y. (1994). *Making Democracy Work: Civic Traditions in Modern Italy*. Princeton University Press.

Rigg, J. (2006). Land, Farming, Livelihoods, and Poverty: Rethinking the Links in the Rural South. *World development*, 34(1), 180–202.

Robinson, A., & Tormey, S. (2012). Beyond the State: Anthropology and 'Actually-Existing-Anarchism'. *Critique of Anthropology*, 32, 143.

Rogaly, B. (2009). Spaces of Work and Everyday Life: Labour Geographies and the Agency of Unorganised Temporary Migrant Workers. *Geography Compass*, 3(6), 1975–1987.

Rudie, I. (1995). The Significance of 'Eating': Cooperation, Support and Reputation in Kelantan Malay Households. In W. J. Karim (Ed.), *'Male' and 'Female' in Developing Southeast Asia* (pp. 227–247). Oxford: Berg.

Rudolph, R. L. (1992). The European Family and Economy: Central Themes and Issues. *Journal of Family History, 17*(2), 119–138.

Sen, A. (1999a). *Development as Freedom*. Delhi, India and Oxford: Oxford University Press.

Sen, A. (1999b). *Beyond the Crisis: Development Strategies in Asia*. Pasir Panjang, Singapore: ISEAS.

Shah, A. (2010). *Shadows of the State. Indigenous Politics, Environmentalism and Insurgency in Jharkhand*. Durham: Duke University Press.

Staples, J. (2007). *Livelihoods at the Margins: Surviving the City*. Walnut Creek, CA: Left Coast.

Tilly, C. (1988). Solidary Logics. *Theory and Society, 17*(3), 451–458.

Trouillot, M.-R. (2001). The Anthropology of the State in the Age of Globalization: Close Encounters of the Deceptive Kind. *Current Anthropology, 42*(1), 125–138.

Vermaak, J. (2009). Reassessing the Concept of 'Social Capital': Considering Resources for Satisfying the Needs of Rural Communities. *Development Southern Africa, 26*(3), 399–412.

Wood, G. (2003). Staying Secure, Staying Poor: The 'Faustian Bargain'. *World Development, 31*(3), 455–471.

Wood, G. D. (2005). Poverty, Capabilities and Perverse Social Capital: The Antidote to Sen and Putnam. In J. Seeley & A. Khan (Eds.), *Making a Living: The Livelihoods of the Rural Poor in Bangladesh*. Dhaka: University Press Limited.

Glossary

Adivasis	indigenous people
Anna	a smaller ancient Indian currency
Atta	sacred offering to Gond goddesses
Barakha	forest guard
Bcc	road made out of cement, a terminology only used amongst people of Panna
Beedi	indigenous source of tobacco
Begar pratha	traditional patron–client relationship
Bengalis	an ethnic group that speaks Bengal; refugees from Bangladesh
Bidaayi	farewell
Dabloodukariya	an obese older woman
Des	nation
Dhams	monastery
Dhanda	trade/ occupation
Didi	elder sister
Dihadi	wages
Durga	Indian goddess
Galla utahana	to collect their rationing supplies from local ration shops
Garibi	poverty
Garibi rekha	below poverty
Ghar	a house
Gharjamayee	a son-in-law who resides in his wife's village

Glossary of Terms

Gora	white man
Gram	a village
Guniya	shamans
Gutkha	indigenous tobacco
Jammadar	labour supplier
Jan sunwayee	public grievances/redressal hearings
Jhariya	branches
Kalyug	doomsday
Kamayee	income
Khadaan	stone quarries
Kher Mata	a Gond goddess
Kucca	made out of mud/clay
Kunthi	a soft head-pad made out of worn-out sarees
Lagan	marriage
Lekha padhi	literacy
Lippai pottai	removing and replacing worn-out paint walls mase out of cow dung and clay
Mahua	a wild fruit
Maistry	professional stone miner
Majdoors	workers/labourers
Majoori	labouring/waging
Mitti ka tel	kerosene oil
Munshi	accountant
Nyaarpanna	gradual household separation due to independent cooking hearths
Paan	betel nut
Paaths	devotional songs
Paisa	a small unit of coin of ancient Indian currency
Palayan	migration
Panchayat	a village-level governing body
Panchnama	a traditional justice system where five witnesses can testify the person to be guilty of the said charge either drinking or gambling
Patwari	land gazetteer
Pucca	made out of bricks
Rajah	king

Rajaswa	postcolonial state
Roji	livelihood
Roti	Indian bread
Rukjana	to stay back, to not return
Sachiv	secretary
Samaj	society
Samajik sewa	social service
Samooh	communal
Sarpanch	head of five council member
Swami	lord
Tasla	an elliptical-shaped plastic bucket used as a unit of work done in crushing stones
Thakurs	landed elites
Thekedaari	labour contractor
Tilak	a sacred symbol on the forehead signifying marital status for a Gond woman
Vides	international

Bibliography

Abrar, C., & Seeley, J. (Eds.). (2009). *Social Protection and Livelihoods: Marginalised Migrants of South Asia*. Dhaka: The University Press.

Acharya, J. (2003). Embodying Craftswomen's Workspace and Well-Being in Orissa, India. *Norsk Geografisk Tidsskrift—Norwegian Journal of Geography, 57,* 173–183.

Addison, T., Hulme, D., & Kanbur, R. (2008). Poverty Dynamics: Measurement and Understanding from an Interdisciplinary Perspective.

Adler, P. S., & Kwon, S. (1999). *Social Capital: The Good, the Bad, and the Ugly*. Modified Version of a Paper Presented at the 1999 Academy of Management Meeting, Chicago, IL.

Agar, M. H. (1986). *Speaking of Ethnography*. Beverly Hills: Sage.

Agarwal, B. (1990). Social Security and the Family: Coping with Seasonality and Calamity in Rural India. *Journal of Peasant Studies, 17,* 341–412.

Agarwal, B. (1997). Bargaining and Gender Relations: Within and Beyond the Household. *Feminist Economics, 3*(1), 1–51.

Agarwal, B. (1998). Disinherited Peasants, Disadvantaged Workers: A Gender Perspective on Land and Livelihood. *Economic and Political Weekly, 33*(13), A2–A14.

Agarwal, B.(2003). Gender and Land Rights Revisited: Exploring New Prospects Via the State, Family and Market. *Journal of Agrarian Change, 3*(1–2), 184–224.

Agarwal, R., Breman, J., & Das, A. (2000). *Down and Out: Labouring Under Global Capitalism*. New Delhi: Oxford University Press.

Ali, A. (2005). *Livelihood and Food Security in Rural Bangladesh: The Role of Social Capital.* Ph.D. Thesis, Wageningen University, the Netherlands, p. 203.

Appadurai, A. (2004). The Capacity to Aspire: Culture and the Terms of Recognition. In V. Rao & M. Walton (Eds.), *Culture and Public Action* (pp. 59–84). Stanford: Stanford University Press.

Arun, S. (2012). 'We Are Farmers Too': Agrarian Change and Gendered Livelihoods in Kerala, South India. *Journal of Gender Studies, 21*(3), 271–284.

Asad, T. (1973). *Anthropology and the Colonial Encounter.* New York: Humanity Books.

Atkinson, P., & Hammersley, M. (1994). *Ethnography and Participant Observation. Handbook of Qualitative Research.* Thousand Oaks, CA: Sage.

Atkinson, P., & Hammersley, M. (2007). *Ethnography: Principles in Practice.* London: Routledge.

Baboo, D., Mahapatra, A., &. Tewari, K. (2015). Displacement, Deprivation and Development: The Impact of Relocation on Income and Livelihood of Tribes in Similipal Tiger and Biosphere Reserve, India. *Environmental Management, 56*(2), 420–432.

Baey, G., & Yeoh, B. (2015). *Migration and Precarious Work: Negotiating Debt, Employment, and Livelihood Strategies Amongst Bangladeshi Migrant Men Working in Singapore's Construction Industry.* Migrating Out of Poverty Working Paper, 26.

Bahuguna, V. K. (2001). Forests in the Economy of the Rural Poor: An Estimation of the Dependency Level. *Ambio, 29*(3), 126–129.

Ballet, J., Bhukuth, A., & Guérin, I. (2007). Social Capital and the Brokerage System: The Formation of Debt Bondage in South India. *Journal of Economic Studies, 34*(4), 311–323.

Bardhan, P., & Rudra, A. (1978). Interlinkage of Land, Labour and Credit Relations: An Analysis of Village Survey Data in East India. *Economic and Political Weekly*, 367–384.

Bates, C. N. (1985). Regional Dependence and Rural Development in Central India: The Pivotal Role of Migrant Labour. *Modern Asian Studies, 19*(3), 573–592.

Baviskar, A. (1998). Tribal Politics and Discourses of Environmentalism. *Contributions to Indian Sociology, 31*(2), 195–223.

Beazley, K. (2011). Spaces of Opportunity: State-Oustee Relations in the Context of Conservation-Induced Displacement in Central India. *Pacific Affairs, 84*(1), 25–46.

Behera, B., Mishra, P., & Nayak, N. C. (2010). A Development Delivery Institution for the Tribal Communities: Experience of the National Rural Employment Guarantee Scheme in India. *Development Policy Review, 28*, 457–479.

Benei, V., & Fuller, C. J. (2009). *The Everyday State and Society in Modern India.* London: Hurst.

Bennike, R. (2017). Frontier Commodification: Governing Land, Labour and Leisure in Darjeeling, India. *South Asia-Journal of South Asian Studies, 40,* 256–271.
Beteille, A. (1998). The Idea of Indigenous People. *Current Anthropology, 39*(2), 187–191.
Béteille, A. (2000). *Antinomies of Society: Essays in Ideologies and Institutions.* New Delhi: Oxford University Press.
Bhagat, R., B. & Keshri, K. (2012). Temporary and Seasonal Migration: Regional Pattern, Characteristics and Associated Factors. *Economic and Political Weekly, 47*(4), 81–88.
Bhukuth, A. (2005). Child Labour and Debt Bondage: A Case Study of Brick Kiln Workers in Southeast India. *Journal of Asian and African Studies, 40*(4), 287–302.
Bhushan, C., Bhushan, C., & Banerjee, M. Z. H. S. (2008). *Rich Lands Poor People: IssustainableMining Possible* (Vol. 6). Chicago: Centre for Science and Environment.
Biehl, J., & Petryna, A. (2013). *When People Come First: Critical Studies in Global Health.* Princeton, NJ: Princeton University Press.
Biswas, J., Coppard, D., Rana, K., Rogaly, B., Safique, A., & Sengupta, A. (2002). Seasonal Migration and Welfare/Illfare in Eastern India: A Social Analysis. *Journal of Development Studies, 38*(5), 89–114.
Blanc-Szanton, C. (1990). Collision of Cultures: Historical Reformulation of Gender in the Lowland Visayas. In J. Atkinson & S. Errinston (Eds.), *Power and Difference* (pp. 345–348). Stanford, CA: Stanford University Press.
Bliss, C. J., & Stern, N. H. (1984). *Palanpur, the Economy of an Indian Village.* New Delhi: Oxford University Press.
Bouchard, M. (2011). The State of the Study of the State in Anthropology. *Reviews in Anthropology, 40*(3), 183–209.
Bourdieu, P. (1977). *Outline of a Theory of Practice* (Vol. 16). Cambridge: Cambridge University Press.
Bourdieu, P. (1986). The Forms of Capital. In *Handbook of Theory and Research for the Sociology of Education.* New York: Greenwood.
Bourdieu, P., & Passeron, J. C. (1990). *Reproduction in Education, Society and Culture.* Beverly Hills: Sage.
Breman, J. (1974). *Patronage Exploitation: Changing Agrarian Relations in South Gujarat, India.* Berkeley: University of California Press.
Breman, J. (1976). A Dualistic Labour System? A Critique of the 'Informal Sector' Concept: I: The Informal Sector. *Economic and Political Weekly, 11*(48), 1870–1876.
Breman, J. (1985). Of Peasants Migrants and Paupers: Rural Labour Circulation and Capitalist Production in West India. In J. Breman (Ed.), *Footloose Labour: Working in India's Informal Economy.* Cambridge: Cambridge University Press.

Breman, J. (1996). *Footloose Labour: Working in India's Informal Economy*. Cambridge: Cambridge University Press.
Breman, J. (2003). *The Labouring Poor in India: Patterns of Exploitation, Subordination and Exclusion*. Oxford: Oxford University Press.
Breman, J. (2007a). *The Poverty Regime in Village India: Half a Century of Work and Life at the Bottom of the Rural Economy in South Gujarat*. New Delhi: Oxford University Press.
Breman, J. (2007b). *Labour Bondage in West India: From Past to Present*. Oxford: Oxford University Press.
Breman, J. (2010). *Outcast Labour in Asia: Circulation and Informalization of the Workforce at the Bottom of the Economy*. New Delhi: Oxford University Press.
Breman, J. (2016). *At Work in the Informal Economy of India: A Perspective from the Bottom Up* (OIP). Oxford: Oxford University Press.
Breman, J., & Mundle, S. (Eds.). (1991). *Rural Transformation in India*. Oxford: Oxford University Press.
Breman, J., Guérin, I., & Prakash, A. (Eds.). (2009). *India's Unfree Workforce*. New Delhi: Oxford University Press.
Breman, J., Kloos, P., & Saith, A. (Eds.). (1997). *The Village in Asia Revisited*. New Delhi: Oxford University Press.
Bruner, E. M. (1997). Ethnography as Narrative. In *Memory, Identity,Community: The Idea of Narrative in the Human Sciences* (pp. 264–280). Albany, NY: State University of New York Press.
Buitelaar, M. (1995). 'Widows' Words: Representations and Realities. In J. Bremmer & L. Van Den Bosch (Eds.), *Between Poverty and the Pyre: Moments in the History of Widowhood* (pp. 1–18). London: Routledge.
Camfield, L., & Copestake, J. (2009). *Measuring Subjective Wellbeing in Bangladesh, Ethiopia, Peru and Thailand Using a Personal Life Goal Satisfaction Approach* (Wed Working Paper 09/45). www.welldev.org.
Camfield, L., Choudhury, K., & Devine, J. (2009). Well-Being, Happiness and Why Relationships Matter: Evidence from Bangladesh. *Journal of Happiness Studies, 10*(1), 71–91.
Carswell, G. (2002). Farmers and Following: Agricultural Change in Kigezi District, Uganda. *Geographical Journal, 168*(2), 130–140.
Carswell, G., & De Neve, G. (2013). Labouring for Global Markets: Conceptualising Labour Agency in Global Production Networks. *Geoforum, 44*, 62–70.
Carswell, G., & De Neve, G. (2014). MGNREGA in Tamil Nadu: A Story of Success and Transformation? *Journal of Agrarian Change, 14*(4), 564–585.
Celtel, A. (2004). *Categories of the Self: Louis Dumont's Theory of the Individual*. London: Berghahn Books.

Chamarbagwala, R. (2008). Regional Returns to Education, Child Labour and Schooling in India. *Journal of Development Studies*, 44(2), 233–257.
Chambers, R. (1989). Vulnerability, Coping and Policy. Institute of Development Studies, University of Sussex. *IDS Bulletin*, 37(4), 1–8.
Chambers, R., & Conway, G. (1992). *Sustainable Rural Livelihoods: Practical Concepts for the 21st Century* (IDS Discussion Paper 296). Brighton, UK: Institute of Development Studies, University of Sussex.
Chandavarkar, R. (1994). *The Origins of Industrial Capitalism in India: Business Strategies and the Working Classes in Bombay, 1900–1940*. Cambridge: Cambridge University Press.
Chant, S. (1997). *Women-Headed Households: Diversity and Dynamics in the Developing World*. Basingstoke: Macmillan.
Charmaz, K., & Mitchell, R. G. (1996). The Myth of Silent Authorship: Self, Substance, and Style in Ethnographic Writing. *Symbolic Interaction*, 19(4), 285–302.
Chaturvedi, V. (2007). *Peasant Pasts: History and Memory in Western India*. Berkeley and Los Angeles: University of California Press.
Cleaver, F. (2005). The Inequality of Social Capital and the Reproduction of Chronic Poverty. *World Development* 33(6), 893–906.
Clifford, J., & Marcus, G. E. (1986). *Writing Culture: The Poetics and Politics of Ethnography*. Berkeley: University of California Press.
Colson, E. (1979). The Harvey Lecture Series. In Good Years and in Bad: Food Strategies of Self-reliant Societies. *Journal of Anthropological Research*, 35(1), 18–29.
Colson, E., Foster, G. M., Scudder, T., & Kemper, R. V. (1976). Long-Term Field Research in Social Anthropology. *Current Anthropology*, 17(3), 494–496.
Coppard, D., & Rogaly, B. (2003). 'They Used to Go to Eat, Now They Go to Earn': The Changing Meanings of Seasonal Migration from Puruliya District in West Bengal, India. *Journal of Agrarian Change*, 3(3), 395–433.
Corbett, M. (2007). *Learning to Leave: The Irony of Schooling in a Coastal Community*. Halifax, NS: Fernwood.
Corbridge, S. (1988). The Ideology of Tribal Economy and Society: Politics in the Jharkhand, 1950–1980. *Modern Asian Studies*, 22(1), 1–42.
Corbridge, S., & Harriss, J. (2000). *Reinventing India: Liberalization, Hindu Nationalism and Popular Democracy*. Cambridge: Polity Press.
Corbridge, S., & Shah, A. (2013). Introduction: The Underbelly of the Indian Boom. *Economy and Society*, 42(3), 335–347.
Corbridge, S., Srivastava, M., Veron, R., & Williams, G. (Eds.). (2005). *Seeing the State: Governance and Governmentality in India*. Cambridge: Cambridge University Press.

Cross, J. (2010). Neoliberalism as Unexceptional: Economic Zones and the Everyday Precariousness of Working Life in South India. *Critique of Anthropology, 30,* 355–373.

Da Costa, D. (2010). *Development Dramas: Reimagining Rural Political Action in Eastern India.* New Delhi: Routledge.

Das, R. J. (2004). Social Capital and Poverty of the Wage Labour Class: Problems with the Social Capital Theory. *Transactions of the Institute of British Geographers, 29*(1), 27–45.

Das, S., Jain-Chandra, S., Kochhar, M. K., & Kumar, N. (2015). Women Workers in India: Why so Few Among so Many? IMF Working Paper. Asia and Pacific Department. Wp/15/55. Jel Classification Numbers: J16, J48, O17. https://www.imf.org/external/pubs/ft/wp/2015/wp1555.pdf. Downloaded December 2015.

Davala, S., Jhabvala, R., Standing, G., & Mehta, S. K. (2015). *Basic Income: A Transformative Policy for India.* London: Bloomsbury Publishing.

De Haan, A. (1999a). The Badli System in Industrial Labour Recruitment: Managers' and Workers' Strategies in Calcutta's Jute Industry. *Contributions to Indian Sociology, 33,* 271–301.

De Haan, A. (1999b). Livelihoods and Poverty: The Role of Migration a Critical Review of the Migration Literature. *Journal of Development Studies, 36*(2), 1–47.

De Haan, A. (2002). Migration and Livelihoods in Historical Perspective: A Case Study of Bihar, India. *Journal of Development Studies, 38*(5), 115–142.

De Haan, A., & Rogaly, B. (2002). Introduction: Migrant Workers and their Role in Rural Change. *Journal of Development Studies, 38*(5), 1–14.

De Haan, L., & Zoomers, A. (2005). Exploring the Frontier of Livelihoods Research. *Development Change, 36*(1), 27–47.

De Neve, G. (1999). Asking for and Giving Baki: Neo-Bondage, or the Interplay of Bondage and Resistance in the Tamilnadu Power-Loom Industry. *Contributions to Indian Sociology, 33,* 379–406.

De Neve, G. (2005). *The Everyday Politics of Labour: Working Lives in India's Informal Economy.* Oxford: Berghahn Books.

De Neve, G. (2006). Hidden Reflexivity: Assistants, Informants and the Creation of Anthropological Knowledge. In *Critical Journeys* (pp. 77–100). Chicago: Routledge.

De Wispelaere, J. (2016). The Struggle for Strategy: On the Politics of the Basic Income Proposal. *Politics, 36,* 131–141.

Deb, U., Rao, M., Rao, N., & Slater, R. (2001). *Diversification and Livelihood Options: A Study of Two Villages in Andhra Pradesh, India 1975–2001.* London: Overseas Development Institute.

Desai, A. R. (1969). *Rural Sociology in India*. Bombay: Popular Prakashan.
Desai, S. (1993). The Impact of Family Size on Children's Nutritional Status: Insights from a Comparative Perspective. In C. B. Lloyd (Ed.), *Fertility, Family Size and Structure: Consequences for Families and Children* (pp. 155–191). New York: Population Council.
Deshingkar, P. (2006). Internal Migration, Poverty and Development in Asia: Including the Excluded. *IDS Bulletin, 37*(3), 88–100.
Deshingkar, P. (2008). Circular Internal Migration and Development in India. In J. Dewind & J. Holdaway: International Organization for Migration (Eds.), *Migration and Development Within and Across Borders: Research and Policy Perspectives on Internal and International Migration* (pp. 161–187). Geneva: Hammersmith Press.
Deshingkar, P., & Farrington, J. (2009). *Circular Migration and Multi Locational Livelihoods Strategies in Rural India*. New Delhi: Oxford University Press.
Deshingkar, P., & Start, D. (2003). *Seasonal Migration for Livelihoods in India: Coping, Accumulation and Exclusion* (Working Paper 220). Overseas Development Institute, UK. *Developing Societies, 25*(4), 457–480.
Deshpande, R. (2017). India's Demonetisation: Modi's 'Nudge' to Change Economic and Social Behaviour. *Asian Affairs, 48*, 222–235.
D'espallier, B., Guérin, I., & Venkatasubramanian, G. (2013). Debt in Rural South India: Fragmentation, Social Regulation and Discrimination. *Journal of Development Studies, 49*(9), 1155–1171.
Dey, N., Drèze, J., & Roy., A. (2008). Finish the Job | India | Hindustan Times. Available at www.hindustantimes.com, http://m.hindustantimes.com/india/finish-the-job/story-85t97oxyruvapzt9wzo9mk.html. Accessed 29 December 2013.
Drèze, J. (2007, November 20). Nrega: Dismantling the Contractor Raj. *The Hindu*. Available at http://www.hindu.com/2007/11/20/stories/2007112056181000.htm. Downloaded on 17 January 2014.
Drèze, J., & Kingdon, G. G. (2001). School Participation in Rural India. *Review of Development Economics, 5*(1), 1–24.
Drèze, J., & Sen, A. (2013). *An Uncertain Glory: India and Its Contradictions*. Princeton, NJ: Princeton University Press.
Duffield, M. (2007). *Development, Security and Unending War: Governing the World of Peoples*. Cambridge: Polity.
Ellis, F. (1998). Household Strategies and Rural Livelihood Diversification. *Journal of Development Studies, 35*, 1–38.

Ellis, F. (2000). *Rural Livelihoods and Diversity in Developing Countries.* New York: Oxford University Press.

Epstein, T. S., Suryanarayana, A. P., & Thimmegowda, T. (1998). *Village Voices: Forty Years of Rural Transformation in South India.* New Delhi: Sage.

Fafchamps, M., & Gubert, F. (2007). Risk Sharing and Network Formation. *American Economic Review, 97,* 75–79.

Ferguson, J. (1990). *The Anti-politics Machine: Development, De-politicisation and Bureaucratic Power in Lesotho.* Cambridge: Cambridge University Press.

Ferguson, J., & Gupta, A. (2002). Spatializing States: Toward an Ethnography of Neoliberal Governmentality. *American Ethnologist, 29,* 981–1002.

Folbre, N. (1984). Market Opportunities, Genetic Endowments, and Intrafamily Resource Distribution: Comment. *American Economic Review, 74*(3), 518–520.

Fortes, M. (1949). *The Web of Kinship Among the Tallensi: The Second Part of an Analysis of the Social Structure of a Trans-Volta Tribe.* London: Oxford University Press.

Froerer, P. (2008). Learning, Livelihoods, and Social Mobility: Valuing Girls' Education in Central India. *Anthropology and Education Quarterly, 43*(4), 344–357.

Froerer, P. (2012). Education, Inequality and Social Mobility in Central India. *European Journal of Development Research, 23*(5), 695–711.

Frota, L. (2008). Securing Decent Work and Living Conditions in Low-Income Urban Settlements by Linking Social Protection and Local Development: A Review of Case Studies. *Habitat International, 32,* 203–222.

Fuller, C. J. (1996). Introduction. In C. J. Fuller (Ed.), *Caste Today.* New Delhi: Oxford University Press.

Gaiha, R., Jha, R., & Shankar, S. (2008). Reviewing the National Rural Employment Guarantee Programme. *Economic and Political Weekly, 42*(11), 44–48.

Gaiha, R., Jha, R., Pandey, M. K., & Shankar, S. (2013). Targeting Accuracy of the Nreg: Evidence from Madhya Pradesh and Tamil Nadu. *European Journal of Development Research, 25*(5), 758–777.

Gardner, K. (1995). *Global Migrants, Local Lives: Travel and Transformation in Rural Bangladesh.* Oxford: Oxford University Press.

Gardner, K. (2009). Lives in Motion: The Life-Course, Movement and Migration in Bangladesh. *Journal of South Asian Development, 4*(2), 229–251.

Gardner, K., & Osella, F. (2003). Migration, Modernity and Social Transformation in South Asia an Overview. *Contributions to Indian Sociology, 37*(1–2), v–xxviii.

Garikipati, S., & Harriss-White, B. (2008). India's Semi-Arid Rural Economy: Livelihoods, Seasonal Migration and Gender. *European Journal of Development Research, 20*(4), 547–548.

Garikipati, S. & Pfaffenzeller, S. (2012). The Gendered Burden of Liberalisation: The Impact of India's Economic Reforms on Its Female Agricultural Labour. *Journal of International Development, 24*(7), 841–864.

Garikipati, S. (2009). Landless but Not Assetless: Female Agricultural Labour on the Road to Better Status, Evidence From India. *The Journal of Peasant Studies, 36,* 517–545.

Geertz, C. (1973). *The Interpretation of Cultures: Selected Essays* (Vol. 5019). New York: Basic Books.

Gidwani, V. (2008). *Capital Interrupted: Agrarian Development and the Politics of Work in India.* Minneapolis: University of Minnesota Press.

Gidwani, V., & Sivaramakrishnan, K. (2003). Circular Migration and the Spaces of Cultural Assertion. *Annals of the Association of American Geographers, 93*(1), 186–213.

Gill, L. (1997). Relocating Class: Ex-miners and Neoliberalism in Bolivia. *Critique of Anthropology, 17,* 293–312.

Giri, A. K., & Singh, S. P. (2015). Primitive Accumulation, Informality and Precarious Work in Neoliberal India: A Review of Arguments and Evidences. *Journal of Economic & Social Development, 11*(1), 25–40.

GoI. Ministry Of Law and Justice. (2005). National Rural Employment Guarantee Act 2005. *The Gazette of India,* 7 September 2005. New Delhi: Government of India Press.

Gold, A. G., & Raheja, G. G. (1994). *Listen to the Heron's Words: Reimagining Gender and Kinship in North India.* Los Angeles: University of California Press.

Gooptu, N., & Harriss-White, B. (2001). Mapping India's World of Unorganized Labour. *Socialist Register, 37,* 89–118.

Gough, K. (1981). *Rural Society in Southeast India.* Cambridge: Cambridge University Press.

Green, L. (2003). Notes on Mayan Youth and Rural Industrialization in Guatemala. *Critique of Anthropology, 23,* 51–73.

Guérin, I., Kumar, S., Roesch, M., & Venkatasubramanian, G. (2013). The Social Meaning of Over-Indebtedness and Creditworthiness. In *The Context of Poor Rural South Indian Households (Tamil Nadu). Microfinance, Debt and Over-Indebtedness. Juggling with Money* (pp. 125–150). London: Routledge.

Guérin, I., Roesch, M., & Venkatasubramanian, G. (2009). Bonded Labour in Rice Mills: Fate or Opportunity. In Breman et al. (Eds.), *India's Unfree Labour Workforce: Of Bondage Old and New.* New Delhi: Oxford University Press.

Guha, A. (2009). Labour Market Flexibility: An Empirical Inquiry into Neoliberal Propositions. *Economic and Political Weekly, 44,* 45–52.

Gulzar, S., & Pasquale, B. J. (2017). Politicians, Bureaucrats, and Development: Evidence from India. *American Political Science Review, 111*(1), 162–183.

Gupta, A. (1998). *Postcolonial Developments: Agriculture in the Making of Modern India*. Durham: Duke University Press.
Gupta, D. (2010). *The Caged Phoenix: Can India fly?* New Delhi: Penguin and Viking.
Gupta, S., Mehta, M., Mosse, D., Shah, V., Rees, J. F., & Team, K. P. (2002). Brokered Livelihoods: Debt, Labour Migration and Development in Tribal Western India. *Journal of Development Studies, 38*(5), 59–88.
Hamann, T. H. (2009). Neoliberalism, Governmentality, and Ethics. *Foucault Studies*, 37–59.
Hamilton, K., & Swift, J. (2001). Household Food Security. In S. Devereux & S. Maxwell (Eds.), *Food Security in Sub-Saharan Africa* (pp. 67–92). London: ITDG Publishing.
Handel, G. (2000). *Making a Life in Yorkville: Experience and Meaning in the Life-Course Narrative of an Urban Working-Class Man*. Westport, CT: Greenwood Press.
Hardiman, D. (1981). *Peasant Nationalists of Gujarat. Kheda District, 1917–1934*. New Delhi: Oxford University Press.
Hardt, M. (1999). Affective Labor. *Boundary, 2*(26), 89–100.
Harihar, V., & Macmillan. (2015). Beyond Compensation: Integrating Local Communities' Livelihood Choices in Large Carnivore Conservation. *Global Environmental Change, 33*, 122–130.
Harris, K., & Scully, B. (2015). A Hidden Counter-Movement? Precarity, Politics, and Social Protection Before and Beyond the Neoliberal Era. *Theory and Society, 44*, 415–444.
Harris, O. (2007). *What Makes People Work?* London: Berg.
Harriss-White, B. (2003). *India Working: Essays on Society and Economy* (Vol. 8). Cambridge: Cambridge University Press.
Harriss-White, B. (2010). Work and Wellbeing in Informal Economies: The Regulative Roles of Institutions of Identity and the State. *World Development, 38*(2), 170–183.
Harriss-White, B., & Gooptu, N. (2009). Mapping India's World of Unorganized Labour. *Socialist Register, 37*(37), 89–129.
Hart, G. (1995). Gender and Household Dynamics: Recent Theories and Their Implications. In M. G. Quibria (Ed.), *Critical Issues in Asian Development: Theories, Experiences, Policies* (pp. 39–67). Oxford: Oxford University Press.
Hart, K. (2000). Industrial Labour in India: The View from 19th-Century Lancashire. *Critique of Anthropology, 20*, 439–446.
Hensman, R. (2009). Organizing Against the Odds: Women in India's Informal Sector. *Socialist Register, 37*, 249–258.
Hetlar, C., & Youssef, N. (1983). Establishing the Economic Condition of Women-Headed Households in the Third World: A New Approach. In M. Buvinic, M. Lycette & W. Mcgreevey (Eds.), *Women and Poverty in the Third World* (pp. 216–243). Baltimore: John Hopkins University Press.

Hewison, K., & Kalleberg, A. L. (2013). Precarious Work and the Challenge for Asia. *American Behavioral Scientist, 57*(3), 271–288.
Hirth, K. G. (1996). Political Economy and Archaeology: Perspectives on Exchange and Production. *Journal of Archaeological Research, 4*(3), 203–239.
Hoffmaster, C. B. (Ed.). (2001). *Bioethics in Social Context*. Philadelphia: Temple University Press.
Homi, K. (2012). Loss in Rural Incomes, Children's Education, and Child Labor Simulation Estimates with Indian Data. *Journal of Developing Societies, 28*(4), 403–417.
Hossain, M., Khan, A., & Seeley, J. (2003, April). Surviving on their Feet: Charting the Mobile Livelihoods of the Poor in Rural Bangladesh. In *Conference Staying Poor: Chronic Poverty and Development Policy* (Vol. 7). University of Manchester.
Hulme, D. (2004). Thinking 'Small' and the Understanding of Poverty: Maymana and Mofizul's Story. *Journal of Human Development, 5*(2), 161–176.
Hussein, K., & Nelson, J. (1998). *Sustainable Livelihoods and Livelihood Diversification* (IDS Working Paper No. 69), Brighton, UK: Institute of Development Studies, University of Sussex.
Ishwaran, K. (Ed.). (1970). *Change and Continuity in India's Villages*. New York: Columbia University Press.
Jeffrey, C. (2002). Caste, Class, and Clientelism: A Political Economy of Everyday Corruption in Rural North India. *Economic Geography, 78*(1), 21–41.
Jeffrey, C. (2008). *Degrees Without Freedom?: Education, Masculinities, and Unemployment in North India*. Stanford, CA: Stanford University Press; London: Eurospan Distributor.
Jeffrey, C., Jeffery, P., & Jeffery, R. (2008). *Degrees Without Freedom? Education, Masculinities and Unemployment in North India*. Stanford: Stanford University Press.
Jeffery, P., & Jeffery, R. (1996). *Don't Marry Me to a Plowman! Women's Everyday Lives in Rural North India*. Colorado: Westview Press.
Jeffery, P., & Jeffery, R. (2006). *Confronting Saffron Demography: Religion, Fertility, and Women's Status in India*. New Delhi: Three Essays Collective.
Jeffery, R., & Jeffery, P. (1997). *Population, Gender and Politics: Demographic Change in Rural North India*. Cambridge: Cambridge University Press.
Jeffery, R., Jeffrey, C., & Jeffery. P. (2004). Degrees Without Freedom: The Impact of Formal Education on Dalit Young Men in North India. *Development and Change, 35*(5), 963–986.
Jeffrey, P., Jeffery, R., & Lyon, A. (1989). *Labour Pains and Labour Power: Women and Child-Bearing in India*. London: Zed Books.
Kabeer, N. (1994). *Reversed Realities: Gender Hierarchies in Development Thought*. London: Verso.

Kabeer, N. (1999). Resources, Agency, Achievements: Reflections on the Measurement of Women's Empowerment. *Development and Change, 30*(3), 435–464.

Kabeer, N. (2000). Inter-Generational Contracts, Demographic Transitions and the 'Quantity-Quality' Tradeoff: Parents, Children and Investing in the Future. *Journal of International Development, 12*(4), 463–482.

Kabeer, N. (2001). Resources, Agency, Achievements. Discussing Women's Empowerment. Conference Paper at 'Power, Resources And Culture in a Gender Perspective: Towards a Dialogue Between Gender Research and Development Practice', Arranged by *The Council for Development and Assistance Studies, Uppsala University, Sweden in Cooperation with Swedish International Development Agency*, October 2000, pp. 16–54. Downloaded 2014, http://www.sida.se/globalassets/publications/import/pdf/sv/discussing-womens-empowerment-theory-and-practice.pdf#page=19.

Kalleberg, Arne L. (2009). Precarious Work, Insecure Workers: Employment Relations in Transition. *American Sociological Review, 74*, 1–22.

Kambhampati, U. S. (2009). Child Schooling and Work Decisions in India: The Role of Household and Regional Gender Equity. *Feminist Economics, 15*(4), 77–112.

Kanbur, R., & Squire, L. (1999). The Evaluation of Thinking About Poverty: Exploring the Interactions. Internet Site: http://www.worldbank.org/poverty/wdrpoverty/evolut.htm. Accessed on 25 January 2014.

Kandiyoti, D. (1988). Bargaining With Patriarchy. *Gender And Society, 2*(3), 274–290.

Kapadia, K. (1996). Property and Proper Chastity: Women's Land Rights in South Asia Today. *Journal of Peasant Studies, 23*(4), 166–173.

Kapila, K. (2008). The Measure of a Tribe: The Cultural Politics of Constitutional Reclassification in North India. *Journal of the Royal Anthropological Institute, 14*(1), 117–134.

Kar, S., & Marjit, S. (2001). Informal Sector in General Equilibrium: Welfare Effects of Trade Policy Reforms. *International Review of Economics & Finance, 10*(3), 289–300.

Karlsson, B. G. (2003). Anthropology and the 'Indigenous Slot': Claims to and Debates About Indigenous Peoples' Status in India. *Critique of Anthropology, 23*(4), 403–423.

Katona-Apte, J. (1988). Coping Strategies of Destitute Women in Bangladesh. *Food and Nutrition Bulletin, 10*(3), 42–47.

Kennedy, M. (1985). *The Criminal Classes in India*. New Delhi: Mittal Publications.

Khan, I., & Seeley, J. A. (Eds.). (2005). *Making a Living: The Livelihoods of the Rural Poor in Bangladesh* (pp. 207–220). Dhaka: The University Press.

Khan, S., & Seeley, J. (2005). Accessing a Living: The Roles Organisations and Institutions Play in Poor People's Livelihoods. In J. A. Seeley & I. Khan

(Eds.), *Making a Living: The Livelihoods of the Rural Poor in Bangladesh*. Dhaka: The University Press.

Khera, R., & Muthiah, K. (2010, April 24). Slow but Steady Success. *The Hindu*. Available at: http://www.thehindu.com/arts/magazine/article409087.ece.

Kingdon, G. G. (1998). Does the Labour Market Explain Lower Female Schooling in India? *Journal of Development Studies*, 35(1), 39–65.

Kingdon, G. G. (2002). The Gender Gap in Educational Attainment in India: How Much Can Be Explained? *Journal Of Development Studies*, 39(2), 25–53.

Kis-Katos, K. (2007). Does Globalization Reduce Child Labor? *Journal of International Trade and Economic Development*, 16, 71–92.

Kolenda, P. (2003). *Caste, Marriage and Inequality: Essays on North and South India*. New Delhi: Rawat.

Kologlugil, S. (2010). Michel Foucault's Archaeology of Knowledge and Economic Discourse. *Erasmus Journal for Philosophy and Economics*, 3, 1–25.

Krishnaraj, S. (2005). Gender Dimensions in Rural–Urban Migration. In *India: Policy Imperatives*. International Union for the Scientific Study of Population Xxv International Population Conference Tours, France, 18–23 July 2005. Downloaded 20 November 2010. http://iussp2005.princeton.edu/abstractviewer.aspx?submissiond=51757.

Kumar, R., & Pandey, A. (2012). Women's Work Participation in Labour Market in Contemporary India. *Jurnalul Practicilor Comunitare Pozitive*, (1), 18–35. https://s3.amazonaws.com/academia.edu.documents/33558351/index.pdf?AWSAccessKeyId=AKIAIWOWYYGZ2Y53UL3A&Expires=1522982352&Signature=VkpeqnTtftb9Blo9AGlw0e2Exk0%3D&response-contentdisposition=inline%3B%20filename%3DWOMENS_WORK_PARTICIPATION_IN_LABOUR_MARK.pdf.

Lahiri-Dutt, K., & Samanta, G. (2006). Constructing Social Capital: Self-help Groups and Rural Women's Development in India. *Geographical Research*, 44(3), 285–295.

Lambert, R., & Herod, A. (Eds.). (2016). *Neoliberal Capitalism and Precarious Work: Ethnographies of Accommodation and Resistance*. Cheltenham: Edward Elgar.

Lanjouw, P., & Stern, N. H. (1998). *Economic Development in Palanpur over Five Decades*. Oxford: Clarendon Press.

Lanjouw, P., & Shariff, A. (2004). *Rural Non-farm Employment in India: Access, Incomes and Poverty Impact* (Working Paper No. 81). New Delhi: National Centre for Applied Economic Work (NCAER).

Lerche, J. (2010). From Rural Labour to Classes of Labour Class Fragmentation, Caste and Class Struggle at the Bottom of the Indian Labour Hierarchy. In B. Harriss-White & J. Heyer (Eds.), *The Comparative Political Economy of Development Africa and South Asia* (pp. 66–87). London: Routledge.

Lerche, J. (2013). The Agrarian Question in Neoliberal India: Agrarian Transition Bypassed? *Journal of Agrarian Change*, 13(3), 382–404.

Levy, R. (1984). Mead, Freeman, and Samoa: The Problem of Seeing Things as They Are. *Ethos, 12*, 85–92.

Lewis, D. J. (1993). Going It Alone: Female-Headed Households, Rights and Resources in Rural Bangladesh. *European Journal of Development Research, 5*(2), 23–42.

Lewis, H., Dwyer, P., Hodkinson, S., & Waite, L. (2014). Hyper-Precarious Lives: Migrants, Work and Forced Labour in the Global North. *Progress in Human Geography, 39*(5), 580–600.

Li, T. M. (2010). To Make Live or Let Die? Rural Dispossession and the Protection of Surplus Populations. *Antipode, 41*, 66–93.

Lloyd, C. B. (1994). *Investing in the Next Generation: The Implications of High Fertility at the Level of the Family* (Research Division Papers No. 63). New York: Population Council.

Locke, C., Rao, N., & Seeley, J. (2013). Migration and Social Reproduction at Critical Junctures in Family Life Course. *Third World Quarterly, 34*, 1881–1895.

Lofland, J. (1976). *Doing Social Life: The Qualitative Study of Human Interaction in Natural Settings*. New York: Wiley.

Luke, N., & Munshi, K. (2011). Women as Agents of Change: Female Income and Mobility in India. *Journal of Development Economics, 94*(1), 1–17.

Macip, R. F. (2012). For the Turtles' Sake: Miracles, the Third Sector and Hegemony on the Coast of Oaxaca (Mexico). *Critique of Anthropology, 32*, 241–260.

Madan, V. (Ed.). (2002). *The Village in India*. New Delhi: Oxford University Press.

Maiti, D. (2013). Precarious Work in India Trends and Emerging Issues. *American Behavioral Scientist, 57*(4), 507–530.

Major, A. J. (1999). State and Criminal Tribes in Colonial Punjab: Surveillance, Control and Reclamation of the 'Dangerous Classes'. *Modern Asian Studies, 33*(3), 657–688.

Maletrud, K. (2001). Qualitative Research: Standards, Challenges, and Guidelines. *The Lancet, 358*(9280), 483–488.

Mandelbaum, D. G. (1970). *Society in India: Continuity and Change* (Vol. 1). Berkeley: University of California Press.

Margold, J. A. (1999). From 'Cultures of Fear and Terror' to the Normalization of Violence: An Ethnographic Case. *Critique of Anthropology, 19*, 63–88.

Marriott, M. (Ed.). (1955). *Village India: Studies in the Little Community*. Chicago: Chicago University Press.

Martin, Josh. (2016). Universal Credit to Basic Income: A Politically Feasible Transition? *Basic Income Studies, 11*, 97–131.

Massey, D. (2009). Staying Behind and Undergoing Ill Health: Seeking Informal Support in West Bengal, India. In J. Seeley & C. Abrar (Eds.), *Social Protection and Livelihoods: Marginalised Migrants of South Asia*. Dhaka: The University Press.

Mayer, A. C. (1960a). *Caste and Kinship in Central India: A Village and Its Region.* London: Routledge and Kegan Paul.
Mayer, A. C. (1960b). *Caste and Kinship in Central India: A Study of Fiji Indian Rural Society.* Oxon: Routledge.
Mayer, A. C. (1989). Anthropological Memories. (Presidential Address) *Man* (NS), *24,* 203–213.
Mayer, A. C. (1996). Caste in an Indian Village: Change and Continuity 1954–1992. *Caste Today,* 32–64.
Mcguigan, J. (2016). *Neoliberal Culture.* Houndmills, Basingstoke, Hampshire. New York, NY: Palgrave Macmillan.
Mcintyre, M., & Nast, H. J. (2011). Bio (Necro) Polis: Marx, Surplus Populations, and the Spatial Dialectics of Reproduction and Race. *Antipode, 43,* 1465–1488.
Meher, R. (2009). Globalization, Displacement and the Livelihood Issues of Tribal and Agriculture Dependent Poor People the Case of Mineral-Based Industries in India. *Journal of Developing Societies, 25*(4), 457–480.
Mehrotra, S. (2008, August 2). NREG Two Years on: Where Do We Go from Here? *Economic and Political Weekly,* 27–35.
Middleton, T. (2015). *The Demands of Recognition: State Anthropology and Ethnopolitics in Darjeeling.* Palo Alto: Stanford University Press.
Miklian, J. (2009). The Purification Hunt: The Salwa Judum Counterinsurgency in Chhattisgarh, India. *Dialectical Anthropology, 33*(3–4), 441–459.
Mills, M. B. (1999). Enacting Solidarity: Unions and Migrant Youth in Thailand. *Critique of Anthropology, 19,* 175–192.
Mitchell, T. (1990). Society, Economy, and the State Effect. In G. Steinmetz (Ed.), *State/Culture: State-Formation After the Cultural Turn.* Ithaca and London: Cornell University Press.
Molé, N. J. (2010). Precarious Subjects: Anticipating Neoliberalism in Northern Italy's Workplace. *American Anthropologist, 112,* 38–53.
Mollona, M. (2009). *Made in Sheffield: An Ethnography of Industrial Work and Politics.* New York: Berghahn Books.
Moser, C. O. N. (1998). The Asset Vulnerability Framework: Reassessing Urban Poverty Reduction Strategies. *World Development, 26*(1), 1–19.
Mosoetsa, S., Stillerman, J., & Tilly, C. (2016). Precarious Labor, South and North: An Introduction. *International Labor and Working-Class History, 89,* 5–19.
Mosse, D. (2007). *Power and the Durability of Poverty: A Critical Exploration of the Links Between Culture, Marginality and Chronic Poverty* (Chronic Poverty Research Centre Working Paper No. 107).
Mosse, D. (2010). A Relational Approach to Durable Poverty, Inequality and Power. *The Journal of Development Studies, 46*(7), 1156–1178.
Munger, F. (2002). *Laboring Below the Line: The New Ethnography of Poverty, Low-Wage Work and Survival in the Global Economy.* New York: Russell Sage Foundation.

Nagarajan, K. (2017). India's Demonetisation Drive Is Affecting Access to Medical Care. *Lancet, 389,* 32–33.
Niehof, A. (2004). The Significance of Diversification for Rural Livelihood Systems. *Food Policy, 29*(4), 321–338.
Niehof, A., & Price, L. (2001). *Rural Livelihood Systems: A Conceptual Framework.* Wageningen-Upward Series and on Rural Livelihoods No. 1. Wageningen, the Netherlands: Wu-Upward.
Nigam, S. (1990). Disciplining and Policing the 'Criminals by Birth', Part 1: The Making of a Colonial Stereotype—The Criminal Tribes and Castes of North India. *The Indian Economic & Social History Review, 27*(2), 131–164.
Olsen, W. K. & Ramanamurthy, R. V. (2000). Contract Labour and Bondage in Andhra Pradesh (India). *Journal of Social and Political Thought, 1*(2). http://www.yorku.ca/jspot/2/wkolsenrvramana.htm.
Omvedt, G. (1993). *Reinventing Revolution: New Social Movements and the Socialist Tradition in India.* New York: M. E Sharpe.
Palriwala, R. (1998). *Changing Kinship, Family and Gender Relations in South Asia: Processes, Trends and Issues.* Leiden: Women and Autonomy Centre, Leiden University.
Parajuli, P. (1996). Ecological Ethnicity in the Making: Developmentalist Hegemonies and Emergent Identities in India. *Identities Global Studies in Culture and Power, 3*(1–2), 14–59.
Parker, M. (2007). Ethnography/Ethics. *Social Science and Medicine, 65*(11), 2248–2259.
Parkin, R. (2009). *Louis Dumont and Hierarchical Opposition.* London: Berghahn Books.
Parry, J. P. (1979). *Caste and Kinship in Kangra.* London: Routledge.
Parry, J. P. (1999). Lords of Labour: Working and Shirking in Bhilai. *Contribution to Indian Sociology, 33*(1–2), 107–140.
Parry, J. P. (2007). Afterword: A Note on the "Substantialisation" of Caste and its "Hegemony". In D. Gellner & H. Ishii (Eds.), *Northern South Asia: Political and Social Transformations.* New Delhi: Manohar.
Patnaik, U. (2007). Neoliberalism and Rural Poverty in India. *Economic and Political Weekly, 42*(30), 3132–3150.
Patterson, T. C. (1998). Flexible Accumulation, Flexible Labor and Their Consequences. *Critique of Anthropology, 18,* 317–319.
Phirth, K. (2009). Craft Production, Household Diversification, and Domestic Economy in Prehispanic Mesoamerica. *Archeological Papers of the American Anthropological Association, 19*(1), 13–32.
Picherit, D. (2009). 'Workers, Trust Us!': Labour Middlemen and the Rise of the Lower Castes in Andhra Pradesh. In J. Breman, I. Guérin, & A. Prakash

(Eds.), *India's Unfree Labour Workforce: Of Bondage Old and New* (pp. 259–283). New Delhi: Oxford University Press.

Picherit, D. (2012). Migrant Labourers' Struggles Between Village and Urban Migration Sites: Labour Standards, Rural Development and Politics in South India. *Global Labour Journal, 3*(1), 143–162.

Pinto, S. (2004). Development Without Institutions: Ersatz Medicine and the Politics of Everyday Life in Rural North India. *Cultural Anthropology, 19*(3), 337–364.

Prakash, A. (2009). How (Un)Free are the Workers in the Labour Market? A Case Study of Brick Kilns. In Breman et al. (Eds.), *Indian Unfree Workforce of Bondage Old and New* (pp. 198–232). New Delhi: Oxford University Press.

Putnam, R. D. (1995). Bowling Alone: America's Declining Social Capital. *Journal of Democracy, 6*, 65–78.

Rabinow, P. (2007). *Reflections on Fieldwork in Morocco*. Berkeley: University of California Press.

Rafique, A., & Rogaly, B. (2003). Struggling to Save Cash: Seasonal Migration and Vulnerability in West Bengal, India. *Development and Change, 34*(4), 659–681.

Rahman, L., & Rao, V. (2004). The Determinants of Gender Equity in India: Examining Dyson and Moore's Thesis with New Data. *Population and Development Review, 30*(2), 239–268.

Rammohan, A. (2014). The Trade-Off Between Child Labour and Schooling in India. *Education Economics, 22*(5), 484–510.

Rangarajan, M. (2005). Fire in the Forest. *Economic and Political Weekly. Commentary, 40*(47), 4888–4890.

Rao, N. (2003). Life and Livelihood in Santal Parganas: Does the Right to a Livelihood Really Exist? *Economic and Political Weekly, 38*(39), 4081–4084.

Rao, N. (2005). Displacement from Land: Case of Santhal Parganas. *Economic and Political Weekly, 40*(41), 4439–4442.

Rao, N. (2006). Land Rights, Gender Equality and Household Food Security: Exploring the Conceptual Links in the Case of India. *Food Policy, 31*, 180–193.

Raventós, D. (2007). *Basic Income: The Material Conditions of Freedom*. London: Pluto Press.

Rawal, V. (2008). Ownership Holdings of Land in Rural India: Putting the Record Straight. *Economic and Political Weekly, 43*(10), 43–47.

Robinson, A., & Tormey, S. (2012). Beyond the State: Anthropology and 'Actually-Existing-Anarchism'. *Critique of Anthropology, 32*(2), 143–157.

Rogaly, B. (1995). Contractual Arrangements for Rural Workers in Asia. *Development in Practice, 5*(2), 165–169.

Rogaly, B. (1997). Linking Home and Market: Towards a Gendered Analysis of Changing Labour Relations in Rural West Bengal. *IDS Bulletin, 28*(3), 63–72.

Rogaly, B. (2003). Who Goes? Who Stays Back? Seasonal Migration and Staying Put Among Rural Manual Workers in Eastern India. *Journal of International Development, 15*(5), 623–632.

Rogaly, B. (2009). Spaces of Work and Everyday Life: Labour Geographies and the Agency of Unorganised Temporary Migrant Workers. *Geography Compass, 3*(6), 1975–1987.

Rogaly, B., & Thieme, S. (2012). Experiencing Space-Time: The Stretched Lifeworlds of Migrant Workers in India. *Environment and Planning A, 44*(9), 2086–2100.

Rossi, A. (2016). *The Labour of Subjectivity: Foucault on Biopolitics, Economy, Critique*. London and New York: Rowman & Littlefield International.

Rudie, I. (1995). The Significance of 'Eating': Cooperation, Support and Reputation in Kelantan Malay Households. In W. J. Karim (Ed.), *'Male' and 'Female' Developing Southeast Asia* (pp. 227–247). Oxford: Berg.

Sapkal, R., & Shyamsundar, K. R. Precarious Work and Less Well Paid? Wage Differential Between Regular and Temporary Contract Workers in India. http://www.iariw.org/India/sapkal.pdf.

Schmink, M. (1984). Household Economic Strategies: Review and Research Agenda. *Latin American Research Review, 19*(3), 87–101.

Schneider, J. (2002). Reflexive/Diffractive Ethnography. *Cultural Studies—Critical Methodologies, 2*(4), 460–482.

Scoones, I. (1998). *Sustainable Rural Livelihoods: A Framework for Analysis* (Working Paper No. 72). Brighton: Institute of Development Studies, University of Sussex.

Scott, J. C. (2009). *The Art of Not Being Governed: An Anarchist History of Upland Southeast Asia*. New Haven: Yale University Press.

Scully, B. (2016). Precarity North and South: A Southern Critique of Guy Standing. *Global Labour Journal, 7*(2).

Searle-Chatterjee, M. (1981). *Reversible Sex Roles: The Special Case of Benares Sweepers*. Oxford: Pergamon Press.

Self, S. (2011). Market and Non-market Child Labour in Rural India: The Role of the Mother's Participation in the Labour Force. *Oxford Development Studies, 39*(3), 315–338.

Sen, A. (1981). *Poverty and Famines: An Essay on Entitlement and Deprivation*. Oxford: Oxford University Press.

Sen, A. (1999a). *Development as Freedom*. New Delhi and Oxford: Oxford University Press.

Sen, A. (1999b). *Beyond the Crisis: Development Strategies in Asia*. Pasir Panjang, Singapore: ISEAS.

Shah, A. (2006). The Labour of Love: Seasonal Migration from Jharkhand to the Brick Kilns of Other States in India. *Contributions to Indian Sociology, 40*(1), 91–118.

Shah, A. (2007). The Dark Side of Indigeneity: Indigenous People, Rights and Development in India. *History Compass*, 5(6), 1806–1832.
Shah, A. (2010). *Shadows of the State: Indigenous Politics, Environmentalism and Insurgency in Jharkhand*. Durham: Duke University Press.
Sharma, A. (2005). *Tribes in Transition: A Study of Thakur Gonds*. New Delhi: Mittal Publications.
Sharp, L. A. (2003). Laboring for the Colony and Nation: The Historicized Political Consciousness of Youth in Madagascar. *Critique of Anthropology, 23*, 75–91.
Shibata, K. (2008). Neoliberalism, Risk, and Spatial Governance in the Developmental State: Japanese Planning in the Global Economy. *Critical Planning, 15*, 92–118.
Siddiqui, T., & Sikder, M. (2005). Rural to Urban Migration for Domestic Work in Bangladesh. In C. Abrar & J. Seeley (Eds.), *Social Protection and Livelihoods: Marginalised Migrant Workers of India and Bangladesh* (pp. 57–81). Dhaka: The United Press.
Silverman, D. (1985). *Qualitative Methods and Sociology: Describing Social World*. Aldershot: Gower.
Sinha, A. (2005). *The Regional Roots of Developmental Politics in India: A Divided Leviathan*. Bloomington: Indiana University Press.
Sivaramakrishnan, K., & Agrawal, A. (2003). *Regional Modernities: The Cultural Politics of Development in India*. Stanford: Stanford University Press.
Skeldon, R. (2003). Migration and Poverty, Conference Paper, Princeton: Program in Urbanization and Migration, Princeton University Press.
Smith, A. D. (1973). *The Concept of Social Change: A Critique of the Functionalist Theory of Social Change*. London: Routledge and Kegan Paul.
Smith, R. C. (2017). *Society and Social Pathology: A Framework for Progress*. London: Springer.
Smith, V. (2002). *Crossing the Great Divide: Worker Risk and Opportunity in the New Economy*. Ithaca: Cornell University Press.
Solinski, T. (2012, June 14). NREGA and Labour Migration in India: Is Village Life What the 'Rural' Poor Want? *The South Asianist, 1*(1), 17–30.
Srinivas, M. N. (Ed.). (1955). *India's Villages*. London: Asia Publishing House.
Standing, G. (2012). The Precariat: Why It Needs Deliberative Democracy. Open Democracy.
Standing, G. (2014a). *A Precariat Charter: From Denizens to Citizens*. London: A&C Black.
Standing, G. (2014b). Understanding the Precariat Through Labour and Work. *Development and Change, 45*(5), 963–980.
Standing, G. (2016). *The Precariat: The New Dangerous Class*. London: Bloomsbury.

Staples, J. (2007). *Livelihoods at the Margins: Surviving the City*. Walnut Creek, CA: Left Coast.

Strauss, K., & Mcgrath, S. (2016). Temporary Migration, Precarious Employment and Unfree Labour Relations: Exploring the 'Continuum of Exploitation' in Canada's Temporary Foreign Worker Program. *Geoforum, 78*, 199–208.

Surendra, L. (1986). *The Ethnic Origins of Nations*. London: Basil Blackwell.

Talib, M. (2010). *Writing Labour: Stone Quarry Workers in Delhi*. Oxford: Oxford University Press.

Tambiah, S. (1992). Environmental Implications (Seminar No. 395: 44–48).

The Challenge of Employment in India an Informal Economy Perspective, Vol. 1 (Main Report. D.O.No.Aks/Ncues /2009). Available at www.ncuesgov.in. Downloaded October 2015.

Thieme, S. (2008). Sustaining Livelihoods in Multi-local Settings: Possible Theoretical Linkages Between Transnational Migration and Livelihood Studies. *Mobilities, 3*(1), 51–71.

Tilley, C. (1997). Performing Culture in the Global Village. *Critique of Anthropology, 17*, 67–89.

Tolen, R. J. (1991). Colonizing and Transforming the Criminal Tribesman: The Salvation Army in British India. *American Ethnologist, 18*(1), 106–125.

Touraine, A. (1989). A Class Act: Anthropology and the Race to Nation Across Ethnic Terrain. *Annual Review of Anthropology, 18*, 401–444.

Tripathi, R. K., & Verma, M. K. (2013). Social Sustainable Rural Housing in India: An Urgent Need. *International Journal of Social Sustainability in Economic, Social and Cultural Context, 8*(3), 71–83.

Tripathy, S. N. (2005). *Tribal Migration*. New Delhi: Sonali Publication.

Trouillot, M.-R. (2001). The Anthropology of the State in the Age of Globalization: Close Encounters of the Deceptive Kind. *Current Anthropology, 42*(1), 125–138.

Udupa, S. (2016). Fast Time Religion: News, Speculation, and Discipline in India. *Critique of Anthropology, 36*, 397–418.

Unnithan-Kumar, M. (1997). *Identity, Gender and Poverty: New Perspectives on Caste and Tribe in Rajasthan*. Providence, RI and Oxford: Berghahn.

Unnithan-Kumar, M. (2000). The State Rajput Identity and Women's Agency in 19th and 20th Century Rajasthan. *Indian Journal of Gender Studies, 7*(1), 49–70.

Veenhoven, R. (2006). The Four Qualities of Life: Ordering Concepts and Measures of the Good Life. In M. Mcgillivray & M. Clarke (Eds.), *Understanding Human Well-Being* (pp. 74–100). Tokyo: United Nations University Press.

Venkatesh, S. A. (2013). The Reflexive Turn: The Rise of First-Person Ethnography. *Sociological Quarterly, 54*(1), 3–8.

Venn, C. (2009). Neoliberal Political Economy, Biopolitics and Colonialism: A Transcolonial Genealogy of Inequality. *Theory, Culture & Society, 26*, 206–233.

Vera-Sanso, P. (2012). Gender, Poverty and Old-Age Livelihoods in Urban South India in an Era of Globalisation. *Oxford Development Studies, 40*(3), 324–340.

Von Fürer-Haimendorf, C. (1982). *Tribes of India: The Struggle for Survival.* Berkely: University of California Press.

Vosko, L. F. (2010). *Managing the Margins: Gender, Citizenship and the International Regulation of Precarious Employment.* Oxford: Oxford University Press.

Wafer, A. (2015). Precarity and Intimacy in Super-Diverse Hillbrow. In *Diversities Old and New* (pp. 156–168). London: Palgrave Macmillan.

Waite, L. (2005). How Is Labouring Enabled Through the Body? A Case Study of Manual Workers in Rural India. *Contemporary South Asia, 14*(4), 411–428.

Walia, H. (2007). Increasing Precarity: The Politics of Migrant Labour. *Left Turn, 9.*

Warner, C. (2014). Foreword. In J. Morris & A. Polese (Eds.) (2013), *The Informal Post-Socialist Economy: Embedded Practices and Livelihoods* (pp. xvi–xix). Oxford and New York: Routledge.

Webster, E., Joynt, K., & Sefalafala, T. (2016). Informalization and Decent Work: Labour's Challenge. *Progress in Development Studies, 16*, 203–218.

Whitehead, A. (2002). Tracking Livelihood Change: Theoretical, Methodological and Empirical Perspectives from North-East Ghana. *Journal of Southern African Studies, 28*(3), 575–598.

Witsoe, J. (2012). Everyday Corruption and the Political Mediation of the Indian State. *Economic & Political Weekly, 47*(6), 47.

Wolf, M. (1992). *A Thrice-Told Tale: Feminism, Postmodernism, and Ethnographic Responsibility.* Stanford, CA: Stanford University Press.

Wood, G. (2003). Staying Secure, Staying Poor: The 'Faustian Bargain'. *World Development, 31*(3), 455–471.

Wood, G. D. (1998, January 14–18). *Investing in Networks: Livelihoods and Social Capital in Dhaka Slums.* Paper Presented at the National Workshop on Urban Livelihoods, Institute of Development Policy Analysis and Advocacy (Idpaa), Dhaka.

Wood, G. D. (2005). Poverty, Capabilities and Perverse Social Capital: The Antidote to Sen and Putnam. In J. Seeley & A. Khan (Eds.), *Making a Living: The Livelihoods of the Rural Poor in Bangladesh.* Dhaka: University Press.

Wuttke, M., & Vilks, A. (2014). Poverty Alleviation Through CSR in the Indian Construction Industry. *Journal of Management Development, 33*, 119–130.

Xaxa, V. (1999). Tribes as Indigenous People of India. *Economic and Political Weekly, 34*(51), 3589–3595.

Index

A
Aditya, 1, 7, 36, 69, 83, 92, 98, 100, 104, 109, 110, 126, 150–152, 154, 168, 171, 173, 175, 177, 178, 182–184
Adivasis, 56, 57, 72, 179, 185, 203, 205. *See also* Indigenous people; Tribal people
Anarchy, 3, 83–85, 209

B
Begari pratha, 63, 65. *See also* Feudal order
Below Poverty Line (BPL), 93, 97, 146, 171
Bengalis (an ethnic group that speaks Bengali; refugees from Bangladesh), 20, 70, 77, 93, 99, 102, 103, 126, 158, 173, 174, 187
Bondage, 62, 63, 65, 67, 104, 120, 155, 166, 195
Breman, J., 110, 136, 137, 200, 202, 205, 207, 208

Bundelkhand, 20, 58, 60, 74
Bureaucratic-mineowner syndicate, 75
Bypass, 32, 102

C
Communal, 11, 13, 26, 46, 86, 104, 127

D
Debts, 67, 88, 93
Development, 14, 16–18, 56, 76, 108, 111, 113, 129, 152, 165, 167, 170–172, 176, 186, 187, 190, 194, 213
Dihadi (wages), 3, 8, 29, 53, 64, 74, 75, 84, 85, 88, 94, 96, 97, 122, 125, 136, 144, 145, 147, 148, 150, 155, 157, 158, 165, 186, 189–193, 195, 200, 202, 205, 208, 211, 215, 217
Disenchantment, 40, 213
Disengagement, 40

F

Ferguson, J., 4, 87, 88, 101
Feudal order, 5
Forests, 15–18, 20–23, 25, 35, 56, 57, 59–61, 63, 65, 67, 72, 77, 111, 113, 120, 123, 127, 132, 151, 153, 165, 173, 174, 177, 181, 192, 194, 212

G

Gram, 44, 62, 101, 174, 188, 191

H

Homestead, 107–109, 111, 152
Households, 8, 20, 24, 25, 56, 61, 64, 73, 79, 80, 89, 90, 92, 97, 98, 104, 108–114, 117, 119–121, 123–129, 132, 145–159, 168, 170–172, 174, 175, 178–181, 183, 185–189, 192, 193, 213, 215–218

I

Indigenous, 15–17, 22, 29, 31, 32, 50, 55, 61, 84, 103, 173, 219
Indigenous people, 14–16, 28, 40, 41, 54, 56, 57, 172, 218, 225

K

Khadaan. See Stone quarry
Kher Mata (a Gond goddess), 104, 108

L

Labour contractor, 21, 34, 40, 53, 63, 78, 96, 98, 146, 153, 195, 214, 218
Labouring/waging, 6, 7, 30, 39, 40, 64, 80, 84–87, 90, 96, 97, 123, 126, 138, 148, 150, 152, 153, 157, 171, 176, 177, 184, 199, 206, 208, 210, 213, 215, 217–219
Landed elites, 16, 18, 54, 61, 78, 93, 167, 169
Land grab, 91, 92
Life-course, 213
Livelihood, 2, 3, 6, 13–17, 20, 24, 27, 39, 44, 52, 53, 62–67, 76–78, 81, 85, 86, 89, 92, 94, 97, 102, 108, 110, 113, 121, 125, 131–137, 139, 143, 145, 149–154, 159, 160, 165, 175, 184, 186, 188, 200–202, 204–207, 209–211, 213, 214, 216, 217

M

Maistry, 53, 94, 96, 209. See also Professional stone miner
Majdoors, 53, 96. See also Workers/labourers
Majoori, 6, 7, 84, 85, 96, 126, 146, 152, 154, 159, 175, 177, 178, 192. See also Labouring/waging
Migration, 1–3, 6, 10, 16, 18, 25, 30, 38, 39, 44, 52, 53, 73, 76, 78, 89, 90, 92–95, 102, 113, 114, 133–135, 144, 147, 148, 171, 173–175, 180, 181, 186, 188, 190–192, 202
Mineowners, 74
Mines, 19, 20, 37, 51, 53, 54, 63, 67, 68, 71–75, 93, 99, 125, 148, 154, 155, 174, 206, 213
Mining, 13, 17, 18, 20, 22, 24, 27, 34, 36, 46, 50, 53, 62, 63, 65, 71–74, 77, 78, 90, 92, 98, 100, 101, 124, 150–152, 154, 169, 185, 191, 210
Munshi, 75, 96

INDEX 253

N
National Rural Employment Guarantee card (NREGA), 8, 9, 19, 21, 53, 69, 76, 79, 101, 167, 168, 172, 174, 186–193, 195, 203
Nyaarpanna, 109–112

P
Panchayat, 8, 20, 21, 24, 37, 44, 62, 64, 69, 72, 74, 79, 92, 121, 147, 149, 153, 166, 167, 171–175, 188–193, 195, 204
Panchnama, 126
Poverty, 16, 18, 20, 22, 40, 68, 88, 93, 103, 104, 111, 149, 166, 167, 169–171, 176, 178, 186, 188, 195, 212, 213, 215, 216
Precarious, 62, 93, 104, 132, 148, 150, 165, 171, 195
Professional stone miner, 96, 150

R
Rajputisation, 56, 58, 87, 89
Roji, 6, 85. See also Livelihood

S
Samaj, 55, 165. See also Society
Samooh, 182. See also Communal
Sanskritisation, 55, 56, 58, 156
Social capital, 132, 177, 214–218
Society, 9, 14, 15, 26, 30, 31, 55, 57, 60, 63, 66, 77, 78, 88, 108, 114, 132, 139, 157, 159, 160, 165, 169, 185, 194, 199, 201, 204, 205, 207, 214
State, 1–9, 14–18, 22, 24, 25, 28–32, 35, 37, 40, 41, 43, 47, 48, 52, 54, 56, 58, 59, 65, 67–69, 71–74, 77–79, 81, 84–88, 91–94, 101, 102, 105, 110, 111, 115, 126, 129, 131, 133, 134, 139, 140, 149, 151, 153, 160, 165–169, 171–173, 176–178, 181, 184, 186, 187, 193–195, 199, 200, 203–210, 212–214, 217–219
Stone quarry, 1, 2, 9, 18, 20, 27, 51, 61, 72–74, 76–78, 85, 89–91, 94–98, 113, 124, 125, 127, 132, 135, 136, 144, 149–151, 154, 165, 175, 183, 185, 187, 194, 202. See also Mines
Sur Gonds, 3–5, 13, 14, 43, 48, 55–57, 59–62, 66, 67, 69, 70, 84, 132

T
Tania Li, 4, 27
Thakurs, 44, 52, 67, 68, 75. See also Landed elites
Thekedaar, 40. See also Labour contractor
Thekedaari, 96
Tiger, 22, 23, 25, 26, 63, 72, 77, 78, 99, 185, 213
Tiger Reserve, 1, 4–6, 22, 23, 27, 43, 45, 46, 63, 74
Tribal people, 3, 9, 13–15, 18, 132

W
Withdrawal, 17, 40, 41
Workers/labourers, 1, 2, 4, 13, 36, 38, 43, 51–53, 71, 73, 75, 78, 84, 85, 95, 96, 105, 136, 140, 142, 150, 153, 157, 174, 177, 186, 189, 193, 200, 205, 206, 208, 209, 211, 212, 216, 217

The manufacturer's authorised representative in the EU is Springer Nature Customer Service Centre GmbH, Europaplatz 3, 69115 Heidelberg, Germany. If you have any concerns regarding our products, please contact ProductSafety@springernature.com

Printed and bound by CPI Group (UK) Ltd, Croydon, CR0 4YY
23/03/2026
02076738-0004